Charles Ernest Smith

Religion Under the Barons of Baltimore

Charles Ernest Smith

Religion Under the Barons of Baltimore

ISBN/EAN: 9783744660969

Printed in Europe, USA, Canada, Australia, Japan

Cover: Foto ©Lupo / pixelio.de

More available books at **www.hansebooks.com**

RELIGION
UNDER
THE BARONS OF BALTIMORE.

RELIGION
UNDER
THE BARONS OF BALTIMORE

BEING A SKETCH OF ECCLESIASTICAL AFFAIRS

FROM THE

Founding of the Maryland Colony in 1634 to the formal establishment of the Church of England in 1692, with special reference to the claim that Maryland was founded by Roman Catholics as the seed plot of Religious Liberty.

BY

C. ERNEST SMITH, D. D.,

RECTOR OF THE CHURCH OF ST. MICHAEL AND ALL ANGELS,
BALTIMORE, MARYLAND.

AUTHOR OF "THE OLD CHURCH IN THE NEW LAND,"
"IN THE HOUSEHOLD OF FAITH," ETC.

TO THE
CONGREGATION
OF THE
CHURCH OF ST. MICHAEL AND ALL ANGELS,
BALTIMORE,
WHO ARE ALREADY FAMILIAR WITH MANY OF THE STATEMENTS MADE IN ITS PAGES, THIS BOOK IS AFFECTIONATELY DEDICATED BY THE AUTHOR, WHO THINKS IT NO SLIGHT PRIVILEGE TO BE THEIR RECTOR.

PREFACE.

Students are well aware that much which passes current in Maryland for reliable history, is utterly unworthy of credit. This is especially the case with Maryland's ecclesiastical history. But this fact need occasion little or no surprise. That error should have been very largely incorporated in the story of Maryland's past, was as natural and inevitable as are the storms of March or the shortening of the days in winter, seeing that imagination had been called upon to fill up many and large gaps in her records.

Now, however, it is altogether different. Increased historical research; the publication of the Maryland Archives; above all, the recovery and publication of the *Calvert Papers* after many years disappearance, have solved questions once apparently insoluble, removed difficulties long considered insuperable, and reconciled seemingly hopeless contradictions. Happily, through the patriotic zeal of the Maryland Historical Society, there is nowadays such a wealth of material at our command, that not only is a hearty tribute of praise due the Society from every lover of truth, but there is due also the frank acknowledgement that its successful labors have rendered comparatively easy the task of the future historian of Maryland.

A very fascinating subject for study is the account of the work of Maryland's Historical Society, apart altogether from its splendid results. In fact, second only in interest to the story they enshrine, is the history of the precious documents themselves. Strange and romantic have been the ways in which these documents have been rescued from oblivion. Not more wonderfully indeed was the famous Old Testament manuscript *Aleph* saved by Constantine Tischendorff, when the monks of the monastery in which he was tarrying for the night had already laid it aside for the kindling of the next day's fire, than have some of Maryland's literary treasures escaped entire destruction. As recently as the year 1894 the Society acquired, from a most unexpected source, several documents which constitute a very valuable addition to its collection. The story of the acquisition of these papers is thus told by a member of the Society:
"It was in May, 1894, that I received a letter from Mr. John Roland Phillips, dated Lincoln, Nebraska, advising me that he had in his possession several old and rare documents relating to the

earliest settlement of Maryland, which he would be glad to dispose of.

"A correspondence ensued which developed the fact that the papers came to Mr. Phillips' possession from his father, who died in 1887.

"The elder Phillips was the author of a work entitled, *Memoirs of the Civil War in Wales and the Marches, 1642–1649*, by John Roland Phillips, of Lincoln's Inn, Barrister-at-Law, in two volumes, London: Longmans, Green & Co., 1874.

"In the preparation of this work the author collected a considerable mass of papers bearing on the subject of his investigations, among which these appear to have been preserved because of their particularly interesting character. Whence the papers were obtained by his father the present Mr. Phillips does not know. They were, at my request, sent to us for examination, and their value as genuine originals being readily recognized by our experts, they were purchased by the Society and form a most interesting series, illustrating transactions immediately preceding the embarkation from London, the events of the voyage over, and the occurrences of the short interval between the arrival in Maryland and the despatch of the ship '*Ark*' on its return to London."

Thus documents of the very highest importance to the historian of Maryland, "which have been for more than two hundred and fifty years without the care of an official guardian," have happily been preserved. What hopes may not be founded on such a discovery as this? Other literary treasures may yet be forthcoming. Two large chests marked *Calvert Papers* seen in the British Museum in 1839, could not be found twenty years later. Probably they were there only temporarily, perhaps offered unsuccessfully for sale. But if so, where was their next resting place? Was it at the country seat, near Windsor, of a descendant of the Calverts, where the recovered papers were actually found, and where a tradition still lingers that a chest full of similar papers had been given to the gardener to be buried? Who shall venture to decide? Meanwhile, although some may still live in hope of seeing that lost chest at a future day, most of us will be thankful for our present possessions, and seek to learn the lessons they teach.

It will, perhaps, be seen that to give an account of religion in the province of Maryland in its early days is a task attended with some special difficulties and no little responsibility, in that it involves the rejection of views as entirely worthless, which have both enjoyed the support of great names, and attained something like universal assent. This is necessarily an ungrateful duty. Beliefs which have become entwined with the heart's affections, even when destitute of all warrant, cannot but be respected. To any one, however, who may be tempted to resent the publication of views distasteful to him, I would say that they have only been published in the full belief that the facts herein recorded are true, and deserve to be fully known. And I would therefore suggest that ere such an one makes a way for his indignation, it would be well for him to examine the records to see whether these distasteful views are or are not well founded. If he will do this, I shall be fully satisfied ; for I am sanguine enough to believe that a thorough examination, and an honest interpretation of the records, will lead him to make the frank confession : *I have not conquered the evidence, but the evidence has conquered me.*

We may not willingly dwell in darkness. Our fathers thought Galileo guilty of impiety in maintaining the true theory of the universe. They likewise believed in ghosts and burned witches. We neither burn witches, believe in ghosts, nor maintain that the earth stands still in the midst of the heavens. We walk in the light, and must prove ourselves worthy of the light. And I trust that the time is not far distant when reputable citizens will be found no more willing to talk about Maryland as having been founded as a refuge for men persecuted for conscience sake, and as the seed-plot of religious liberty than they are now to plead for the burning at the stake of some poor, harmless old woman as a witch.

In my endeavors to further the cause of truth I am sure of the approval of the noble-minded everywhere, whatever their sentiments may be, but I trust that no just fault can be found by any with the spirit in which I have discharged my task.

TITLES OF CHAPTERS.

	PREFACE.	
I.	MARYLAND'S LEGENDARY ORIGIN.	1
II.	SIR GEORGE CALVERT AT THE COURT OF KING JAMES I.	19
III.	THE CHARTER OF AVALON.	37
IV.	LORD BALTIMORE (SIR GEORGE CALVERT) IN NEWFOUNDLAND.	58
V.	LORD BALTIMORE IN VIRGINIA.	77
VI.	THE DEATH OF LORD BALTIMORE.	95
VII.	THE CHARTER OF MARYLAND.	113
VIII.	THE ADVENTURERS, AND HOW THEY WERE GATHERED TOGETHER.	129
IX.	THE JOURNEY OF THE ADVENTURERS TO MARYLAND, AND THEIR ARRIVAL.	150
X.	FOUNDING A CITY TO DWELL IN.	171
XI.	SHEEP WITHOUT A SHEPHERD—THE BEGINNINGS OF THE MARYLAND CHURCH.	191
XII.	"WHILE THE GOVERNMENT IS CATHOLIQUE."	209
XIII.	WORKING THE LEGISLATURE.	225
XIV.	THE APPEAL TO THE LORD PROPRIETARY	244
XV.	BATTLES WITH THE JESUITS—THE DEFEAT OF LORD BALTIMORE.	258
XVI.	GATHERING CLOUDS.	276
XVII.	THE STORM.	294
XVIII.	A NEW DEPARTURE—THE PROGRAMME.	309
XIX.	MARYLAND UNDER PURITAN RULE.	329
XX.	LORD BALTIMORE ENJOYS HIS OWN AGAIN.	348
XXI.	THE CHURCH OF ENGLAND ESTABLISHED AND ENDOWED.	362

CHAPTER I.

MARYLAND'S LEGENDARY ORIGIN.

" But faith, fanatic faith, once wedded fast
To some dear falsehood, hugs it to the last."
—MOORE.

It has long been claimed for Maryland that she owes her existence to the desire to found a colony where religious liberty, sternly proscribed and lying under a ban elsewhere, should find, in at least one place in all the world, protection and a home. Nothing less than this, we are told, was the purpose of Sir George Calvert, first Baron of Baltimore, as he sought and obtained from King Charles the First his Charter of Maryland. Although stricken down himself by the hand of death ere he could fulfil his splendid purpose, that purpose still lived on, destined to a glorious fulfilment. Its perfect accomplishment, we are assured, was the one aim of the men who, in the winter of 1633-34, under the leadership of Leonard Calvert, crossed the Atlantic and founded the Province of Maryland ; the one desire that influenced them to leave home and friends, and to brave the perils of the deep and the hardships of early colonial life. From this point of view, these men are certainly entitled to be regarded as pilgrims seeking a country where, in all questions of conscience, Ephraim should no more vex Judah, nor Judah vex Ephraim, but where peace and harmony should bear unbroken rule; pilgrims, moreover, who were solely intent upon building up in the wilderness a home for religious freedom, and whose watchword was, "Liberty to worship God." That this was the character of their mission, seemed even to be proclaimed by the very names of the fragile boats in which they sailed: the *Ark*, and the *Dove!* What else could such names signify, than that the deluge was everywhere, and that the voyagers were seeking a place where, safe from the raging waters, they might, in peace and safety, after the manner of their fathers and the dictates of their consciences, offer up the sacrifice of prayer and praise to God continually?

Thus considered, the expedition of the "pilgrims" is full of pathetic interest. Nor is it without its own striking parallel in history. It is, in fact, singularly like the traditional account which relates how Joseph of Arimathea, and his twelve companions, fleeing from the intolerable bigotry of their countrymen, came to Britain, bearing the Holy Grail and the tidings of the Gospel. Like that, too, the story of the Maryland pilgrimage is beautiful. It is rich also in lofty purposes and spiritual aims; in steadfastness of heart and a ready willingness to suffer for the Truth's sake. And that in Maryland many are sincerely attached to it will create no astonishment. Maryland, by means of it, has a glory all her own. Here is the beginning of her greatness, the source of her power. Here the proof that starting with a distinctly religious motive, she was "the brightest gem in the American cluster of provinces or states," justly entitled in consequence to a proud pre-eminence among them all. Here is the authority for the lofty claim that her foundation marks the epoch that gave birth to the idea of absolute religious liberty, the first step in that direction on this continent, aye, the first in the world.[1] Surely no greater distinction than this could have been hers.

[1] McSherry, *History of Maryland.* Page 24. McMahon P. 193. The statement in the text is made under the belief that the Act of Toleration, (see chapter xviii) passed in 1649 by the Maryland House of Assembly, was the first of its kind. As a matter of fact this statute was not passed until thirteen years after Roger Williams and others who had suffered persecution in Massachusetts, had established at Providence, as Arnold says, "A pure Democracy, which for the first time guarded jealously

Had not religious liberty on her soil "obtained a home, its only home in the wide world?"[2] If this be true, then let us indeed salute Maryland, and exclaim, All hail to Maryland, the first of all lands to proclaim that a man's faith is a matter between himself and his Maker.

But should we bethink ourselves to ask from what persecutions these "pilgrims" were fleeing, whose flight had so glorious a termination, we shall be answered, from the fines, the confiscations, and the imprisonments which were then the common portion of the English Roman Catholics. Now that the English Romanists of that day did suffer "the odium and disabilities of a political ostracism and some of the rigors of a downright persecution,"[3] must be confessed; though at the time of the sailing of the *Ark* and the *Dove*, their lot, it must also be acknowledged, was so much brighter than

the right of conscience by ignoring any power in the body politic to interfere with those matters that alone concern man and his Maker." It was not, however, until March 14, 1643, but yet six years before the Maryland Act of Toleration was passed, that the "Patent for Providence Plantations" was issued, prior to which time the legislation of the colony was without royal sanction. See "Patent for Providence Plantation," and foot note to the same, in "Charters and Constitutions," vol. ii, p. 1594.

[2] Bancroft, vol. i, chapter vii, page 247—10th edition.

[3] Md. Hist. Society Pamphlet.

it had been for many years, that it really seemed as if the long day of tribulation had for ever passed away. Still, "a code which embodied the howl of terror, indignation and vengeance, raised throughout England by the recollections of Philip and Mary, of Alva and Parma, of St. Bartholomew's, of the Inquisition, the Armada, and the Gunpowder Plot, was the stern law of the realm."[4]

Yet a careful and impartial inquiry into the origin of the expedition which Leonard Calvert led to Maryland, will show that neither the odium and the disabilities of political ostracism, nor even the rigors of religious persecution, had anything whatever to do with that expedition. Sufferings for conscience' sake contributed nothing to the issue either immediately or remotely. Had England been as much a stronghold of the Roman Church as is Spain today the Calvert expedition would have sailed to Maryland. Although this is happily nowadays a matter quite capable of satisfactory proof, there was a time when it was not so easy to satisfy the sceptical, with the result that men came to accept without question a wholly untenable

[4] Oration of General Charles E. Phelps, page 30. *Proceedings of the Maryland Historical Society in connection with the 150th anniversary of the settlement of Baltimore*, F. P. No. 15. See also Donaldson, pamphlet of Md. Hist. Soc., page 14.

theory of Maryland's origin; a mere legendary tale at the best. And so it has come to pass, that Leonard Calvert and his fellow travelers appear in history as a band of heroes bearing freedom to man's mind, and their landing place in Maryland, as the most sacred spot on this continent, if not in all the world.

By those who accept this legendary account as a true and faithful description of the beginnings of Maryland, Sir George Calvert, the originator of the enterprise, is regarded as a man sent from God, as almost another Elijah or John the Baptist. And indeed if their judgment is just, it were a crime to regard him otherwise. To but few has it been permitted to be benefactors of all Christendom. Yet it is nothing less than this which is claimed on Calvert's behalf. Of him it is written, that his mission was to open the eyes of men to "the enormity of persecuting men for their religious tenets;" and that "it seemed to be sent to him like an inspiration, that this great evil, this perennial scourge of Christendom, could and should be redressed at once and forever."[5] To accomplish this, he "discarded, so we are assured, the emoluments of earth for the rewards of heaven, and

[5] *United States Catholic Magazine*, April 1842.

exchanged the bright hopes of the present for the unfading certainties of the future."⁶ "He was the first," wrote Bancroft·in language afterwards repudiated by him, though frequently quoted since as if it had never been withdrawn, "in the history of the Christian world to seek for religious security and peace, by the practice of justice, and not by the exercise of power; to plan the establishment of popular institutions with the enjoyment of liberty of conscience."⁷ "It is," says Cardinal Gibbons, "with no small degree of satisfaction, that I point to the State of Maryland as the cradle of civil and and religious liberty, and the land of the sanctuary. Of the thirteen original American Colonies, Mary-

⁶ The *United States Catholic Magazine*, April 1842.
⁷ Bancroft. vol. i, chapter vii, page 244, 10th edition. Surely it is an unfortunate cause which needs the support of words repudiated by their author, (page 158, author's last revision,) and that author George Bancroft, a historian of whom it has been said that his "usual trespasses" are "mis-statements, omission, garbling, perversion and suppression." (See *Critical and Political Essays*, Wallis, page 46, vol. ii.) Indeed, were it not for the prodigal use made of Mr. Bancroft's opinions, I should apologise for quoting him at all, for of all historians he is the worst. Concerning Maryland in particular it is said "that Mr. Bancroft seems to have dedicated himself with particular solicitude to the falsification of her historical record." (Wallis, *Critical and Political Essays*, vol. ii, page 55.) And yet this is the historian whose self-repudiated words are quoted again and again as an authority. See especially Cardinal Gibbons, *Faith of Our Fathers*, p. 230.

land was the only one that was settled by Catholics. She was also the only one that spread aloft over her fair lands the banner of liberty of conscience, and that invited the oppressed of other colonies to seek an asylum beneath its shadow."*

Nor are these merely the opinions of men interested in Maryland, either as her sons or her historians. With remarkable unanimity they are shared by other men, dwelling beyond her borders and having no special interest in her history. George W. Childs, one of the most generous and enlightened of Churchmen whom recent years have seen, assures us that "Calvert and his companions should be at least as widely renowned as the New England Pilgrims, for their Maryland colony was freer than Massachusetts Bay. When Calvert planted Maryland, his infant state stood first and far in advance of all the world. It was built upon the immutable principles of human freedom—the honest heritage of all men, just law, equality before the law, no restraint upon the conscience, no disability on account of religious faith, and absolute self-government."⁹ "Maryland," says John Greenleaf Whittier, "like Pennsylvania, has reason to be

---

* *Faith of Our Fathers*, page 272, edition of 1893.
⁹ Baltimore *Sun*, May 20th, 1897.

proud of Calvert and her first emigrants who built up their state on the sure foundation of religious freedom."[10] Benjamin F. Butler writes, "No character in our colonial history has, in my maturer years, more attracted my admiration, than that of Lord Baltimore. With far-reaching sagacity, and out-growing the general intelligence of his time, he was broad-minded enough to establish for the first time in America, a colony accompanied by absolute religious toleration."[11]

Now next to the question how or when it was first proclaimed that the true genesis of Maryland lay in the desire to found a refuge from the storms of persecution, it would prove a most interesting subject of inquiry, under what circumstances Sir George Calvert made his debut as the advocate of the doctrine of religious toleration. For in his day the duty of tolerating religious error was a part of no man's creed. No preacher of true toleration had yet arisen among men. Nor was the world ready for such a prophet. "Neither the Church of England, the Puritans, nor the (Roman) Catholics believed in religious liberty at that time. Each believed in a state church established by law, and each was intent on establishing its own faith to

[10] *Ibid.* [11] *Ibid.*

the exclusion of every other."[12] Speaking of the religious disputants of Henry the Eighth's time, James Anthony Froude says: They "clamored against persecution, not because it was persecution, but because truth was persecuted by falsehood; and, however furiously the hostile factions exclaimed each that the truth was with them and the falsehood with their enemies, neither the one nor the other disputed the obligation of the ruling powers to support the truth in itself."[13] It was precisely the same in James the First's time. Then, too, men considered it the business of the government to prescribe a religion for its subjects. They also held that the more perfect the government, the more conscientiously and effectually it would do this. Whatever a man's private opinions might be, he had no right outwardly and publicly to assert them, and should he be so unreasonable as to do so, he deserved to be severely punished. Accordingly, Sir George Calvert himself, when Secretary of State, Roman Catholic though he was, made no scruple of sending even his own co-religionists to prison, because they either could

[12] Fisher, vol. ii, page 156. *Men, Women and Manners in Colonial Times.*

[13] Froude, *History of England, Henry the Eighth*, vol. ii, chapter 12, page 480.

not or would not bow down and worship in what was to them the House of Rimmon, with the same facility with which he himself did.[14]

Sir George Calvert's appearance as a 17th Century preacher of religious toleration can therefore only be regarded as a pleasant fiction. It is a fiction, however, which has proved an unexpected piece of good fortune to his co-religionists. His glorious deeds have shed lustre on them. By what process, indeed, our Roman Catholic brethren have come to be regarded as, so to speak, residuary legatees in any glory rightly pertaining to the hero is not manifest. For to the uninitiated they would seem to have been as innocent of any complicity in his doings, as was the Grand Llama of Thibet or the Mikado of Japan. Yet a traditional belief in his great services to humanity, has wrought their Church lasting good. Probably nowhere else in the world among English speaking people, is the Roman Church more kindly thought of than she is in Maryland. Maryland owes much to her, so it is thought, and she has her reward.

[14] Wilhelm. *Maryland Historical Society, Fund Publication*, No. 19, page 77. "The Secretary was named a special commissioner by the King to arrest and punish Seminary Priests and other recusant clergy remaining in the country contrary to the law."

But even some Anglican Churchmen have been quite as zealous in contending for the theory of Sir George Calvert's services to religion as have the Roman Catholics themselves. One has only to consult the pages of Wilberforce, Anderson, Hawks and other church writers to be fully assured of this. When exactly fifty years ago Josiah Polk, a student of Maryland history and a member of the Protestant Episcopal Church, on the authority of the slender stock of materials then at his command, asserted that Sir George Calvert was no religious hero at all, but simply a politician and a merchant, he was pitied even by the members of his own church as being the victim of a narrow-minded and ungenerous spirit; and doughty champions forthwith appeared from among Churchmen themselves, to prove the fallacy of his statements, and so preserve for Rome what was regarded as her due; a very remarkable instance, by the way, of Anglican fair-mindedness.[15]

> Semper ego auditor tantum? numquamne
> reponam . . . . ?

[15] William Meade Addison, of whose defence a Roman Catholic writer says: "With perfect candor I will now add that the best argument I have seen in favor of the Roman Catholic claim, is from the pen of my good and dear friend, William Meade Addison." Davis, *The Day Star*, page 129, note.

This question is forced upon us. How shall it be answered? Are we to remain silent when called upon to believe as sober truth that which belongs to the region of dreamland—the mere folklore and myths of a nation's infancy? Is there never to come a time when, impatient at hearing what we cannot accept, we may cry out with David: "While I was thus musing the fire kindled, and at the last I spake with my tongue?" Of course ere this, other men recognising the legendary character of the accepted theory of Maryland's history, have become impatient at marking its wide acceptance, and have hastened to freely express their opinions about it. "The grandiloquent phrases," says Mr. Sydney George Fisher, "in which the first settlement of the Maryland (Roman) Catholics at St. Mary's, on the Potomac, is described as the home of religious liberty and its only home in the wide world, can deceive only the ignorant."[16] Unfortunately, the firmest believers in this theory, at any rate the most active propagandists of it, have not come only from the lowest of the people. They are of all sorts and conditions of men, not excluding, as we have seen, the most

[16] Fisher, vol. ii, page 156, *Men, Women and Manners in Colonial Times.*

literary, the most eminent, and the most cultured in the land.

That so many really believe in what I do not hesitate to describe as an unhistorical and apocryphal account is capable of a very simple explanation. What Bancroft says of American history in general, may be said with equal truth of Maryland history in particular: "The early history was often written with a carelessness which seized on rumors and vague recollections sufficient authority for an assertion which satisfied prejudice by wanton perversions, and which, where materials were not at hand, substituted the inferences of the writer for authenticated facts. These early books have ever since been cited as authorities, and the errors, sometimes repeated even by considerate writers, whose distrust was not excited, have almost acquired a prescriptive right to a place in the annals, of America." [17] That this explanation is a sufficiently accurate solution of the problem, Bancroft himself afterwards furnished ample proof, for even he, when he came to deal with Maryland, solemnly retailed as reliable history, the folk-lore and legends of her past. But with all due respect for the probity and integrity of these eminent men, and

[17] Bancroft, vol. i, preface, page 6, 10th edition.

of the many others who have expressed the same views, and have published them to the world, I may not fail to ask attention to the fact that the evidence of historical writers who depend upon each other is not cumulative. An echo adds nothing of value to the voice. It is a sound only. Yet every one of these voices is only an echo of other and earlier voices proclaiming without examination and without adequate authority to an uncritical and uninformed age, Sir George Calvert's remarkable services to humanity and to religion.

When Bancroft wrote of Maryland in subsequent editions he made it abundantly clear that he recognized his mistakes. Yet in nothing is his enlightenment more observable than in his treatment of Sir George Calvert. In his first edition he had glorified him as "the first in the history of the Christian world to seek for religious security and peace by the practice of justice, and not by the exercise of power ; to plan the establishment of popular institutions with the enjoyment of liberty of conscience.[18] In his last edition he is content to acknowledge him as deserving " to be ranked among the wisest and most benevolent of lawgivers, for he con-

---

[18] Bancroft, vol. i, page 244, 10th edition. Compare preface, page 6, same vol.

nected his hopes of the aggrandizement of his family with the establishment of popular institutions; and, being a Papist, wanted not charity towards Protestants." Even Calvert's enemies could have taken no exception to so mild a commendation. "But how has the gold become dim and the most fine gold changed."[19] Yet this was Bancroft's latest utterance on the subject.

The religious toleration theory, however, once given to the world, its subsequent propagation has been a matter of course. With the rise among us of a colonial cult, with its societies of colonial dames and its sons of revolutionary sires; its revival of colonial forms and reverence for lengthy pedigrees; there has come upon us as a side developement, a Calvert cult. The offspring, like its parent, serves a useful, though widely different purpose. It owes no apology for its existence. It has a work to do. And by special societies formed for the purpose, by frequent addresses from distinguished men, accorded through its influence generous space and a prominent place in the columns of a sympathetic press, it carries on this work, at once thoroughly practical, and eminently successful.[20]

[19] Lam. iv, 1.
[20] The orator at the jubilee of "The Maryland Pilgrims' Association" did full justice to his theme as he eloquently

We need not therefore marvel greatly at the successful work of the cult; indeed, we shall marvel still less if we remember that in addition to these agencies it has one auxiliary at its command which exceeds in wide-spread influence all other agencies combined. The use in our schools of untrustworthy histories[21] is doing its work grandly and effectively. When once a child has imbibed teaching which is thus given under the sanction of the state, the cult has little to do beyond safe-guarding the impression made. Its aim has in fact been largely accomplished by the state herself. No doubt as soon as the true character of these lesson-books becomes more widely known, the state will refuse its sanction to them.

What evidence do I offer as I challenge with

---

told his hearers that no sooner were the colonists, who, two hundred and sixty-three years ago, "left their homes because of persecution, planted on Maryland soil, than they declared that intolerance and persecution should have no existence among them." (Baltimore *Sun*, March 25th, 1897.) Was even this eulogy considered as altogether too poor a tribute for a jubilee gathering? It would appear so, for shortly afterward another declared, that Calvert as a ruler was the first in the history of the world to declare civil and religious liberty to all men alike. (D. J. Scully in Baltimore *Sun*, May 25th, 1897.) Here we may presume the cult is in full bloom. After this, what more remains to be said?

[21] Cp. Onderdonk's *History for the Use of Schools,*—a mere summary of McSherry's Roman Catholic History. *History of the United States for Schools*, E. Johnstone.

such sweeping statements, the cherished history of a great state? This it will be my object in the following pages to show. I am of course sure to be misrepresented.[22] But then I am also sure of the kindly judgment of those whose opinions I value. "Every one admits," wrote Severn Teackle Wallis, "that if the interests of truth demand at any time a reversal of the judgments of the past, neither prejudice, nor prescription, nor sentiment, can be permitted to stop the way."[23] In this line have we an unconscious prophecy? Did the writer foresee the passing of the "pilgrims?" It may be so. Yet none contended more zealously than he did for the pilgrim theory and the honor due to the Calverts. With such men, however, truth is always the first consideration.

[22] Note the following: "Scepticism has often united with bigotry in the feeble and inglorious attempt to overthrow the facts of external history." . . . "It goes upon the assumption that man is mean; that he has no generous or noble spring of action." Davis, *The Day Star*, page 254.

[23] Wallis, *Critical and Political Essays*, vol. ii, page 105.

CHAPTER II.

SIR GEORGE CALVERT AT THE COURT OF KING JAMES I.

"Oh! that a dream so sweet, so long enjoyed
Should be so sadly, cruelly destroy'd."
MOORE : " Lalla Rookh."

An unpopular effort at royal matchmaking, doomed from the first to failure, and resulting in the politic retirement from office of a prominent state official as a salve to a nation's wounded pride ; a fruitless attempt to achieve wealth where a barren soil and a rigorous climate alike made it almost impossible to produce even the necessaries of life ; a coasting voyage in search of a more genial climate and a kindlier soil, extending from the rocky shores of Newfoundland to the entrance of the James River in Virginia ; a distinct refusal on the part of the Virginians to violate their laws in order to bestow citizenship upon a stranger ; a journey back to England for the purpose of appealing to the king in person for a share of that goodly land which the Virginian colonists were enjoying ; followed by the royal gift of a large portion of the Virginian territory; these were the somewhat inauspicious beginnings which culminated in the founding of the Province of Maryland.

These events carry us back to the days and the court of King James, the Sixth of Scotland and First of England. But if we would understand the history of Maryland aright, and especially her ecclesiastical history, we must go futher back still—to the reigns of Elizabeth and her father Henry, if not even to Henry VII, the first of the Tudor line. We must not disregard the importance of thus looking far away from Maryland herself if we would find the true genesis of her history, and possess the key to many of her problems. For just as it would be useless for one to attempt to form an accurate judgment of a man's character, without knowing anything of his early environment and training, so it would be vain to expect to properly appreciate Maryland's ecclesiastical beginnings without knowing something of those old-world influences which so manifestly contributed towards making her what she is today. Consequently our researches will naturally take us across the seas to England, to Spain, to Italy, and even to wild and rocky Newfoundland in this western world.

Maryland history, whether civil or ecclesiastical, properly opens at the court of King James. There we first meet with George Calvert, to whose instrumentality Maryland owes her political existence. And yet there was another man, a contemporary of Sir George, who, though at the time a prisoner, was bearing no inconsiderable part in the making of the province. This was Sir Walter Raleigh, "that prince of courtesy," the foremost statesman of his age, "and founder of the English Empire in America,"[1] as the tablet erected by Americans in Westminster Abbey justly bears witness, a man of such brilliant and varied gifts that we may say of him as of Shakespeare : " We shall not look upon his like again." Such a man even in prison could not be without influence ; and when in after years Calvert sought to plant a colony in Newfoundland, and, failing to achieve success there, turned his face with like intent towards prosperous Virginia, he was in truth but following the lead of the great statesman to whom he had been already largely indebted for valuable information and advice, and for important sea-charts and very helpful manuscripts on the art of war, and on the sea-ports of the world.[2]

[1] *A History of the Protestant Episcopal Church in America*, Wilberforce, page 9.
[2] *Terra Mariæ*, Neill, page 16.

George Calvert was born about 1578 in the little Yorkshire town of Kipling, some twenty miles from Durham, where now, as then, Cuthbert's Cathedral

> "huge and vast
> Looks down upon the Wear."

It was perhaps the proximity of his home to Durham, which accounted for his entering Trinity College, Oxford, a College which owed its foundation and maintenance to the princely munificence of the Bishops of Durham. He remained at Oxford until he graduated, when he became private secretary to Sir Robert Cecil, then Secretary of State, and afterwards Earl of Salisbury, one of the most influential men in England. It was an auspicious beginning for any young aspirant for political honors. Soon afterwards young Calvert came under the notice of the king himself, by whom he was appointed clerk to the Privy Council. It then seemed as if his ultimate success was assured. Promotion so rapidly followed that at forty years of age he had actually succeeded his patron in the secretaryship. What might have been his future, and what in that event the future of Maryland, had the affairs of the nation gone smoothly on, it is impossible to say. He might have become Prime Minister of England, and Maryland might never have known him. But the king whom Calvert served was not distinguished for the possession of tact, or even of common sense, and his new Secretary of State unfortunately eventually came to stake upon one of the worst of his errors of judgment his own political future. All England was against James. "Consider," wrote an intelligent foreigner, "for pity's sake what must be the state and condition of a prince whom Parliament braves and despises, and who is universally hated by the whole people."[3]

Awkward in address and slovenly in appearance, of excessive vanity, ridiculous prejudices and infinite littleness of soul, and yet withal possessed of such overweening notions of his own kingly prerogatives, it is not to be wondered at that James' subjects regarded him more as a buffoon than as a king. This was, however, the man under whom Calvert had come to the front as the exponent in Parliament of his follies, and the minister to put them into practice. It need hardly be stated that to have been the obsequious follower of such a monarch as this, will scarcely tend, in the opinion

[3] *Ibid*, page 22. Vide also, *History of the English People*. Green, vol. iv, page 15.

of those most competent to judge, to exalt Calvert to the level of the world's greatest benefactors.

King James had for years set his heart upon marrying his son Charles, then heir to the throne, to the Infanta of Spain.[4] One marvels that even by him so foolish a design could have been entertained, notwithstanding the fascinating vision of the flowing into his depleted treasury of 2,000,000 crowns in Spanish gold, which went with the princess as dowry.[5] No doubt Spain, with an empire extending over both the old and the new worlds, loomed large in the eyes of the man who, as James VI. of Scotland, had merely been king of "the smallest and meanest of European realms," and whose "actual power had been less than that of an English peer."[6] Dazzled, however, as he was by his unexpected elevation to the English throne, the alliance of his house to the first power in Europe seemed the last prize of greatness. But Spain was not what she had been. The destruction of the Armada had ruined forever both her naval prestige and her naval supremacy, while her long and impotent struggle with the Netherlands had greatly weakened her army. She was a falling

[4] Green, vol. iv, page 30.
[5] *Ibid*, vol. iv, page 31; Smollet, vol. v, page 58.
[6] Green, vol. iii, page 438.

state. Even Buckingham was fully prepared "to prove the actual penurie and proud beggarie" of Spain.

But it was not this which weighed with Englishmen, as they considered the question of the Spanish marriage. There might be negotiations of peace between the nations, but the English people had not forgotten that if Spain had had her way, their country would have been reduced to a condition little better than that of a Spanish province, and their national Church, which *Magna Charta* had declared should be forever free, again brought into bondage. Naturally, therefore, a country which had thus perilously assailed their liberties as Englishmen and their faith as Churchmen, and which still cherished her ancient spirit, was hateful in their eyes, and any treaty of peace with her must have been as a wall built with untempered mortar.

Nor was this all. Men still lived who had seen the fires of Mary's reign, fires which it was more than suspected had been kindled by that misguided queen under the influence of her Spanish husband. Rightly or wrongly, the English people regarded Philip as guilty, and they breathed more freely when, unwilling to live longer among a nation which so evidently detested him, the gloomy husband of Queen Mary shook the dust of England off his feet, and returned to his own land. The English nation had had, in fact, too recent experience of a Spanish match to view another with equanimity.

Neither did the Spaniards themselves desire such an alliance. They, too, had had their experience, and it was not a happy one. They had not forgotten the wrongs of the Infanta of Aragon. Perhaps another English king might also find it convenient to repudiate his Spanish wife while retaining her Spanish dowry. Moreover, the utter defeat of their comrades at the hands of Drake and his brave sailors, had filled them with bitterness. Its memory rankled in their breasts, and until they had obtained satisfaction for the national disgrace, they wanted, not peace, but a sword.

Then, too, they had in reality nothing to gain by the marriage. After all, it was only a one-sided affair. Consequently, the stars might sooner be expected to fall from heaven at the bidding of King James than that, with their consent, this matrimonial alliance should be made. Nevertheless they had no objection to dally with the proposals made to them. But their negotiations were all a blind, a mere pretense, a veritable chasing of shadows, a device to gain time for the exigencies of Spanish politics, "a stratagem in fact of the court of Spain."[7] A suspicion that he and his father were being duped, seems at length to have crossed the mind of Prince Charles himself. And so in part, though it may have been, in a spirit of gallantry, but certainly in part imbued with the determination that an end of all this dallying should be reached, attended only by Buckingham, he suddenly left England in disguise and appeared in person at Madrid. What this act meant to the national feeling in England—the shame and wounding of the nation's spirit and pride—we cannot fathom. All men, in the words of Constance to King John, cried out:

"Gone to be married!
Gone to swear a peace!
It cannot be."

At once the rumor of the prince's visit flew to Newmarket. The Council knelt to implore the king to tell them if it were true. They were told it was true. For Sir George Calvert it was the beginning of the end.

The tedious prosecution by Prince Charles of his suit, closing with the visit to the Spanish court.

[7] Smollet, vol. v, page 38.

somewhat recalls the visit paid by Ethelbert, King of Kent, and Bretwalda of Britain, to Charibert, King of Paris, as a suitor for the hand of the Princess Bertha. Before Charibert would consent to the marriage, he required that his daughter should have liberty to practise her own religion, and to have her own chapel and priests. And in this the French king did wisely, for Ethelbert was only a pagan, while Bertha was a Christian. That Prince Charles was a member of the same Holy Catholic Church as themselves, howbeit of another land, did not apparently occur to the Spaniards. Like Bertha, their princess was to have her own chapel, priests, religious household, and perfect freedom of conscience, all of which Charles readily promised her.[8] She was furthermore, to have the right of directing the religious education of her children. This, too, was granted. But the Spaniards, following the leadership of the Pope,[9] were still unsatisfied. Something yet hindered. The truth was that Charles had been too complaisant. The Spaniards would have been better pleased if he had stood out against granting some of their conditions. So gracious, however,

---

[8] Smollet, vol. v, page 62.
[9] Hume, vol. vi, page 133.

had he been, that they were in a dilemma. Yet what excuse for any further delay could they offer? Apparently none. Judging Prince Charles from the standpoint of narrow-minded and bigoted men, they had asked for perfect religious liberty for the princess, and he had pledged it. Beyond this no loyal and upright Christian could go; and whatever were the faults of Charles, whether as man or prince, disloyalty to his own National Church was not one. It was indeed his loyalty to that Church which, twenty-two years later, cost him his life, when it was easily within his power to have saved it. Even the influence of the Roman Catholic princess he afterwards married, devotedly attached to her as he was, never weakened his earnest attachment to his own Church. In this at any rate Charles was consistent throughout his whole career.

The next request which the Spanish court made, shows the desperate straits to which Charles' unexpected liberality had reduced the Spaniards. He must become a Roman Catholic, or the infanta could not be his.[10] This was the climax. Angry and mortified at such unreasonable treatment, the prince abruptly returned to England, where the

[10] Smollet, vol. v, page 63.

ringing of bells and firing of guns testified to the relief of the nation. The Spanish party, as the few court sympathizers were called, among whom Calvert was conspicuous, fell into immediate disgrace.

Probably as a Roman Catholic, Calvert looked forward to the advent of a queen of his own faith as likely to be of considerable advantage to him. It is true that he had not always been openly of the Roman obedience, having outwardly been for many years a member of the Church of England; in fact, ever since he obtained court preferment. But, like many other secret Romanists, he had withheld the revelation of his religious belief until the time should come when it would not be disadvantageous to acknowledge it.[11] Of course Calvert could not have been possessed of very deep spiritual feelings. Politicians are very rarely men of markedly devout minds, or of strongly formed religious habits, and this particular politician was no better than his class. His religion had never been burdensome. When it appeared likely to become so, he readily dispensed with it; all too readily, if Archbishop Abbott's remark that he had turned papist three times be correct; and as

[11] He avowed himself a Romanist after his fall from power.

a contemporary the Archbishop knew more of Calvert than we do, and as an Archbishop of Canterbury he was not likely to be found making reckless statements, easy of refutation, concerning the public men of his day. The truth about Calvert appears to be that he was an ambitious man who had placed the reaching of the goal of his ambition before everything else. With this in view, he was ready to barter away the civil liberties of his countrymen, the best interests of his country, and even his own religious and spiritual welfare. The seals of office glittered in his eyes. Prompted then by ambition he had conformed to the National Church, and had not been found afraid to use even religion itself as the ladder by which he might rise to wealth and fame. So it came about that to the world he was an Anglican, providing Anglican ministrations for his emigrants, laying his Roman Catholic wife to rest in the Anglican church-yard at Hertingfordbury, and setting up a tablet to her memory in the little village church ;[12] even holding official positions which required him to administer English laws against Roman Catholics, while all the time, so far as he was anything at all, a mem-

[12] *Md. Hist, Soc., F. P., No. 20.* page 77, Wilhelm.

ber of the Holy Roman Church. Well may the satirist say:

> "All live by seeming.
> The beggar begs with it, and the gay courtier
> Gains land and title, rank and rule, by seeming."

Had the prince brought back his Spanish bride, Calvert's political aspirations would have had a fair chance of success. As it was, his political future was wrecked. Placing his resignation in the hands of the king whom he had obsequiously served, as Wolsey hath it, "Not wisely, but too well," he retired from official life with six thousand pounds obtained by the enforced sale of his office, a pension of one thousand pounds per annum, and the title of Baron of Baltimore[13] in the peerage of Ireland.[14] This was not much for what Calvert had

---

[13] Fiske, *Old Virginia and Her Neighbours*, vol. i, page 255, appears to be in error in identifying the Baltimore in County Cork with the place which gave Sir George Calvert his title. See *Md. Hist. Soc., F. P., No. 20*, page 118, Wilhelm. Sir George Calvert's barony was in Longford County, and cannot be seen "from the deck of a steamer passing the southwest coast of Ireland, not far from Cape Clear."

[14] McMahon, Page 9; Hawks, page 18. The statement often made that Calvert resigned his office because he had become a Roman Catholic is inconsistent with admitted facts: (1) Roman Catholics were not debarred from employment at Court under James I. (2) It was known that Calvert himself was a Roman Catholic when he received his appointment. "The

done, for his Irish peerage did not carry with it
the privileges of the peerage of England.[15] Indeed,
there he was a commoner still, and his pension was

office of treasurer was put in commission, and Secretary Win-
wood dying about the same time, his place was divided between
Naunton and Calvert, the first of whom was a Protestant and
the other a Papist." This was in 1616. See Smollet, vol. v,
page 40. Moreover, in 1620 he is expressly mentioned by name
along with the Earls of Arundel and Worcester, Lord Digby
and others, as "popishly affected." Kennedy, page 38. Why
should he have thought it necessary to resign, even if he had
been recently converted? The only motive that could compel
him to such a course for conscience' sake was the necessity
of taking the oaths of supremacy and allegiance, and these
he had already taken. (3) When Calvert avowed his Romanism
in 1625 Archbishop Abbott said of him : " He apparently turneth
Papist, which he now professeth, this being the third time he
hath been to blame that way." See Wilhelm, page 112. (4) In
1624 Calvert's eldest son, Cecil, was in his 18th year ; Leonard,
who came next, in his 16th. They were both Roman Catholics, so were all his children. When did they become so?
Was Cecil "converted" when his father was? Was Leonard?
This allegiance of all his family to Rome, together with the
fact that his mother was of the Roman obedience, and that his
own adherence to it was well-known long before his acknowledgement of it, has even suggested the question : Was he
ever anything else than a Roman Catholic? (5) Again, the
king, who entertained the most violently unreasonable feelings
of hatred towards " perverts " but who was kind and considerate for those who were born Roman Catholics, always retained
his attachment for Calvert to the last, even making him a peer
of the realm only a few months after his supposed conversion,
and willingly granting to him on his own terms the charter of
his Newfoundland plantation.

[15] Green, vol. iv, pages 19, 20. Baronies in this reign, and
especially Irish baronies, were very cheap affairs. They were
actually put up to sale.

on paper only. Yet the Secretary's devotion to to his master's interests in other matters than that of the Spanish marriage had been unquestioned, and he was clearly entitled to his gratitude. "As a Parliamentary tool, to bribe, bully and argue in the House of Commons against the great Coke, and the noble band of patriots who strove to give England a free parliament,[16] James had had no more faithful henchman.

But it is through this contemplated marriage that we know Calvert well. We see him as he was, and he was not one whom Americans can honor for his works' sake. Doubtless he was sincere in all he did, but he was at heart an imperialist. His aims were those of Strafford in the next reign, or of Bismarck in our own day. He sought to concentrate all power in the hands of the king. "The justice of history must avow," writes Bancroft, "that he misconceived the interests of his country and his king, and took part in exposing to danger civil liberty and the rights of the Parliament of England."[17] Surely a heavy indictment this of a benefactor of the human race. For less than this statesmen have been impeached as enemies of their country.

[16] Prowse, *Hist. of Nfld.*, page 92.
[17] Bancroft, *U. S. History*, last edition, page 158.

But is it not passing strange that the man who was against all personal liberty, whose voice and vote alike, whose secret bribes and potent threats were all on the side of unconditional surrender to the extremest of monarchical pretensions, whose colonial charters drawn up by himself,[18] destitute of a single democratic element and sanctioned by two complacent kings, clothed him with powers never before and never since, to the same extent, conferred on any British subject, so that it was in no mere figure of speech but in accurate and well-chosen phrase that his successor described himself as "true and absolute lord of Maryland and Avalon; whose thorough-going advocacy of royal measures in defiance of popular opinion brought his public career in England to an untimely end; who, on the ground that it was the name of the Spanish historian who taught the heresy that "the will of the people is higher than the law of tyrants," objected to the name Marianna for Maryland, suggested by King Charles, and who hesitated not to claim in Parliament that the American territory, having been acquired by conquest, was subject

---

[18] McMahon, vol. i, page 10; Anderson, vol. ii, page 113; Bancroft, vol. i, page 241, says: "The nature of the document itself, and concurrent opinion, leave no room for doubt that it was penned by Lord Baltimore himself."

exclusively to the royal prerogative;[19] is it not strange that, by a unique irony of fate here, in America, the land of all others furthest removed from sympathy with all such principles and ambitions, this man should have come to be widely regarded as a benevolent lawgiver, a patron of religious liberty, and a lover of popular institutions? Certainly it is not out of such material that great religious reformers and popular leaders are commonly made.

[19] Quoted by John P. Kennedy, page 22.

CHAPTER III.

THE CHARTER OF AVALON.

1624-1627.

"O! let your honour cheerfully go on,
End well your well begun plantation."
—ROBERT HAYMAN.

When Sir George Calvert, in 1624, found himself, like Othello, with occupation gone, he had no intention of settling down to a life of idleness. Those who describe him as a man of restless energy, possessed of an endless capacity for work, are probably right. Idleness to such a man is unbearable. He must work, or he will die. But what was he to do? As a statesman he was discredited. His countrymen had repudiated his policy. Public life in England was closed against him. For ordinary business he was now, of course, totally unfitted. Moreover, the fascination which political life always exercises over those once drawn within the vortex of its influence, was upon him. Immediately following our last presidential campaign, a keen-sighted observer of men and things wrote concerning the defeated candidate: " Hereafter life in glorious ease becomes impossible; he must continue whirling about at high pressure and seek excitement."[1] It is ever thus. It is living death to the senator, the prime minister, the president, to go back to the obscurity of private life. But it was this hard fate which now clouded the horizon of King James' late Secretary of State.

There was, however, for Sir George Calvert, a way of escape. Across the seas, in the Island of Newfoundland, was a door of hope. He could there take possession of land which was already his; establish a prosperous plantation; retrieve his fallen fortunes, and at the same time work out his own peculiar ideal of what a true government should be. He had owned land there since 1621. In that year a certain Sir William Vaughan had sold to him a part of an immense territory which he held in the southeast corner of the island.[2] Vaughan and Calvert had been friends and fellow-students at Oxford, and quite in a natural way, as one palms off a worthless horse on a friend, Sir William disposed of a large portion of his unprofitable grant to his old friend of Oxford days.[3]

---

[1] Mr. Andrew Carnegie, *North American Review*, January, 1897.
[2] Prowse, Second Edition, Chapter 5, Page 111.
[3] *Ibid.*

Here, however, was a haven of refuge from the storms now threatening his future. Deeming that the time had come to seek this haven, on the 16th of March, 1625, he publicly announced his intention of migrating to Newfoundland. But the death of King James on the 25th of March, only twelve days afterwards, threw all his plans into confusion. In consequence of that event, Calvert did not actually arrive in the colony until the last week in July, 1627; more than two years afterwards.

Newfoundland is not nowadays regarded as a very desirable place, whether for settlement or investment. The most ancient of English colonies, it is certainly the most unfortunate of them all; a land of "historic misfortune," in the phrase of the present Prime Minister of England, Lord Salisbury, the heir of Calvert's early patron. There is now little to attract anyone to its shores, if we except the lover of picturesque nature, the fisherman and the sportsman. These will not be disappointed. But for all others, that country can hold out few inducements. The patriotism of its hardy people will, I know, not hesitate to dispute this, for the Newfoundlander dearly loves his island home, and can ill brook that any should think little of it. But then patriotism always sees through rose-colored glasses. And the Newfoundland immigrant, if such there be, after a brief experience of the leanness of the country, will be very apt to agree with me.

Such at least was my own conclusion when some years ago I first found myself off the Newfoundland coast. We had but just come out of a latitude where the warm, sunny air of May had made an ocean voyage delightful, into a latitude where the sun indeed still shone brightly, but the air was cold and bracing, and the fog was everywhere. Soon isolated pans of ice appeared dazzlingly white in the cold, black water; then

> "It grew wondrous cold;
> And ice, mast-high, came floating by,
> As green as emerald."

At last immense ice-fields hove in sight and completely surrounded us. Then the dark, misty sky, catching from them a luminous appearance, flashed as with the trembling light of the aurora. Our environment was altogether Arctic. Two days later we reached land. It was not prepossessing. Dark red cliffs, barren as rocks could be, and for the most part covered with snow, rose up precipitously before us. Presently, through an opening cleft in the rocky coast line, appropriately termed "The Narrows," we discerned the city of St. John's, clinging to the steep hill-sides as if it were an Alpine village.

The country we were looking upon had once been known to the Northmen, who as early as the year 1000, under the leadership of a son of Eric the Red, had coasted along its shores and explored its resources. Strangely enough, those hardy sailors of the Northern seas have left traces of their presence behind them. At a spot[4] not far from St. John's where at times the wildest waves of the Atlantic break on an iron-girt shore, their Scandinavian runes, cut in the solid rock, may still be seen. But the visit of the Northmen had long been as a dream when one awaketh, and as a tale that is told. All knowledge even of the existence of the island had entirely passed away, when Sebastian Cabot came in 1497, and revealed it to the world a second time. Notwithstanding, however, Cabot's rediscovery, it remained for more than a century a veritable no-man's land, "without law, religion or government." On the coming in 1583, of Sir Humphrey Gilbert, half brother of Sir Walter Raleigh, there dawned a hope of better days, as Gilbert, with pompous ceremonial, claimed

[4] Grates Cove, Trinity Bay.

the island for Queen Elizabeth. But it was a mere ceremony, nothing more; and when it was performed, Gilbert embarked for his native land, which he was destined never to see again. His death in mid-Atlantic left Newfoundland to continue without interruption on her chaotic way.

Yet poor and of no reputation as she is, Newfoundland possesses unique honors of which more favored American lands cannot boast. Hers is a glorious heritage. On her shores Englishmen held their first Christian service in the new world. There also was celebrated for the first time the Holy Communion. There, too, long before the settlers on the banks of the James or the Potomac had come from their English homes, or Drake and his chaplain had carried the Book of Common Prayer within the Golden Gates of California, the prayers of the old English Church, uttered by her own clergy, had been offered up to God.[5]

Newfoundland can also claim honors of another kind. For over a hundred years, she was England's one and only colony. On her soil England first obtained a foothold in the New World; there laying the foundation of her colonial empire.

[5] Lanslot Thirkill, of London, received £20 "upon a prest for his shipp going towards the new Ilande, 22nd March, 1498;" See Prowse, Page 12.

The mother country has not always been mindful of her debt to her eldest daughter, yet Newfoundland has always been loyal to her. It was she who in the dark days of 1649, when men's hearts were failing them for fear, boldly offered King Charles a place of refuge from the men who were seeking his life.[6] Aye, even to the early American settlers Newfoundland has not been without honor. She was the parent colony which supplied New York with men and appliances when the younger settlement sought to establish a fishery at Sandy Hook, and she it was who, at an earlier date, in 1623, saved the "kingdom of Virginia" from semi-starvation by a timely cargo of fish.[7]

It is thus evident that Newfoundland, two and a half centuries ago, occupied a very different position from that which she now occupies, and unless we bear this in mind, we may go astray and fail to appreciate the situation. Did Englishmen then think of foreign adventure, there was no land which presented so favorable an opportunity as their only colony. In other lands they met the foreigner, and lived under his flag; but there they lived under their own, and were amid their own

[6] Prowse, Second Edition, Page 135.
[7] *Ibid*, Page 151.

kith and kin. Nowhere else could they do this, for the fond colonization dreams of Elizabeth's reign had all come to naught; having vanished like shadows. Gone was Raleigh's El Dorado. Perished, too, his settlement at Roanoke. An Indian raid had quenched it in blood. Drake's voyage, so full of promise, had borne no fruit. England, notwithstanding the auspicious beginnings of her colonial policy, had not a single settlement left on all the American coast. There was small encouragement for Englishmen to go forward in colonization ventures, and nothing at all to suggest their future greatness as the actual planters of this vast continent—the true founders and ancestors of this now mighty American nation.

After the peaceful settlement of King James upon the English throne, when England and Scotland at last recognized the same sovereign, the passion for colonial adventure broke out again, and public attention in England was inevitably centred first upon Newfoundland. Why should not the island become the centre of British trade in America, and a lesser England? Its waters, in treasures of fish inexhaustible, were richer than gold-mines— and such treasures! No inland mines famed for wealth were like those around her coast. Bacon spoke but the simple truth when he said that the Newfoundland fishing grounds were "richer than the mines of Peru." Immense tracts of fertile land awaited the coming of the husbandman, while primeval forests stood there in lonely grandeur. In the same latitude as France, it was naturally supposed that its climate was far superior to that of the mother country. Here assuredly great fortunes might easily be made, and life itself be passed amid genial influences and pleasant surroundings. Moreover, popular rumour had it that it was about to become a naval station for the great northwest passage to the Indies, soon to be opened. A book entitled *Westward Ho* had just been published, describing the advantages of the country in the most glowing terms, and a copy of it had been sent to the Privy Council. Newfoundland had thus loomed up out of the fog as a newer and better El Dorado.

At once many chartered companies, like the Royal Chartered Company of South Africa today, sprang into existence, whose business it was to open up so favored an island for immediate occupation and commerce. The first of these companies was that of John Guy, alderman and merchant of the city of Bristol. Taking several men with him Guy first went to Newfoundland in 1610. Well satisfied with what he saw, he returned to England to make preparations for colonizing on an extensive scale. In 1612 he again arrived in Newfoundland with a very large company, "all of civil life, artizans and traders," accompanied also by the Rev. Erasmus Stourton, the first clergyman of the Church of England to settle in that colony.[8] Other traders soon followed. In a few years there were not less than six regularly constituted trading companies, which had parcelled out the whole island among themselves. One of the latest to arrive of these companies was that of Sir George Calvert, under the spiritual care of the Rev. Richard James, a clergyman, like Stourton, of the National Church, whom Calvert had sent out with his emigrants.[9]

The Rev. Richard James, an Oxford graduate, seems to have been intimately connected with the fortunes of Sir George Calvert. His death took place in England in 1638.[10] Later on we shall read of a

---

[8] Stourton's headquarters were at Cupids, but his parish or mission extended completely around Conception Bay, and from Cape St. Francis to Ferryland, the estate Sir George Calvert was eventually to purchase from Sir William Vaughan.

[9] Neill, *Terra Mariæ*, Page 46.

[10] *Athenæ Oxoniensis*, and *Gentleman's Magazine* 1767 and 1768, Vol. i, Pp. 524, 525.

Rev. Richard James on Kent Island, in Chesapeake Bay, who made his appearance in the "Great Bay" about the time that Sir George himself appeared there. He also was an Oxford man, and died in England in 1638. It would seem, therefore, a reasonable supposition, that the Richard James of Avalon was the Richard James of Kent Island. If so we have here an interesting proof that Sir George Calvert had not entirely forsaken the profession of politics, and that his right hand had not forgotten its cunning. Though then a professed Roman Catholic, and having clergy of his own faith in his province yet, as we shall see, he took care when the time came for him to migrate from Newfoundland to Virginia, to leave the Roman priests behind him, and sail in company with the Church of England clergyman to the Church of England colony. On their arrival in Virginia the clergyman and the ex-Secretary seem to have parted company, the one settling down to minister in spiritual things to the settlers on Kent Island, in Chesapeake Bay; the other to secure through his influence at court as large a portion of the Virginians' territory as he possibly could, including Kent Island itself, on the plea that it was unoccupied territory.

It is not without good and sufficient reason that I draw attention to the Newfoundland experiences of Sir George Calvert. Of the Privy Council, to whom had been sent all those wonderful accounts of Newfoundland's possibilities as a field for lucrative investment and colonization, Sir George was the clerk. That fact indeed explains all. It makes his motives perfectly transparent. Like most public men of his age, he had become interested in plans for colonizing. Already a member of the Virginia Company, and also of the New England Company, he bought his Newfoundland property in 1621, when he had apparently no more expectation of ever seeing it than an ordinary citizen among us has of settling in Dahomey or Pekin; for at the time of that purchase he was high in the royal favor as a principal Secretary of State, and a member ostensibly of the Anglican Church. As such he needed no sympathy; he desired no protection; he was a victim of no intolerance; he was looking for no place of refuge. He was not in any sense a sufferer from the fines and confiscations which were occasionally inflicted on the obscure and unimportant members of his Church. On the contrary, he was one of those who wore soft clothing, and were in kings' houses. Yet it was to this very circumstance he owed it that he had become a colonial landowner. He had been anxious to eke out his income, all too slender for his requirements as a courtier, by judicious investments abroad. With this in view, he had purchased that plantation on the peninsula which eventually received the name of Avalon, but whether from himself or another is unknown.[11]

Having acquired his transatlantic property, Calvert at once took steps to develop it by sending out a certain Captain Wynne as agent, or governor, with twelve men under him. In the following year he dispatched twenty-two more men, under the leadership of one Daniel Powell. With this latter company it was that the Rev. Richard James went as chaplain.[12]

In the meantime, political affairs in England had taken such a turn, that Calvert had probably begun to think of Avalon, not only as a region bought in

---

[11] "The name Avalon is derived from Avalon in Somersetshire, England, the traditional site of the first preaching of the Gospel in Britain, where Avalonius is supposed to have converted the British King Lucius, and all his Court, to Christianity." The Charter of Avalon is dated 1623. See Belknap, Vol. II, Page 365, and authorities there cited.

[12] That Calvert himself dated his letters from Ferryland is a presumption against his having given Avalon its name. That name in fact described the whole peninsula, and not the slice of it which Calvert bought.

the way of a mere business speculation, but also as a place of refuge in his declining years, and as a home where he could find shelter when he should be put out of the stewardship. The marriage negotiations had evidently failed. With the return of the prince, Calvert's worst fears were realized. Some months after the failure of the scheme, Abbott, Archbishop of Canterbury, wrote: "Secretary Calvert hath never looked merrily since the coming of the Prince out of Spain."[13] And no wonder! He was a ruined man, and he was now contemplating exile as a painful necessity. To Avalon his thoughts were turning. Under these circumstances it was manifestly desirable that he should have a better title to his property than that which he had derived from Sir William Vaughan. Accordingly he now had his grant re-confirmed, and passed under the Great Seal of England. In doing this he was acting wisely. He would have, so far as it was possible to obtain it, a secure dwelling place which none could take away from him. On the seventh of April, 1623, the charter was issued, and there is little doubt that royal sympathy with Calvert in his misfortunes explains

---

[13] From Abbott to Sir T. Roe. *Roe Letters*, Page 372. Quoted by Walpole in his *Noble Authors*, and by Kennedy, Page 39.

satisfactorily the remarkably favorable terms granted to him.[14]

This charter has, so we are informed, a unique interest attached to it, inasmuch as it was "one of the earliest instruments prepared as a basis of social, civil and religious organization of English colonists on the North American Coast."[15] Yet after all it was destitute of a single democratic element. It was an instrument which solely looked to the establishment of ancient feudalism in the new world. By it Sir George Calvert became absolute lord of all persons within his province, clothed with powers greater than those possessed by the King of England himself, the nearest approach to them being the powers granted by William the Conqueror to the Counts Palatine of Durham, Chester, and Kent. In fact, Sir George Calvert's province in Newfoundland was confessedly modelled after the ancient feudal palatinate of Durham; while he himself was declared to be in his palatinate, what the former Prince Bishops of Durham had ever been in theirs. This was no slight honor. Counts Palatine were the deputies of the king, commissioned to act in his name, and generally to

[14] Sloan MSS, 170. Vide Prowse, Page 131.
[15] *Md. Hist. Soc.*, F. P. No. 20, Wilhelm, Page 129.

be his vice-gerents. Within their own boundaries they possessed *quasi* regal rights as complete as those which the king exercised in his own palace, and hence indeed the title of Palatinate bestowed on the places of their jurisdiction. But Calvert could not well have received like powers with those of the English Counts Palatine without having received greater. Durham was not far from Westminster; whereas an ocean rolled between the absolute lord of Avalon and the court of the English king. It was precisely this danger which was pointed out, and effectually guarded against, when the Maryland Charter was under consideration.[16]

[16] *Considerations to the Patent to the Lord Baltimore dat. 20 Junij Octavo Car.* (1632).
"There is intended to bee granted the Liberties of a County Palatine and there is noe exception of Writts of Error or of the last appeale to the King as by Lawe ought to bee.
INCONVENIENCES.
[1] "That the Lord Baltimore hath power to grant any part in fee to whom hee please which may bee Aliens, Savages, or Enemies of the Kingdome, and yet their children born there shall bee denizens by express words of the Patent. fol. 7 and 8.
"It is inconvenient that the Lord Baltimore should have power to make peace or entertaine warre with any att his or his heires pleasure and soe to engage all the rest of the English Colonies (which as to strangers cannot bee distinguished the One Colonie from the other) by his and his heires owne voluntary Acts which matter is of that importance as concernes the utter ruine or essentiall safety of the whole English Plantation in all that Country of America.
"There is no restraint in the Patent of furnishing the Sav-

THE CHARTER OF AVALON. 53

To a certain extent this menace to the liberties of the settlers existed in all English colonies. The governors, being men of rank and fortune, had generally sufficient influence to shield themselves from punishment in the somewhat improbable event, considering the distance from the mother country, and the tedious and uncertain means of communication and transport thither, of an impeachment at home, on the charge of playing the tyrant. Spain, whose colonial experiences had begun earlier than those of England, had found it necessary " to hold these petty tyrants in check by means of regular tribunals, or Royal Audiences,

ages with Armes &c and such like if in case they should invade the other Colonies.

"The power of giving Honors, Lands, Privileges, and other Franchises to such as will take of him will bee in short tyme an Occasion to dispeople the King's Colonie and to people his with persons of all sorts whatsoever from the other Colonies in Religion Assertion or otherwise.

"Royall and Imperiall Power which is granted in all things of Sovraignty saving only an Allegiance to the King's Majesty, to the Lord Baltimore to be granted to any Person in ffee Simple in Places soe remote and where the King's Subjects are soe neare Neighbors may prove very dangerous by exalting the One and decreasing the other, the Counsells reliefe and Actions of all the other Colonies beeing to depend on soe great distance as England from Virginia, and Lord Baltimore's Colonie having power in themselves to manage their affaires free from all dependency on others.

Archives of Maryland, Council Vol. 3, Page 18.

as they were termed, which, composed of men of character and learning, might interpose the arm of the law or at least the voice of remonstrance, for the protection of both colonist and native." Here was a safeguard wholly wanting in Calvert's case. How necessary such a safeguard was, the hard fate of Vasquez Nunez de Balboa, the illustrious discoverer of the Pacific, abundantly shows;[17] for at the early age of forty-two he was beheaded through jealousy of his growing reputation, and by an extraordinary abuse of his power on the part of one of the colonial governors of Spain. And it it was because of charges brought against him of similar mal-administration as Governor-General of India, that Warren Hastings, notwithstanding his splendid services in that country, was impeached before the Lords at Westminster. Nay, even in these days of rapid communication, we have had in the doings in Africa of a German High Commissioner, a signal instance of what a petty tyrant, living at a distance from the mother country, can be guilty of in the way of oppressive dealings towards those unfortunate enough to live under his rule.[18] Now Calvert's case differed in nothing

[17] Prescott, *Mexico*, Vol. 1, Page 231.

[18] Dr. Carl Peters, sometime German High Commissioner, and a well-known African explorer, was dismissed from the

from that of any other colonial governor save in this: that he had a more despotic and irresponsible position; for in the case of a controversy between himself and his subjects no appeal could be taken to any British court.[19] So far as the King of England could do it, he had established a czar in the new world.

Knowing Newfoundland only through misleading reports Calvert thought at once of taking full advantage of his opportunities, and beginning without delay the work of reconstructing his shattered fortunes. His province promised abundant returns. Unfortunately he was to pay dearly for his experience. With life politically wrecked in England, entailing the loss of his secretaryship, with its official status, accompanying income, and pleasant associations at court, there was trouble enough for one day. But troubles do not come singly. Presently evil tidings began to reach him from beyond the seas. All was not well in Avalon. His choice of Wynne and Powell as his stewards was soon to be recognized as a most unfortunate one.

German Imperial Service in April, 1896, after having been convicted of grossly abusing his authority in being guilty of extreme cruelty, and even worse offenses, to natives while he was Commissioner.

[19] Fiske, *Old Virginia and Her Neighbors*, Vol. I, Page 285.

Both men had their counterpart in the unjust steward of the Gospel. Sending to their master glowing reports of work done, and predicting fruitful harvests in the near future, they had so lured on the unwary Sir George, that upon casting up his accounts shortly afterwards, he found he had spent on the acquisition of his estate, and on necessary working expenses, between twenty-five and thirty thousand pounds. It was an immense sum to lose, for its purchasing value was far greater than it is now. It may be that Wynne and Powell, knowing they had got all they were likely to get out of the unfortunate ex-Secretary, had now no longer any reason to hide from him the real state of affairs. At any rate, Calvert soon had an inkling of the truth. His colony was evidently in a very bad way. He had been putting his money into a bag full of holes. Thus for more reasons than even to find a place of refuge for himself and his family, it would be desirable for him to hasten out to his Newfoundland plantation.

Calvert's misfortunes were indeed rapidly multiplying. One cannot help deeply sympathising with him. In his sorrows he reminds us of Jacob, to which venerable Hebrew Patriarch, as having also a keen eye for business, I may not inappropriately compare him, who, when an old and worn out man, and feeling that God's hand had gone out against him, exclaimed in bitterness of soul, "All these things are against me."[20] Nor does the parallel end here; for as Jacob shortly afterwards prepared to go into Egypt under distressing circumstances, so Calvert in great distress made his preparations to go to Newfoundland, there to spend, as he supposed, the remainder of his days.[21] He, too, would seek corn in Egypt. Yet when it came to the point, he was more than loath to go. Willingly would he have avoided the journey; but necessity is a hard master. To his intimate friend, Sir Thomas Wentworth, who could not understand why he should go at all, he explained that he went in order to save his investments. I "must either go" he said, "and settle it in better order, or else give it over and lose all the charges I have been at hitherto, for other men to build their fortunes upon. And I had rather be esteemed a fool by some, for the hazard of one month's journey, than to prove myself one certainly for six years past, if the business be now lost for want of a little pains and care." It is the word of a man who says, Go I must; there is nothing else left for me to do.

[20] Genesis xlii, 26.
[21] Prowse, Page 132. Neill, *Terra Mariæ*, Page 39.

CHAPTER IV.

LORD BALTIMORE (SIR GEORGE CALVERT) IN NEWFOUNDLAND.

1627–1629.

"Great Sheba's wise queen travel'd far to see
Whether the truth did with report agree ;
You, by report persuaded, laid out much,
Then wisely came to see if it were such ;
You came and saw, admired what you had seen
With like success as the wise Sheba queen.
If every sharer here would take like pain,
This land would soon be peopled to their gain."
—ROBERT HAYMAN.

When Lord Baltimore eventually sailed for his new home at Avalon, in harmony with his recent acknowledgement that he was of the Roman obedience, he took with him two priests of the Roman Catholic Church.[1] It is not quite clear in what capacity these gentlemen accompanied the expedition, for the Rev. Richard James[2] was already in the field as the settled pastor of the flock at Ferry-

---

[1] *Founders of Maryland*, Neill, Page 41.
[2] *Terra Mariae*, Neill, Page 46, note. See also *Athenae Oxoniensis*, and *Gentleman's Magazine*, 1767 and 1768,

land. They could therefore hardly expect to find much priestly work to do among the colonists, especially as but few, if any, of their faith were to be found among them. It is probable, however, that Lord Baltimore regarded his priests more in the light of private chaplains, while they, with that apostolic zeal which has so often distinguished Roman Catholic missionaries, chiefly thought of themselves as destined for the spiritual welfare of the "barbarous people" of whom their patron's charter made mention.

On Lord Baltimore's arrival at his new home in Avalon, he was at last in a position to judge for himself of the capabilities of his adopted country. The whole province, of which he had but a small strip on the southeast coast, is only one sixth larger than the eastern shore of Maryland, with Delaware included. Containing some 45,000 square miles in a country rather larger than Ireland, it is the least profitable part of the whole island. Whatever may be the agricultural prospects of the interior of the western portion, they are certainly not shared by Avalon. Prophets indeed predict that it will one day be the Chili of North America, so great is its mineral wealth. But Baltimore was not looking for minerals. All his preparations were for farming; but farming, in a country where great boulders everywhere cover the ground, and where even to make a small garden, soil has not seldom to be brought from a distance, as the German vine growers carry the soil for their vineyards on the Rhine, is never likely to prove either a very lucrative or a very popular undertaking. Yet such is Avalon. In all parts of it there are immense tracts appropriately termed "barrens,' covered only with stunted pines from which masses of lichens hang like banners. No sign of animal life is to be seen. No song of bird is heard. Silence reigns. The great boulders borne hither ages ago on the ice floes, are all around, whilst at intervals the solid rock breaks through the thin layers of soil or moss, as if to proclaim its universal presence, and to bid defiance to the farmer and his plough.[3]

Elsewhere, northwards and westwards, it is different. Broad acres; noble forests; mighty rivers; lakes as beautiful as Como, Loch Lomond or Windermere, with scenes of exquisite beauty, are features of every landscape. But the home of Baltimore was on the poor, storm swept, eastern seaboard, where at certain seasons a cold, clammy

[3] The author knows Avalon well.

fog makes life miserable; a fog so thick and blinding, that once upon a time the penguin on Baccalieu Island, just off the coast, were protected by law because their cries served to protect vessels from being dashed upon the rocks, and where, to serve the same purpose, in the fortress of St. John's a warning gun was fired every half hour.

And yet when Lord Baltimore first saw Avalon in the August of 1627, all things conspired to give it favor in his eyes. The weather is at that season delightful; the growth of vegetation rapid; while the beautiful blue skies and still bluer water remind one of the scenery of southern Europe. Strawberries, raspberries and the much prized capillaire berries, with many others, are to be found in the greatest profusion, while the beauty and endless variety of the native flowers blossoming in the woods, on the ponds, and upon the hills, are remarkable. Indeed, were it not for the occasional visit of an iceberg, as swept along by the current, stately and majestically, within sight of the coast, to be driven aground at last, there to remain for weeks a silent witness to the power of the frost in its northern home, there would be little to indicate the storms and severity of winter. All is so very beautiful.

Newfoundland scenery has in fact a charm which is peculiarly its own. The sea, constantly changing, finds there its most variable moods and its greatest extremes. How soft and limpid the waters appear on a calm summer evening, when the gorgeous colors of the setting sun are reflected in them; how still and motionless, with the little craft scattered about upon them, looking like sea birds taking rest. Then again, how wild and boisterous, and yet how grand the waves, when, with sullen roar, they rush, crowned with foam, upon the rocks, which seem contemptuously challenging them to do their worst. Again, how the icicles cling to the bold headlands, when winter's hand catches the frozen spray and holds it in an iron grasp, and the waters out to seaward, like lakes amid the white expanse of the ice fields, are of a more transparent blue than ever, as they stand out against the dazzling white of ice and snow, which stretches away to the far-distant horizon. Like mighty dissolving views the changing scenes pass before our eyes.

For Baltimore's purpose the time of his visit was the very worst possible. He did not realize that he was looking on Newfoundland in holiday attire, and he came at once to the conclusion that it was a land favorable "to sett and sow." Then after a stay, all too brief, he returned to England, full of plans for the future. He reached England in November.[4] Early in the following year he had again embarked, taking with him a second wife, his family, with the exception of Cecilius,[5] his eldest son, the stay-at-home member of the family; and another Roman Catholic priest. They were all hopeful and enthusiastic. How could they well be otherwise? They were about to retrieve heavy losses, and all things seemed favorable. Alas! the glamour was soon rudely dispelled, and they saw things as they were. True, there were days, and even nights, in the autumn, when the picturesque beauty of nature compelled their admiration as when they first looked upon it. Then came the bright, clear days of winter, when the sky was clearer than they had ever seen it, and the moon like silver and the stars like diamonds shone with a lustre unknown to them before. During the calm, frosty nights, they saw the Northern lights, flashing with a quivering brilliancy, rapid as lightning, beautiful as the sunset, turning night into day, and making fairyland of all the country

---

[4] *Md. Hist. Soc. F. P., No. 20.* Wilhelm, Page 134.
[5] *Founders of Maryland*, Neill, Page 41.

round them, as well as of all the sky above them. All this was inspiring. But on scenery they could neither live nor prosper. Soon came dark days and storms, and the mid-winter weather when the ground was deeply frozen. Was it any wonder, ere that first winter had fled and the dismal Newfoundland spring had come, that all hope had completely forsaken them? They had not seen, neither had their fathers told them, what winter was in America under the Northern lights.

We need not marvel then, that on August 19th, 1629, less than two years afterwards, Lord Baltimore was upon his knees thanking the king for the loan of a "faire shipp" to take him away. His letter to King Charles describing his unfortunate condition and the miserable state of his plantation is truly pathetic. He had met with differences and incumbrances as could no longer be resisted. For his majesty might be pleased to understand that he had there found by a too dearly bought experience, which other men for their private interests always concealed from him, that from the midst of October to the midst of May there is a sad face of winter upon all this land, both sea and land so frozen for the most part of the time, as they were not penetrable, and his house had become a hospital. Out of one hundred persons fifty had been sick at a time, himself included, and nine or ten had died. Hereupon he had strong temptations to leave all proceedings in plantations, and being much decayed in his strength, to retire himself to his former quiet; but his inclination carrying him naturally to these kind of works, and not knowing how better to employ the poor remainder of his days than, with other good subjects, to further the best he may the enlarging his majesty's empire in this part of the world, he is determined to commit this place to fishermen that are able to encounter hard weather and storms, and to remove himself with some forty persons to his majesty's dominion of Virginia, where, if his majesty will please to grant him a precinct of land with such privileges as the king his father, his gracious master, was pleased to grant him here, he will endeavor with the utmost of his power to deserve.[6]

It is a pitiable story this, which he concludes by making request for land in Virginia. He now knew the island better. He knew Avalon better. And now having told the king that he had determined to commit the place to fishermen[7] who could

[6] *Archives of Maryland, Council*, Vol. 3, Pps. 15, 16.
[7] *Founders of Maryland*, Neill, Page 46, quoting State Papers.

endure the storms and bad weather better than he could, without awaiting even an answer to his appeal, leaving his priests behind,[8] or sending them back to England with his children, he sailed away with his wife and dependants, and, as it would appear, the Rev. Richard James, to the settlements on the banks of the James River in Virginia.

Of all those who had sought to colonize the country, he had been the least successful, his work the most ephemeral. A Newfoundland clergyman of the present day, and former Rector of Ferryland, once wrote to me in answer to inquiries: " I cannot remember having heard his name mentioned. I know not where his house stood and, as far as I know, no relic whatever remains. Well may the historian of Newfoundland write: " None of the great patentees, from Gilbert to Baltimore, exercised the least permanent influence on the history of the colony; least of all, Baltimore; he came and stayed an uneasy, discontened stay of two seasons; all his company of forty persons left the colony together, and then his Lordship and his

---

[8] The Southampton records show that one of Lord Baltimore's priests came home under an assumed name in August, 1629. See Southampton Municipal Archives, *Book of Examinations, Informations and Depositions*, No 42, A.D., 1622-1643.

seminary priests and his noble retinue and his Welsh colonists, vanish from our annals,"⁹ From beginning to end, his had been an unfortunate adventure.

It is perhaps only fair to the colony to state that but a few years afterwards—October 2d, 1639—Sir David Kirk, writing to Archbishop Laud, from Lord Baltimore's own homestead at Ferryland, upon the possession of which he had recently entered, as a gift from the king, gave a very different account of the climate from that which Baltimore had sent to the king. "Out of one hundred persons they took over," Kirk tells the Archbishop, "only one died of sickness. The air of Newfoundland agrees perfectly with all God's creatures, except Jesuits and schismatics. A great mortality amongst the former tribe so affrighted my Lord of Baltimore that he utterly deserted the country." As between these two accounts of the climate there is no doubt that the latter is correct. There is no healthier climate known than that of Newfoundland. It agrees perfectly well with everyone.[10]

No Lord Baltimore ever saw Newfoundland

[9] Prowse, 2nd Edition, Pages 112, 113.
[10] *Terra Mariae*, Neill, Page 103, note.

again. The family doubtless heartily wished they had never had anything to do with it. The Baltimores did not, however, resign the hope of getting some of their money back again, and long afterwards they still considered themselves as the rightful Lords of Avalon.[11]

But as the first Lord Baltimore turned his back upon his unfortunate colonial adventure, another chapter of his life was closed. Again all his plans were unsettled. Again he had failed. Again he was a wanderer on the face of the earth. He now set his face southwards. It might be that in Virginia, or in the parts beyond, he could find for himself a home and a resting place on earth. But in what had he failed? What was it that he had unsuccessfully attempted to do in that sea girt isle beside the north Atlantic? For what did he buy his plantation there? For what did he send there three successive expeditions of emigrants? And finally, for what did he himself seek to settle there?

The nature of his attempts precludes any supposition that he failed to found a colony where the profession of religion might be free. For certainly I may without fear of contradiction, quote Bozman's words as signally applicable to Calvert up to

---

[11] *Archives of Maryland, Council,* Page 42.

this time: "Thus far, then, we have not yet found that either religious persecution or political oppression, or even the glory of propagating the Christian faith, however much talked of, were really and truly the prime and original motives."[12] of his colonization schemes. In fact at the very time when Sir George Calvert bought his Newfoundland property, he was a professing Anglican, and during all the six years that he was an absentee landlord his one idea seems to have been to make money out of the estate; while during his less than two year's residence in Newfoundland his time seems to have been equally divided between obtaining a satisfactory answer to these two problems: First, how he was to get his money back again; and secondly, how he and his family were to get out of the country to some more hospitable land.

If it had been ever Lord Baltimore's intention to found a place of refuge from persecution it is evident that this was not known to his contemporaries. Indeed the Rev. Erasmus Stourton, was so little aware of the fact as seriously to complain to the king that the priests at Ferryland said mass every Sunday in the ample man-

---
[12] Bozman, Page 156.

ner used in Spain.[13] Stourton's religious zeal seems to have been of the sort that strains at gnats and swallows camels. It was not apparently the having mass that disturbed his spirit, but the having it openly. But Lord Baltimore's offence does not seem to have gone beyond having mass in his own house, for there was no chapel of the Roman Church in Avalon till the establishment of the French in Placentia in 1662, more than a generation later. But Stourton was so deeply moved that he appealed unto Caesar. Was it possible that the king did not know of the doings of Lord Baltimore's priests at Ferryland? Stourton's action was deemed so serious by Balti-

---

[13] Prowse, Page 101, note. Penn in 1708 brought the same charge against the Secretary of his colony. He was perfectly willing that Roman Catholics should have mass in their own private houses but he objected to his Secretary allowing "Public Mass." See Fisher, *Men, Women and Manners in Colonial Times*, Vol. II, Pages 220-223. "In 1704 there was a complaint that mass was celebrated in the Popish Chapel at St. Mary's in Maryland when the county court was holding its sessions there. For this too public exhibition of the Roman ceremonial the chapel was ordered to be closed by the sheriff, and the Roman Catholics were informed by the Governor. "You might, methinks, be content to live quietly as you may, and let the exercise of your superstitious vanities be confined to yourselves, without proclaiming them at public times in public places." Stourton was therefore in line with later public opinion on this subject—an opinion, however, which I cannot commend.

more, that he sought to justify himself by a personal letter to Charles. He need not have done so, for although in Newfoundland Stourton was apparently popular, in England he was regarded as a busybody in other men's matters.[14] It is, however, quite clear that not only Stourton, but Lord Baltimore himself, must have been entirely ignorant of the colony having been founded as a seed plot of religious liberty; otherwise, how readily would Lord Baltimore have replied, " Yes, I have mass here, and that openly; but what am I here for? Is it not that, free from religious bigotry and intolerance, I may worship God according to my conscience? How came those emigrants of the English Church and that clergyman there? Sir George Calvert himself had sent them. He had in truth actually petitioned the Archbishops of Canterbury and York to use their influence in securing just such emigrants.[15] Now a man who is fleeing from persecution does not ordinarily ask his persecutors to colonize the place of his refuge with their own followers. Elijah fleeing from Jezebel did not ask that some of Baal's worshippers, and a priest or two, might be allowed to come and

[14] See Governor Robert Hayman's *Quodlibets*, quoted by Neill, *Terra Mariæ*, Page 44.
[15] *Md. Hist. Soc. F. P., No. 20.* Wilhelm, Page 130.

live with him on Mount Carmel. But this is precisely what we must credit Baltimore with doing on his Newfoundland plantation, if he had secured it as a refuge for Roman Catholics who were, so we are dramatically told, being "hounded from every hundred in the three kingdoms."[16]

But why say more? Even if at the time of acquiring his Newfoundland property Lord Baltimore had been openly a member of the Roman Church, the case is in no wise altered. The Roman Catholics had never been more hopeful; their prospects had never been brighter. Their conduct at the coming of the Armada had done much to rehabilitate them in the eyes of their countrymen as good citizens, for they had shown themselves in that great crisis as Englishmen first and Romanists afterwards. Much of the irritation and resentment aroused against them in Queen Elizabeth's time, had, in consequence of their patriotic conduct, died away. There was something in the nature of a reaction going on. King James had never been a rabid anti-Romanist, neither was King Charles. Besides, ere Baltimore left England, there was a queen of his own faith. What object, then, could he have in exiling himself? The Roman faith

[16] *Md. Hist. Soc. F. P., No. 18*, Johnson, Page 9.

was rapidly becoming fashionable.[17] A woman of rank is recorded as having apologized to Archbishop Laud for leaving the Anglican church for the Roman, giving as her reason that, as she hated crowds, she wanted to get in before the crush came.[18] It had even been foretold by one familiar with the court circle, that had the Spanish marriage negotiations succeeded, many would have fallen "away from the Church of England, as fall withered leaves in the autumn."[19] Small necessity existed, therefore, for the planting of such a colony. It is quite true that persecuting laws were on the statute books of England which rendered the Roman Catholics at any moment liable to persecution and imprisonment, but for the matter of that they are there still. A law of Edward I or Henry VIII may at this moment be pleaded in court with as much authority as a law made under Queen Victoria. Moreover a section of the Catholic Emancipation Act of 1829 provides "that nothing con-

[17] "There is great complaint of the increase of Popery everywhere." Chamberlain to Carlton, February 10th, 1620. See Neill, *Terra Mariæ*, Page 23, note.

[18] *The claim of the Church of Rome to the Exercise of Religious Toleration during the Proprietary Government of Maryland examined.* By Joshia F. Polk, Washington, 1846, Page 7.

[19] Letter from John Chamberlain, Esq. to Sir Dudley Carleton, April 19th, 1623.

tained in this Act shall be held to legalize in any way the residence in the United Kingdom of any member of any religious body of men," and further enacts "that upon information sworn before any two of His Majesty's Justices of the Peace, the Secretary of State may expel such member of a religious order from the country within forty-eight hours." The situation therefore is this: All the religious orders, and the thousands of Dominican and Franciscan Tertiaries now in England, are liable to summary expulsion at any time. Yet Cardinal Vaughan of Westminster, in a pastoral letter on the occasion of the Queen's jubilee in 1897, took occasion to say to his people, "Our highest and most religious cause for thanksgiving is to be found in the growth of the Catholic Church under the English ægis of civil and religious liberty. Antiquated restrictions and disabilities have, during her Majesty's Reign, given place to freedom of speech and action, the law safe guarding the reputation, person, and property of all. The people of England have said: "We are free-traders, and open wide our markets to the world. If you possess religious truths and medicines that heal the soul, come, preach and administer them as you will." More recently still Archbishop Ireland, of St. Paul,

Minn., addressing the Roman Catholic Union Society of Great Britain on June 27, 1899, said that "the liberty granted by England to Roman Catholicism would, he believed, greatly influence the nations of the world."[20] It was not altogether dissimilar in James' reign. Certainly the first Lord Baltimore did not leave England on account of the laws against Romanism. There is in fact not one word of his which implies that he went to Newfoundland because of any religious differences or conscientious difficulties at all. But if any proof of the entirely non-religious character of his undertaking were lacking, that proof would be found in his dismissing his priests and making his free choice of Virginia as the scene of his next venture; of all places in the world the most undesirable, and indeed impossible, for the purposes of a Roman Catholic colony. That one act alone in his life should shatter forever the theory of his seeking to found a colony as a refuge for the victims of intolerance. Virginia was, be it always remembered, the very hotbed of Anglicanism, the only spot in America where the people were more English than the English themselves, and where Churchmen were more loyal to their Church than

[20] *Baltimore Sun*, June 28, 1899.

they were in Canterbury or York. Yet it was to this place of all others that Lord Baltimore turned when Florida, with her Roman Catholic associations, wonld have opened her doors gladly; when Mexico, more Roman still, would have done the like; and when there was hardly a place in all the world but would have been more suitable for his purpose.

CHAPTER V.

LORD BALTIMORE IN VIRGINIA.

1629.

> Their tents are pitched, their spades have broke the soil,
>   The strong oak thunders as it topples down,
> Their lily-handed youths essay the toil,
>   That from the forest rends its ancient crown.
> Where are your splendid halls, which ladies tread,
> Your lordly boards with every luxury spread,
>   Virginian sires—ye men of old renown?
> Though few and faint, your ever-living chain
>   Holds in its grasp two worlds, across the surging main.
> —LYDIA SIGOURNEY "Pocahontas."

When Lord Baltimore, newly arrived from the bleak shores of Avalon, in the early part of October, 1629, saw for the first time the banks of the James, he must have felt as did Lot of old, when first he saw the beautiful vale of Jordan, well watered everywhere and like the garden of the Lord. Certainly Virginia presented a striking contrast to Avalon. The month of October is the beautiful month for woodland scenery throughout this Western continent, and as Lord Baltimore and his company sailed along as far as James City, the principal settlement of the Virginians, and containing with its adjacent plantations about three thousand settlers, they saw the trees in all their varied shades of green and brown, bright crimson and gorgeous purple, forming for them, as they passed up the river, an avenue of wondrous beauty. Even the least observant among them must have been charmed. The fields were not all harvested. In some the corn was yet ripening. Orchards were still bearing their fruit. On either side of the river, fair pasture lands stretched afar. All was very good. What could man need more? Why go further? Here was a country which might claim the "prerogative over the most pleasant places known, for large and majestic navigable rivers; for beautiful mountains, plains, hills, valleys; for rivulets and brooks running most pleasantly into a fair bay, encompassed, except at the mouth, with such fruitful and delightsome land, that heaven and earth seemed never to have agreed better to frame a place for man's commodious and delightful habitation, were it fully cultivated and inhabited by industrious people."[1] Avalon could not rival this. At last Lord Baltimore had found a place, such as he had dreamed of, where he could build his home

---

[1] Smith, *History of Virginia*, Book I, P. 114.

and permanently settle down. Here his fairest hopes might be realized and fortune prove no longer fickle.

From the acting governor, John Pott, and the various officials of the colony the travelers received a kindly welcome.[2] It is almost unnecessary to say this. The Virginians of today are famous for their hospitality to strangers, so were their fathers before them. Their readiness to entertain strangers is in truth a heritage, the gift of the parents to the children. Yet remembering all the circumstances, it undoubtedly speaks well for the genuine goodness of heart of those early settlers in the Old Dominion, that they were so ready to extend the right hand of fellowship to their visitors. For of course they knew all about Lord Baltimore's parliamentary career, and they must have disapproved of it *in toto*. Moreover, strongly as they objected to his political doings, they must have even more emphatically disapproved of his theological gyrations. If he had ever been a Churchman, they must have regarded him as a faithless son of their own beloved Church. If on the other hand he had always been a Roman Catholic, he had, in their judgment, been guilty of long continued hypocrisy. Perhaps,

---

[2] *Founders of Maryland*, Neill, P. 44.

too, they had heard of his troubles with Stourton. But now that he was their guest, forgetting these unpleasant features in his former career, they gave him a hearty welcome. Still, after all, they candidly acknowledged that they regarded Lord Baltimore as a very desirable person to have among them, "as being of that eminence and degree whose presence and affection might give a great advancement to this Plantation."[3] Those early Virginian settlers were not without a keen eye for the advancement of their colony. Rank and social position had, in their eyes, a certain money value, and they made ready to use his lordship as one of the colony's assets, while Lord Baltimore, on his part, readily reciprocated their sentiments.

From the pathetic letter which Baltimore wrote to the king as he was about to leave Newfoundland,[4] it is evident that when he sailed up the James he had not the remotest idea of settling at Jamestown itself. Probably he himself had not then any very clear ideas of what he wanted to do, having nothing more than an indefinite intention of "planting himself to the southward." It was only after he had actually seen their country, that he forthwith formed his plans, and informed the

[3] *Archives of Maryland, Council*, P. 16.
[4] *Calvert Papers*, Vol. I, P. 222.

colonists of his determination to remain in Virginia. Upon his making this decision known the Virginians naturally asked his acceptance of the country's constitution, to the adoption of which he had been, while in power in England, a consenting party. To their utter amazement he flatly refused to take the usual oaths of supremacy and allegiance which that constitution required, "a thing which," as they afterwards said in a letter to the king, they "could not have doubted, in him whose former employment under his late Majesty had naturally led them to suppose that he could not have refused the loyalty and fidelity which every true subject owes to his sovereign." From this statement it is evident that Baltimore's refusal, either to take the oath himself, or to allow his followers to take it, very greatly perplexed them. What could his action mean? They were dumbfounded, and the more so because they knew that he must have taken the oath before, not only as a professing Protestant, but as an acknowledged Roman Catholic. His objections, therefore, must have been entirely incomprehensible to them, and no wonder! They knew very well that, as an educated Englishman, Baltimore was perfectly familiar with the limitations of the oath, the result of the controversies in Henry's time and their final satisfactory settlement in Elizabeth's; and they also knew that, rightly understood, the oath had never been really objectionable even to the most rigid opponents of kingly intrusion into spiritual matters.[5] But that there might be no plausible ground of complaint when Elizabeth succeeded to the throne, she not only deliberately refused the title of supreme head of the Church,[6] but she even took particular care to define and limit the constitutional meaning of her supremacy.[7] Her objection to the title of 'supreme head,' it was explained, was based on the fact that the word head had been taken to imply an original initiatory power, where-

[5] Hallam, *Constitutional History*, Vol. 1, P. 556 with respect to this oath, says, "that except by cavilling at one or two words it seemed impossible for the Roman Catholics to decline so reasonable a test of loyalty, without justifying the worst suspicions of Protestant jealousy."

When Archbishop Cranmer was charged at his trial with having made "King Henry VIII supreme head" of Christ's Church he replied "that the king was supreme head of all the people of England, as well ecclesiastical as temporal." But that Christ was "the only, Head of His Church." Cranmer, *Works*, Vol. 4, Ps. 116, 117.

[6] Collier, *Church History*, Part II; Book VI.

[7] Cardinal Gibbons informs us "The Church of England acknowledges the reigning Sovereign as its Spiritual Head." *Faith of our Fathers*, P. 26. The Cardinal, who, as a teacher of the doctrines and history of his own church speaks *ex cathedra*, is not of course an authority on Anglican Church affairs.

as the sovereign's power was simply that of an administrative authority according to established laws. The meaning of the headship had in fact been misunderstood. Hence, the adoption of the title of governor. Of course Lord Baltimore knew all this, so that it could not be charitably alleged on his behalf that he was acting under a misapprehension of what was required. Such a plea

Churchmen will naturally prefer to trust to their own official formularies. Thus Article XXXVII, which has also the additional force of an Act of Parliament, defines the queen's position very differently:

ARTICLE XXXVII.—Where we attribute to the Queen's Majesty the chief government, by which Titles we understand the minds of some slanderous folks to be offended; we give not to our Princes the ministering either of God's Word, or of the Sacraments, the which thing the Injunctions also lately set forth by Elizabeth our Queen do most plainly testify; but that only prerogative, which we see to have been given always to all godly Princes in Holy Scriptures by God himself; that is, that they should rule all estates and degrees committed to their charge by God, whether they be Ecclesiastical or Temporal, and restrain with the civil sword the stubborn and evil-doers.

Queen Victoria's official position towards the English Church is here not appreciably different, as may readily be observed, from that which she occupies towards the Roman, and other religious bodies, throughout the dominions. She is over all, supreme governor. An admirable illustration of this may be seen in the circumstances attending the sensational burial some years ago in Montreal of the Roman Catholic Guibord. Guibord had fallen under the ban of his church because of his membership in the Order of Masons, and eventually died under the ban. When burial in consecrated ground was denied him the Queen's government came to the aid of his Roman Catholic relatives and secured for them their rights. For this whole question, calmly and scholarly dicussed, see *The Thirty-Nine Articles*, Browne, Pps. 786 to 802.

might have been put forward effectively on behalf of a foreigner, or an illiterate Englishman, but not for a graduate of Oxford University.

The truth is that the Anglican objects, quite as strongly as his Roman Catholic brother does, and often much more successfully, to any interference by the civil authority in spiritual affairs, and he resolutely refuses to recognize any other supremacy of the secular power than that which is involved in acknowledging its authority over all persons, spiritual or civil, within its jurisdiction. But the Queen's position in the English Church gives her no such authority as that to which the Roman Church in France is subjected. There the Church cannot build a mission chapel, or even a sacristy,[8]

---

[8] See the following pathetic incident recorded by Cardinal Gibbons, "*Faith of our Father's,*" P. 240. "Some years ago, in company with the late Archbishop Spalding, on my return from Rome, I paid a visit to the Bishop of Annecy, in Savoy. I was struck with the splendor of his palace, and saw a sentinel at the door, placed there by the French Government. But the venerable Bishop soon disabused me of my favorable impressions. He told me that he was in a state of gilded slavery. "I cannot," said he, "build as much as a sacristy without obtaining permission of the government." See also Pps. 237 and 238 of same work, for a vivid description of the sad condition of the Roman Church, among its own people on the continent of Europe, even Italy not excepted. In England and America alone does the Roman Church appear to enjoy her own without interference.

unless the government first gives its permission. It is the same in Germany. Only recently the Kaiser sent back to Italy a bishop, and he German born, who had fallen under his displeasure, and this not arbitrarily, but in strict agreement with the Concordat between him and the Pope.

But again, Lord Baltimore's objections to recognising the king as the lawful ruler in all things ecclesiastical as well as civil, must have been more than ever incomprehensible to the Virginians, if they recalled that the qualified headship of the Church which he so stoutly refused the king he had not scrupled to exercise himself. For the charter of Avalon invested him with all power, civil, military, naval, and ecclesiastical. He was thus head of both Church and State; a ruler without a parliament, or even a council of state. The lord of Avalon was consequently in his own demesne a greater man than his royal master was in his kingdom, who was not in any sense absolute. No King of England ever was. The troubles of the Stuarts began when they sought to be absolute; but even the Stuarts, with all their notions of the divine right of kings, never claimed in their own persons such ample powers as were conferred by King James upon the first Baron of Baltimore. Compared, then, with the power which Baltimore had himself exercised in Avalon, the rule over the Church claimed by the Kings of England, and allowed to them as just and right, was a mere shadow. That his opinions had undergone no change in this respect will be evident when we come to deal with the charter of Maryland. Under its provisions he was to be the supreme head of the Church in Maryland, just as he had been in Newfoundland. To be sure there were certain limitations imposed upon him which radically changed his status as head of the Maryland Church. But inasmuch as these changes were not made at his instance we can give him no credit for them.

Lord Baltimore's conduct in Virginia was, therefore, of the nature of straining at a gnat and swallowing a camel. And it seems to have been so regarded by some of the Virginians themselves, who had begun to suspect that it was not citizenship but territory for which their aristocratic visitor was looking in Virginia. It was assuredly due to this supposition that Baltimore was once at least in danger of personal violence at the hands of a stout Virginia patriot, one Tindale, who was "pillori'd for two hours, for giving my Lord Baltimore the lie, and threatening to knock him down." [9]

[9] Anderson, Vol. II, P. 90.

LORD BALTIMORE IN VIRGINIA. 87

The Virginians have been severely arraigned for insisting upon Baltimore's taking the oath. They have even been accused of giving him a "cold reception," and "anything but a cordial welcome," and even of having been "most ungracious."[10] But what else could they have done? They could not lawfully have admitted him to citizenship, any more than our courts now may naturalize an Englishman who should refuse to take the oath of allegiance to the United States. For the last and concluding clause of their charter ran thus: "And lastly because the principal effect which we can desire or expect of this action, is the conversion and reduction of the people in those parts unto the true worship of God and Christian religion, in which respect we should be loath that any person should be permitted to pass, that we suspected to affect the superstitions of the Church of Rome, we do hereby declare, that it is our will and pleasure, that none be permitted to pass in any voyage from time to time, to be made into the said country, but such as shall first have taken the *oath of supremacy.*" Nor was this a dead letter. In the instructions to Governor Yardley, of Virginia, in 1624, he was directed "to administer the oath of allegiance

[10] Fiske, Vol. I, Page 264. Neill, *Founders of Md.*, P. 45.

and supremacy to all such as came there with intention to plant and reside; which if any shall refuse, he is to be returned or shipped from thence."[11] What, then, becomes of all that is urged on Lord Baltimore's behalf? Plainly he was not only arbitrarily refusing to obey the law himself, but was demanding that the Virginian colonists should become law-breakers too; a demand which they very properly refused, and in their refusal we have reason to believe that the King and Privy Council heartily supported them.

Bozman, who deals at some length [12] with this matter of the oath, finds that the Virginia Assembly could have dispensed with it had they been so minded, since noblemen were expressly exempt from its operation. But such a conclusion is inconsistent with Governor Pott's letter to the king, in which he expressly denies the existence in the colony of any dispensing power. Besides, even if Lord Baltimore himself could have pleaded "benefit of peerage" his followers most assuredly could not have done so. However, it is a question whether Lord Baltimore as an Irish baron, had any such privilege of peerage at all, an Irish

[11] Bozman, P. 162.
[12] P. 240.

LORD BALTIMORE IN VIRGINIA.   89

nobleman before the Union—it is different now—being reckoned merely as a commoner.

It is all very well to raise objections, but would those who find fault with the Virginians have thought more highly of them if they had admitted Baltimore without the oath, and so placed themselves in the position of breaking their own laws? Virginia was at that time especially the king's own domain, his "Kingdom of Virginia," and the Virginians had, therefore, especial justification in acting as they did. And yet, that there might be no reasonable opportunity for cavilling, they immediately referred the whole question to the king in council. If his majesty should be pleased to allow Lord Baltimore the privileges of Virginia citizenship without requiring from him the usual oath, they, as loyal subjects, would be well content. In the mean time they could not but obey the law which they had sworn to keep. No treatment could well have been more courteous to their visitors, or more dutiful to their common king.

The letter of Governor Pott, and his advisors, to the king's Privy Council dated November 30th, 1629, details the points at issue. It states: "that about the beginning of October last there arrived in this colony the Lord Baltimore from his plantation of Newfoundland, and that according to the instructions from your lordships and the usual course held in this place, we tendered the oaths of Supremacy and Allegiance to his lordship and some of his followers, who making profession of the Roman religion utterly refused to take the same." His lordship offered, however, to take an oath, a copy of which they were sending to the Council, but they could not imagine that such latitude was left to them to decline from the prescribed form, so strictly executed and so well justified and defended by their late Sovereign Lord King James."[13] Thus they left the case to the decision of the king in council.

Baltimore soon showed that he had no intention of quietly awaiting in Virginia the answer to this appeal. To that letter to the king, written from Ferryland, in which he had asked permission to plant himself to the southward, he had received no answer, owing to his having abandoned the colony shortly after having written it. He now deemed it best to go himself to England and there to plead his cause in person. Once there he would be in a position to answer all questions and meet all diffi-

---

[13] *Archives of Maryland, Council*, P. 16.

culties. The decision was all the more timely, as well as the more necessary, since he had plans of his own to accomplish, which, when publicly known, would set all Virginia in an uproar.

It was in pursuit of these plans that, probably while waiting for a ship to carry him home, he sailed upon a voyage of discovery up the Chesapeake,[14] "the mother of waters," the great bay which divides Maryland into two parts. About 1608, the celebrated Captain John Smith, Governor of Virginia, had explored this magnificent inland sea, and in the account of his voyage there is a beautiful indication of the religious character of the people that should one day dwell on its shores. "Our order," runs the record, "was daily to have prayer with a psalm."[15] Thus when upon the waters of the Chesapeake, there sailed for the first time the ship of a white man, the sound of prayers and hymns offered in the name of Jesus, the Son of the Living God, was borne by the breeze to the densely wooded shores whereon the wild Indians dwelt. Church of England men were these voyagers, Churchmen or Episcopalians, as they are indifferently termed now, who used as their book

[14] *Md. Hist. Soc., F. P., No. 9*, P. 12, Streeter.
[15] Smith, *History of Virginia*, P. 183.

of devotion the Book of Common Prayer. In this way it was that along with the first sail of Anglo-Saxons on the Chesapeake, there went the English Bible and the English Prayer Book. Now for the second time these waters were being plowed by the keel of a vessel bearing white men. It was, however, by this voyage of Baltimore's, that the suspicions of William Clayborne, Virginia's Secretary of State, were aroused. The secretary had a settlement of his own in the bay, on an island lying almost as far north as the Patapsco River, and he feared, only too reasonably as events turned out, that Lord Baltimore might cast covetous eyes upon it. As the result of his suspicions, Clayborne also resolved to visit England, that he might be on hand to protect, if need be, his interests, and safeguard his rights, a course of action the wisdom of which after events fully justified.[16] This Clayborne was the second son of Sir Edward Clayborne, or Cleburne, of Westmoreland. He was one of the colonial officers appointed in 1621 by the London company for Virginia, and the ablest man in the Virginia colony. Accordingly when Lord Baltimore sailed away from Virginia, Clayborne seems to have sailed too.

[16] Neill, *Founders of Md.*, p. 47.

That Lord Baltimore did not anticipate much trouble in gaining his object is evident, since he left wife and dependents behind him, as if confident of a speedy return. Manifestly his relations with the colonists were not unpleasant, notwithstanding the well-grounded suspicions of Clayborne and perhaps a few others.

Had the Virginians known all, there might have been more than one Tindale to put into the pillory for giving my Lord Baltimore the lie, and threatening to knock him down. Meanwhile, as the colonists went down to the ship to bid him God-speed, and to wish him a safe return, they were all innocently wishing prosperity to the man who was coveting their land, and who was destined to be successful in his endeavors to rob them of many thousands of its acres.[17] Little did they imagine, that he was not sailing to England in order to gain citizenship in Virginia without having to take the usual oath, but to secure at their expense a new province of his own. It was this design which was at the back of all his remarkable scruples. The

[17] It is true that the Charter which originally conveyed this property to the Virginians had been annulled since 1624. But both James I. and Charles I. simply abolished the sovereignty guaranteed to Virginia; not interfering at all with the territorial limits of the colony—a very important, and even vital difference, but one often lost sight of.

truth is that had the Virginians been willing to present him with all the land he coveted, even to the half of their inheritance, he would in all likelihood have declined the gift for reasons not difficult to discover. There existed in England an executive committee of the Privy Council called the Star Chamber, which had the charge of all plantations abroad. This committee was absolute. Its will was law; its judgments final. But there cannot be two Star Chambers in one country, and Baltimore's ambition was to be the Star Chamber of his new colony. He had been a monarch in Newfoundland, and he had no intention of becoming anything less in Virginia.[18] He was by nature an autocrat, and his imperialistic tendencies, unchanged by misfortune, untaught by the education of travel or experience, were with him still.

"Cœlum, non animum mutant qui trans mare currunt."

But these tendencies could have no legitimate outlet in Virginia.

[18] See Lodge, *A Short Hist. of Eng. Colonies in America*, P, 94.

CHAPTER VI.

THE DEATH OF LORD BALTIMORE.

1632.

> I think poor beggars court St. Giles,
> Rich beggars court St. Stephen;
> And death looks down with nods and smiles
> And makes the odds all even.
> —PRAED: "*Brazen Head.*"

Back again in England! Back from foreign parts! How lovely would England seem with her trim hedgerows and green fields, like some neat and well-kept garden. How his friends would crowd around him to learn the news of those strange countries of which at that time the wisest knew but little. But he could not afford to tarry among them long. He was intent on business which would take him, either to the historic home of England's kings and queens besides the royal Thames, or to that noble palace which the ambition of Cardinal Wolsey had raised as a dwelling place for himself, and which the king now called his own. He would have private interview with Charles and learn from him his fate. But even had his plans necessitated his making such a request as the Virginians had refused, it is not at all likely that, with his courtier's experience and natural shrewdness, he would have been unwise enough to present it, for it was a request which was not only sure to be refused, but one well calculated to injure, if not even to entirely destroy, his influence at court. No king is apt to look kindly upon a subject who asks him to abate his claims upon his loyalty; more especially when those claims are of matters which touch the very stability of his throne. But no such petition was in Baltimore's mind. Flinging aside all disguise, he boldly asked for a province of his own to be carved out of Virginia, specifying, in accordance with his Newfoundland letter, a portion to the southward.

Here, however, he met with opposition from an unexpected quarter, his opponent being none other than the king himself, who could not endure seeing his old servant and courtier becoming a mere wanderer on the face of the earth, and who therefore urged him to give up his colonization enterprises, with their attendant hardships, as not being suited for men of his quality, and to stay in England. Royal advice may not fall on deaf ears, and so obtaining a ship from the king, he sent to Virginia for his wife and servants, who, not without mishap, for the vessel was wrecked on the homeward voyage, eventually reached England. The incident is thus referred to by Joseph Mead, Chaplain to Archbishop Laud: "Though his Lordship (Baltimore) is extolling that country to the skies, yet he is preparing a bark to send to fetch his lady and servants from thence, because the king will not permit him to go back." [1]

Lord Baltimore himself, in a letter addressed about the same time to Lord Dorchester, Secretary of State, begs that his "Lordship would be pleased to move his Majesty that whereas upon my humble suit unto him from Newfoundland for a portion to be granted unto me in Virginia, he was graciously pleased to signify by Sir Francis Cottington that I should have any part not already granted, that his Majesty would give me leave to choose such a part now, and to pass it unto me, with the like power and privileges as the king, his father of happy memory, did grant me that precinct in Newfoundland, and I shall contribute my best endeavors, with the rest of his loyal subjects, to enlarge his empire in that part of the world, by such gentle-

[1] *Founders of Maryland*, Neill, Page 47. The letter is dated February 12th, 1629-30.

men and others, as will adventure to join with me, though I go not myself in person." [2]

Observe carefully the closing sentence. It shows that although Lord Baltimore could not return to Virginia, he had no intention of abandoning a project on which he had so steadfastly set his heart. It was not, however, until February 1631, fully a year afterwards, that his plans had made any material progress. Then it was that he obtained a grant from the king of a tract of land south of James River. Happily for the Virginians' peace of mind, Clayborne, their secretary, was in London, as was also their ex-Governor Francis West, both of whom made such representations that, at the very last hour, the charter granting it was revoked. Another moment and it would have been too late. The charter had in fact been sealed with the seal of the Privy Council, and only wanted the Great Seal of England to make it effective. As with the revoking of this charter, it now seemed that all danger had passed away, Clayborne sailed to Virginia with the proud consciousness that he had saved his adopted land from dismemberment.

Alas for Clayborne! When his back was turned Lord Baltimore returned to the attack, and since

[2] *Ibid*, Page 46.

he could not have the territory he had applied for, he now asked for those lands to the northward, which he had seen on his voyage up the Chesapeake, stating that they were unoccupied by English subjects, although he knew very well that Clayborne's plantations were there. But perhaps the knowledge of this fact was an additional incentive. Twice had Clayborne crossed his path and thwarted his plans. This new request the king granted. It was indeed unfortunate that the secretary was not now in England to speak for himself. His London partners, however, promptly complained that the grant was within their limits. The Virginians, too, when they heard of it, were up in arms against the charter, and they preferred a petition to the king, in which they complained " that some grants have lately been obtained of a great proportion of the lands and territories within the limits of their colony there, being the places of their traffic, and so near to their habitations, as will give a general disheartening to the planters, if they be divided into several governments, and a bar to that trade which they have long exercised towards their supportation and relief."[3] This petition was acted upon in July, 1633, when, in a very

[3] *Archives of Maryland, Council*, 1636-1667, Page 21.

oracular manner, as if it were really making a most important contribution towards the settlement of the dispute, the Council declared that it had decided to leave Lord Baltimore to his charter and the other party to the course of law.

One hardly knows how adequately to characterize Baltimore's part in this transaction. The Virginians had received him kindly and treated him with the utmost consideration, yet he hesitated not to beg for their land, and to go to very considerable trouble to deprive them of it. But notwithstanding this discreditable incident, and all it implies, he is described as "a truly great and good man," who "discarded the emoluments of earth for the rewards of heaven, and exchanged the bright hopes of the present for unfading certainties of the future."[4]

As regards the king's part in the transaction, it has been rightly characterized by Anderson when he says: "A more iniquitous and unjust piece of business never stained Charles' reign. An English nobleman sets foot upon a colony in which his countrymen are already settled; surveys the vastness and fertility of its territory; finds that he is prohibited, alike by the laws of the province and of

[4] *United States Catholic Magazine*, April, 1842.

his native country, from obtaining his object unless he takes the oath of supremacy; refusing to take that oath, he returns to England, and, secures, through his influence at court and his personal friendship with the king, property and privileges within the borders of the desired land, far greater than had been conferred upon any British subject."[5]

Lord Baltimore had won the day. Plain, honest colonists, three thousand miles away, were no match for the trained politician, who in kings' courts had long ago learned the art of wire-pulling. But victory had come too late. The king's rewards were for another. As it was with the recalled grant, the last stage had been reached. Conditions, limits, terms, had all been agreed upon, and again the seal of the Privy Council had been affixed, when lo! another objector, more terrible than Clayborne and the indignant Virginians, appeared. Death had marked George Calvert for his own, and on the thirteenth of April, 1632, at the early age of fifty-two, a worn out man before his time, he passed away, bequeathing his worthless estates in Newfoundland, and all his Irish and English property, together with his expectations

[5] *History of the Colonial Church*, Anderson, Vol. 2, P. 108.

in Maryland, to Cecilius, his eldest son, the god-son of his early patron, Sir Robert Cecil.[6] The old Church of England which, with that sublime charity which "hopeth all things, endureth all things, believeth all things," buries her children—and all baptized of English birth she reckons her children—"in the sure and certain hope of a joyful resurrection," opened for the son whom she had educated at one of her greatest universities, Roman Catholic though he professed himself to be, the doors of old St. Dunstan's Church,[7] in Fleet Street, London, and in its chancel, with the honors due to his rank, laid the wanderer to rest.

It was fitting that the first Baron of Baltimore should thus find his last resting place, not amid the scenes of his boyhood in the obscurity of a Yorkshire village, but in the heart of great London, with its restless energy and ceaseless activity. His had been a public career. He had lived among statesmen. And it was right the closing scene should not be out of harmony with the scenes that

---

[6] *Calvert Papers*, No. 1, Page 48. His will runs thus:—" I do bequeath my lands, goods and chattels of what nature soever to my eldest sonne Cecil Calvert either in England or Ireland and elsewhere."

[7] Since destroyed by fire. Another church with like dedication, occupies the site of the old one.

had preceded it. More than a generation had gone by since he had come up from the Yorkshire dales to seek his fortune in the great metropolis. He had experienced strange vicissitudes since then. London had opened her doors to receive him, and there he would have been well satisfied to remain. But dark days came. Plans failed. Enemies multiplied. And the great city became no place for him to dwell in. Where, then, should he find a home? In Ireland, Newfoundland, Virginia, Maryland? He had tried all in turn. But none were to him what London had once been, and so he came back to his old home to die. Let him, therefore, lie there, amid the scenes he loved so well, where, beside the church in which they laid him to rest, the traffic of the mighty city rolls on forever. Yet the place of his burial has its own lesson to teach. Notwithstanding its singular appropriateness, why was it that his grave was not made with the graves of his ancestors in the burial place of his race? It is thus oftentimes that they bury dead statesmen, far away from the scenes of victory and the nation's capital.

The question is easily answered. George Calvert, first Baron of Baltimore, had no noble ancestors. He was a plebeian, a new man, the first of his line.[8] We have, it is true, been told of his inherited greatness, of his ancient family, and of his ancestral home.[9] His ancestral home was a farmhouse near the town of Danby Wiske, in the valley of the Swale, in Yorkshire, and his ancestors were probably but Flemish artisans. His very coat of arms had been made to order and delivered to him, just as the tailor had made and delivered the suit of clothes that indicated his new rank as knight. That Lord Baltimore was a new man is not, of course, any ground for objection against him. Indeed, it must ever remain his highest honor. Ten thousand other page boys would have remained servitors to the end. But Baltimore had abilities to succeed, and he did succed. And although his sun went down while it was yet day, full orbed behind the horizon, for a while fortune had seemed to be his own guardian angel. But scion of an ancient house he was not, save in that one sense in which we are all scions of a very ancient house indeed, for he was the actual lineal descendant of that family of landed proprietors who, at the dawning of history, owned and ruled vast estates lying

---

[8] On the roll of students matriculated at Oxford he is described as 'pleb'.

[9] Davis, *Day Star*, Page 162. Sparks, *Biography*, Page 16. Kennedy, Page 23.

somewhere between the Tigris and the Euphrates. But in this sense we are all honorable men.

"The life of Sir George Calvert," says a Maryland historian, "had been one of uninterrupted personal and political success." Baltimore himself was of a different opinion. Very auspicious had been the morning of that life, but the evening shadows had soon begun to fall, and then "one woe did tread upon another's heels," so that he early felt as a man feels who has failed of the goal of life. He had passed through the waters of tribulation and had tasted their exceeding bitterness. Many sorrows had enriched his character. We have a convincing and touching proof of this in a letter to his friend Wentworth, who had just lost his wife. "Were not my occasions," so he writes, "such as necessarily keep me here at this time, I would not send letters, but fly to you myself, with all the speed I could, to express my own grief, and to take part of yours, which I know is exceedingly great, for the loss of so noble a lady, so virtuous and loving a wife. There are few, perhaps, can judge of it better than I, who have been myself a long time a man of sorrows. But all things, my lord, in this world pass away; *statutum est;* wife, children, honor, wealth, friends, and what else is dear to flesh and blood. They are but lent us till God please to call for them back again, that we may not esteem anything our own, or set our hearts upon anything but Him alone, who only remains forever. I beseech His Almighty goodness to grant that your lordship may, for his sake, bear this great cross with meekness and patience, whose only Son, our dear Lord and Saviour, bore a greater for you; and to consider that these humiliations, though they be very bitter, yet are they sovereign medicines, ministered unto us by our heavenly Physician, to cure the sickness of our souls, if the fault be not ours." [10]

It was the letter of one who had found that so far as earthly honors go, all is vanity and vexation of spirit, and that in Christ alone there is perfect rest; of one who, out of the fulness of a ripe personal experience, could now sincerely pray to be permitted

> To leave all disappointment, cares and sorrow,
> To leave all falsehood, treachery and unkindness,
> All ignominy, suffering and despair
> And be at rest forever.

He had found the Golden Fleece, but when he stretchd forth his hand to claim the prize, lo, death came in between. 'Tis often thus: "One sows and

---

[10] Letter of Calvert to Wentworth, October 11th, 1630.

another reaps." One labors, and another enters into those labors.

As the latter chapters of his life were in turn closing, each with its record of failure, sadly must he have realized his own limitations and the limitations of mankind generally. We cannot command success. Nay, for

> Fate holds the strings, and men like children move
> But as they are led; success is from above.

Let us now observe the true place George Calvert fills in history. In this connection there is a circumstance which we cannot fail to remark upon, and at which indeed we justly marvel. To this man who is credited with laying Maryland and the Christian world under such vast and lasting obligations, not a single public memorial exists in Christendom, if we except his picture painted for the Earl of Verulam by the famous artist, Daniel Mytens; no, not even a statue to remind a too forgetful world of one of its greatest benefactors. Most of all are we astonished at this neglect in Maryland; for we remember that it is written of him that he was not only the founder of the State, but the Christian statesman to whom she owes her unique glory as "the land of the sanctuary," "the brightest gem in the American cluster of States," and so forth, *ad infinitum.*

To other men memorials are not wanting. Washington and stars of lesser magnitude are all suitably remembered. But Sir George Calvert—according to the Calvert cult—greatest of them all, for they were great only in the state, whereas he was great with a true greatness in Church as well as in State, as shown in his personal advocacy of those eternal principles without which there had been no sphere of action even for a Washington, inasmuch as in the school of which they were at best but apt pupils, he was first teacher and master; not even, I say, in Maryland, no, nor yet even in the city which takes its name from the title under which his individuality is hidden, is there aught to remind the citizens of him who brought that message from God, but for which the world might longer have remained in darkness and doubt. Go through Baltimore's streets and squares and see if it be not thus. There those who have served their country —orators, statesmen, generals, judges, poets—are all suitably remembered. But Sir George Calvert's memorial is nowhere to be found. He alone is forgotten. Imagine it. The first preacher of liberty of conscience—unhonored in Baltimore! Unhonored by the descendants of the men among whom, and for whose good, he promulgated, for the first time in the history of the world, the eternal principles of religious liberty. How, forsooth can we explain such strange forgetfulness? Not thus have they dealt with William Penn in the State which he founded. As if he were still the guardian of its welfare, in heroic size, to be seen from afar, crowning the lofty dome of the City Hall of Philadelphia, in the quaint old dress of the Quakers, towers his mighty statue. It is the one prominent object in the city and for miles around, being visible far down on the Delaware River; and destitute of all excuse must even the stranger be who remains in ignorance of what Penn has been to Pennsylvania. That statue is a magnificent lesson in bronze. Yet Penn was never to Pennsylvania what Lord Baltimore was to Maryland. The contrast therefore is one which, if the cult be right, makes Maryland's neglect of her hero all the more flagrant, all the more inexplicable. What, I ask again, can adequately explain such neglect as this? Surely even Lord Baltimore's panegyrists must be in a dilemma here. How do they account for it? Is there any possible explanation, other than the

Scriptural one that a prophet is not without honor, save in his own country and among his own kin?

Is it not abundantly evident that in the frank recognition of Baltimore's true position we have the only feasible explanation of an otherwise incredible neglect? History, patient, impartial, inexorable, regardless of conseqences, ruthless in her decisions, regards his place and services very differently. She asserts that he was no benefactor at all; certainly not such as an ill founded sentiment would have us believe. He followed his own good solely, And the world consequently knows him not in the Pantheon of her noblest and best.

Deeply rooted ideas are hard to eradicate, especially when general sympathy is enlisted on their behalf, and we may not therefore expect a very speedy acknowledgment of the truth; yet happily where the truth is working the doom of error is sure. It is so here. Although for the sake of our brethren who see, with eyes of faith, on George Calvert's brow the saintly halo of the preacher of religious toleration, and who really believe him to be all that they so eloquently describe him, we could almost wish that history for once would be less impartial, and that we could see Calvert as they see him. For our sympathies are naturally with the heroic, and with all that sheds a heavenly lustre upon our race and proclaims its lofty origin. We hate to have our own idols shattered, even while confessing that they are but idols, and we would not therefore voluntarily shatter the idols of others. Who willingly would think of Jason and his brave Argonauts as sailing on a voyage of discovery solely to establish new commercial relations? Yet this was all that Jason sought to achieve by his voyage of discovery, so that when at length he had won the Golden Fleece, ever guarded by the sleepless dragon, abundant success had crowned his efforts. Now Lord Baltimore was Maryland's Jason, and commercial prosperity his Golden Fleece. And the world, commonly in its judgments fairly accurate, and always finally impartial, has not misunderstood this. Accordingly the founder of Maryland has found his appropriate place, not among the world's benefactors, the Isaac Newtons, the Francis Bacons, the Gallileos, and the Keplers; the Luthers, Savonarolas, Augustines and the St. Pauls, but among the men of lower rank and inferior aim, the promoters of the mere trading schemes and colonization enterprises, the birth of which every age has witnessed, but in which the sixteenth and seventeenth centuries more especially abounded.

Here then we take our leave of George Calvert—neither sage nor philosopher, pilgrim father nor public benefactor—but politician, merchant, adventurer, whose creed and life alike were no better than the creed and life of many thousands of other Englishmen who lived in his own age.

CHAPTER VII.

THE CHARTER OF MARYLAND.

1632.

> England, our Mother's Mother! Come, and see
> A greater England here! O come, and be
> At home with us, your children, for there runs
> The same blood in our veins as in your sons;
> The same deep-seated Love of Liberty
> Beats in our hearts.
> —R. H. STODDARD, "*Guests of the State.*"

Two months after Lord Baltimore's death, the charter of his new province, written in Latin, "the only one of the colonial charters the original of which is in that language"[1] finally passed the Great Seal of England, with no other changes in its wording than the substitution of the name of Cecilius in place of his father's. The province was named Maryland or Terra Mariæ. It had been the wish of the elder Baltimore to have it called Crescentia, but the king was firm for Maryland. Virginia memorialized the virgin queen, Elizabeth, and Maryland should memorialize his own beloved queen, so that side by side in the new world should be the twin memorials of the two English queens.

The province was of vast extent. Its generous limits were defined in the chapter's opening paragraphs :—

"Charles, by the Grace of God, King of England, Scotland, France, and Ireland, Defender of the Faith, &c.

To all to whom these presents shall come, greeting.

* * * * * * * * *

"Know ye therefore that we favoring the pious and noble purpose of the said Baron of Baltimore, of our special grace, certain knowledge, and mere motion, have given, granted and confirmed, and by this our present charter, do give, grant and confirm, unto the said Cecilius, now Baron of Baltimore, his heirs and assigns, all that part of a Peninsula lying in the parts of America between the ocean on the east, and the Bay of Chesapeake on the west, and divided from the other part thereof by a line drawn from the promontary or Cape of Land called Watkins Point, (situate in the aforesaid bay, near the river of Wighco)[2] on the west, unto the main ocean on the east, and between that bound on the south unto that part of Delaware Bay on the north which lyeth under the fortieth degree of northerly latitude from the equinoctial, where New England ends ; and all that tract of land between the bounds aforesaid that is to say, passing from the aforesaid bay called Delaware Bay in a right line by the degree aforesaid, unto the true meridian of the first fountain of the river Potomack, and from thence tending towards the south unto the further bank of the aforesaid river, and following the west and south sides thereof, unto a certain place called Cinquack,[3] situate near the mouth of the said river, where it falls into the bay of Chesapeake, and from thence by a straight line unto the aforesaid promontary, and place ealled Watkins Point."[4]

[1] Fisher, *Men, Women and Manners*, Vol. II, Page 154.
[2] Now called the Pocomoke.
[3] Now Smith's Point.
[4] This description of the bounds of the Province was framed by the aid of the map in Smith's *History of Virginia*, which

All this, a province large as an empire, was given without money and without price. It was as if King Charles, addressing Cecilius Calvert, had appropriated the language of scripture : "Lift up now thine eyes, and look from the place where thou art northward, and southward, and eastward, and westward : for all the land which thou seest, to thee will I give it, and to thy seed forever. Arise, walk through the land in the length of it and in the breadth of it ; for I will give it unto thee."[5] All, all, in this vast territory, was his which corresponded with the description then given—*hactenus inculta*—"hitherto uncultivated." What a princely gift! What a splendid property! And yet what a tremendous responsibility? A young man, twenty-eight years of age, suddenly finds himself the largest land owner in the king's dominions. Let anyone take one of the Chesa-

"may safely challenge a comparison in point of accuracy with the maps of this day," McMahon, Page 2.

A glance at the map of Maryland, will show that the present boundaries of the state are by no means the same as the boundaries here given. Maryland has, in fact, been deprived of a strip forty miles wide, extending from east to west along her northern border. This loss of a territory now embracing the whole of Delaware, and a large portion of Pennsylvania, including the site of Philadelphia itself, she owes to William Penn who obtained it by perjury. See his letter in the *Md. Hist. Soc's* care.

[5] Genesis XIII, 14, 15, 17.

peake Bay steamers which ply on the great rivers of Maryland, such as the Patuxent on the western, or the Choptank on the eastern shore, and after steaming for hours, and seeing nothing on either side but what was once Lord Baltimore's land, he will be impressed by the magnificence of the gift as he could not be impressed in any other way. Never did any baron of the Conqueror receive so great a territory, or mediæval earl hold such extensive possessions. No scion of even a royal house had ever so splendid a portion. It was a patrimony which almost rivalled that of the king himself, and other than the king no man then living had the like.

Nor was this all of his good fortune. Cecilius Calvert, the second Baron of Baltimore, who thus suddenly appears on the world's stage destined to play thereon no insignificant part, was in some respects in an entirely unique position.[6] As lord Proprietary of Maryland, he was at once sole tenant of the Crown and absolute owner of every foot of

[6] Penn's charter created a government very similar to Lord Baltimore's, but far less independent, for laws passed in Pennsylvania must be sent to England for the royal assent, and the British Government, which fifty years before had expressly renounced the right to lay taxes upon the Marylanders, now expressly asserted the right to lay taxes upon the Pennsylvanians. Fiske, Vol. II, Page 145.

land in the province. All laws passed by the freemen of his province required his assent to become valid. He could coin money and grant titles, subject only to the restriction that they should not be such as were then used in England; he could create courts and pardon criminals; he could dictate war and put to death the captives taken in arms against him, or otherwise dispose of them according to his pleasure. He was even allowed to levy duties on goods imported from the mother country—the only case on record of a colony being given such power.[7] In addition to this remarkable concession the Crown bound itself never to tax the people of his colony— a right not conceded in any other charter given by an English king.[8] It was upon becoming just such a landlord in Virginia that the first Baron of Baltimore had so earnestly set his heart on the day he sailed up the James, three years before.

And yet, absolute lord though he was,[9] there were clauses in the Charter of Maryland of so restricting and limiting a nature, that Cecilius

[7] Fisher, Vol. II, Page 155.
[8] *Ibid.*
[9] The Proprietary of Maryland claimed 'royal' jurisdiction. See *Archives of Maryland, Assembly*, Page 170, September, 1642. This claim caused him trouble later on. See *Archives*, Page 263, April, 1650.

never possessed such absolute powers under it as his father had exercised in Newfoundland under his Charter of Avalon. The two charters are often, spoken of even by reliable writers, as almost the same, and even as absolutely identical,[10] *mutatis mutandis*. But this is only another proof of the accuracy of Bancroft's statement that the early history was often written with a carelessness which seized on rumours and vague recollections as sufficient authority for an assertion which satisfied prejudice by wanton perversions, and which, where materials were not at hand, substituted the inferences of the writer for authenticated facts.[11]

However, the charters are not the same, as anyone may see who chooses to compare them together. In two exceedingly important respects the power of the landlord under the Maryland Charter was very considerably diminished, the patentee being placed in a new and subordinate position by the insertion of clauses for which we look in vain in the earlier charter.

By the first of these clauses the terms on which the grants were held differed. Avalon had been

---

[10] S. T. Wallis, Essays, Vol. II, Page 104. Fisher, Vol. II, Page 154. Kennedy, Page 21. Chalmer's *History of Revolt of American Colonies* Book II, Chap. 3. Sparks, *American Biography*, Vol. XIX, New series IX, Page 23.

[11] Bancroft, Vol. I, Preface, 6, 10th Edit.

held by knight service. Sir George Calvert was in Newfoundland as a feudal lord. Now there was no more honorable nor independent way of holding land than that. Ordinary knight service merely required the knight to render forty days' service in the field to his master the king; to bear a due portion of the expenses when he knighted his eldest son; and the same when he married his eldest daughter. In place of these three forms of service substitutes were not infrequently accepted; an indulgence which was permitted in the case of the first Baron of Baltimore, his substitute being nothing more than the tender of a white horse whenever the king should in person visit the Province of Avalon.

In the Maryland Charter it was expressly declared that the grant to Lord Baltimore was not by knight service, but by "free and common soccage," on payment of an annual rent of two Indian arrows and one fifth of all the gold and silver there found. It is interesting to note that the character of this payment is curiously in accord with some of the old land tenures in England. The Manor of Elston, Nottingham, was held by the rent of one pound of cummin seed, two pairs of gloves and a steel needle. Henry III. gave to Henry de Aldithely, Egmundun and Newport, in the County of

Salop, for the rent of a mewed sparhawk to be delivered into the King's Exchequer every year at the Feast of St. Michael." Today the visitor at Windsor Castle is shown a couple of silk flags, which must be renewed every year to enable the owners to retain possession of the noble estates of Blenheim and Marlborough.

The change was great. The feudal lord[12] had been abolished, and in his place had been put the citizen, with vast powers and rare privileges indeed, but holding his property precisely as we hold ours, subject to the laws and bound by all the responsibilities entailed. The feudal lord of Avalon needed never to go to England, ought not to go, and might even refuse to go; the patentee under the Maryland holding "by free and common soccage" was obliged to go. The one could rule in his distant province, and tyrannize over his subjects without let or hindrance, and without any opportunity afforded of redress, until the king himself came into his demesne; the other year by year had to appear

---

[12] The statement that the charter, "Created a great feudal proprietorship and introduced on the American continent the feudal system, which was gradually disappearing in England" would seem to be incorrect, Fisher, *Men, Women and Manners*, Vol· II, Page 155. For same statement see Sparks, Vol. XIX, new series IX, P. 7.

personally at Windsor, bringing his Indian arrows with him and prepared to give an account of his stewardship. Doubtless this great change was due to the action of the Privy Council, which had all along looked upon the king's favoritism of Lord Baltimore with ill-concealed dislike. Nor was its motive in thus making so radical a change anything difficult to understand or appreciate. When Sir George Calvert received his Charter of Avalon, he was a professing Anglican Churchman. Cecilius Baltimore, on the other hand, was a professing Roman Catholic, and the Privy Council, with the Archbishop of Canterbury as its chiefest member, had no intention of allowing their fellow-countrymen living in a distant land to be subjected to the arbitrary rule of a member of the Roman Church, however excellent a man he might be. Hence the change.

Was it this immense difference, with its entailed obligations on the patentee to regularly appear in person at a certain time and place, and then and there pay his rent, that explains why Cecilius never left England to see the province he held? In part this certainly was the explanation, although it appears that the English government insisted upon his remaining in the country, his presence there being security for his good behavior.[13]

The second clause was even more important. It dealt directly with the religion of the new colony, as the first clause had dealt with it indirectly. In giving the Lord Proprietary of Maryland the same power to license the erection of places of worship which he had already possessed in Avalon it was now stipulated that the churches and chapels were "to be dedicated and consecrated according to the ecclesiastical laws of England"[14]—*a provision wholly wanting in the Avalon Charter.*

---

[13] It is not here implied that Cecilius was never able to visit Maryland. Later on the time came when he could have settled on his property, as his son and successor gladly did, but at first, and for some years while the experiment of a Roman Catholic proprietary with royal jurisdiction was on its trial, he was undoubtedly detained in England as security.

[14] Comments on this important addition to the Maryland Charter are generally noteworthy as tending to evade its real significance. e. g. McSherry, P. 24. "The ecclesiastical laws of England, so far as they related to the consecration or presentation of churches or chapels were extended to the colony, but the question of state religion was left untouched and therefore within the legislative power of the colonists themselves." But if England's ecclesiastical laws were extended to Maryland then England's Church was established there.

Again, Browne, *Maryland*, P. 69. The charter "permitted him to have churches consecrated according to other rituals." And the following by way of proof! "One of the first acts of the missionaries was to consecrate a Roman Chapel." But see the text for quotations from stranger conclusions still.

THE CHARTER OF MARYLAND. 123

That the insertion of such a clause should have been deemed a necessary condition of the issuing of the charter, has, not without reason, sorely perplexed those who see in it an instrument for securing religious liberty. No wonder "the candid inquirer must admit that there is in the charter no advance upon the ideas which then prevailed in England upon this subject," and that it is equally mysterious to the same candid inquirer to see that the "same connection between Church and State is contemplated, which then existed in the mother country."[15] But so obvious are these truths, that we may not unreasonably marvel at certain strange deductions which have been made from the presence of this restricting clause. For we have been told that the proprietary possessed the right to prevent the erection of any church or chapel for the propagation of a faith which he should choose to suppress.[16] We have further been told that having "the patronage and advowson of all churches which should happen to be built, the proprietary had besides the full control of all ecclesiastical affairs"; that "the pastors were to be chosen, not by popular election, but by the appointment of the owner of

[15] Sparks. *American Biography*, Vol. XIX, new series, IX. P. 27.
[16] *Ibid.*

the soil"; and that in fact he might "by the exclusive power of appointment, dictate the faith of the province."[17] But behold the climax: "Thus this clause becomes an additional mark of favor on the part of the sovereign power towards the patentee!"

I am not in the least surprised that one holding these views of Lord Baltimore's powers should confess that, "no little ingenuity is required to explain the fact that such extensive ecclesiastical powers should have been conferred by Charles, himself a Protestant, on Lord Baltimore, an avowed Catholic." Or that he should never be able to comprehend a thing "still more mysterious, how a (Roman) Catholic could consecrate churches according to the ecclesiastical laws of England, when the exercise of that religion was there forbidden under severe penalties, by Act of Parliament."[18] All this is but another illustration of the hopeless confusion which follows neglect to observe carefully the intent of a charter which guaranteed "all the privileges, franchises and liberties of this our Kingdom of England" to the colonists. Perhaps a closer acquaintance with the ecclesiastical system of England would have shown that the difficulties

[17] *Ibid*, Pps. 27 and 28.
[18] *Ibid*.

supposed to be created by the charter were not so
insurmountable. In England the idea of the clergy
being chosen by popular vote is almost unknown.
The lord of the manor is commonly the patron of
the "living," as the parishes are called, and until
Queen Anne's time, even were the patron a Roman
Catholic, he legally exercised the right of appointment.[19] Now Lord Baltimore was simply the patron of the churches to be built and of the parishes
to be founded in Maryland. And while it is con-
ceivable, that disregarding alike the dictates of prudence, the teachings of common sense, the impulses
of common gratitude and the obligations of honor,
that he might have acted in the way suggested, it
is noteworthy that he never did so act. On the
contrary, though by no means always a model patron, he took care to interfere in ecclesiastical affairs
as little as possible. Indeed, although the charter
made provision, as Burnap admits, "for the support
of the clergy, not by the people, but by the rent of
lands, or other property, bestowed upon each individual church by the proprietary, or those to whom

---

[19] Under a statute of the thirteenth year of Queen Anne no Roman Catholic is permitted, "directly or indirectly, mediately or
immediately," to exercise patronage within the Church of England, his right of presentation or nomination lapsing to the
University of either Oxford or Cambridge.

he might convey landed estates,"[20] there is no evidence that Baltimore ever faithfully carried out that part of his contract. Freely he had received; it could scarcely be contended that he had freely given.

But the effect of this clause was even more far-reaching still, even more intolerant. By it every church and chapel built in the province was to be the property of the Church of England. Did the Puritans erect a place of public worship, the Church of England could claim it. Did the Roman Catholics do the same, she could claim that too. Thus the charter virtually prohibited the erection of any place of public worship except that of the Church of England. Moreover, it was not by any means a dead letter. The Jesuits who came to Maryland with the first batch of colonists were so far from thinking it was so, that they built no churches at all. In fact, not till 1661 did they have a place of worship of any substantial character at all, a chapel being then built near Leonardtown, in St. Mary's

[20] Sparks, P. 28.

Baltimore appears to have entered upon his administration of his province with the intention of honestly providing glebes for the English clergy, but the fierce opposition of the Jesuits (See Father Copley's letter in Chapter XIV) coupled with the fact that there were no English clergy to provide for, caused him to let the matter drop.

County. Beside this, for some time after their advent into the colony, the Jesuit priests were contented to hide their ecclesiastical character under assumed names, thereby showing they well knew they were in the enemies' country. Manifestly all understood that the Church of England was to be the Church of the colony, and all public worship was to be in accordance with her standards.

The hands of the Lord Proprietary were indeed tied. They were doubly tied. For as if this were not enough, a portion of the tenth clause of the charter reads: "We will also, and of our more especial grace, for us, our heirs and successors, we do straightly enjoin, constitute, ordain and command, that the said province shall be of our allegiance, and that all and singular the subjects and liege people of us, transported, or to be transported, into the said province, and the children of them, and of such as shall descend from them, *shall be denizens and lieges of us, our heirs and successors of our Kingdoms of England and Ireland.*[21] The

[21] This would seem to be a third restricting clause. But as a matter of fact it is simply the logic result of the first. The change from the feudal lordship to the free and common soccage involved it. As by feudalism all the people in Avalon were also under the over lord—the English king—under the Maryland Charter they were not, save as specially declared to be so. Hence the clause.

settlers in Maryland were still to be Englishmen, with all the rights of Englishmen. Never, then, was man in worse plight if under this instrument [22] the Lord Proprietary of Maryland hoped to found a colony where his countrymen could legally enjoy their proscribed religion in peace and safety, and be beholden to none. With all his absolute lordship and royal jurisdiction there was one thing which he could not do; he could not establish his own creed in Maryland. What a pity it was that Cecilius, on receiving such a charter as this, did not at once send it back to the king, saying that for his purposes it was altogether worthless. That he did not do so, is fair presumptive proof that it suited his purposes and satisfied his wishes.

[22] Davis, *Day Star*, Page 26, speaks of the charter as "a compact between a member of the English and a disciple of the Roman Church" and as being "to the confessors of each faith the pledge of religious freedom," and as having, if not the form, the spirit and substance of a concordat. And he claims that "This is the inference faithfully drawn from a view of the instrument itself; from a consideration of the facts and circumstances attending the grant; and from a study of the various interpretations, essays and histories, of the many discourses and other publications which have appeared upon this prolific theme." The facts revealed in the text show Mr. Davis' inferences to be not well-founded.

CHAPTER VIII.

THE ADVENTURERS, AND HOW THEY WERE GATHERED TOGETHER.

1632-1633.

> Home, kindred, friends, and country—these.
> Are things from which we never part;
> From clime to clime, o'er land and seas,
> We bear them with us in our heart,
>
> —MONTGOMERY.

Although Cecilius Calvert was for over forty-three years Lord Proprietary of Maryland, he never set foot upon her shores. As an Irish baron, he probably saw nothing amiss in following a custom which allowed him, without forfeiting public esteem, to own and draw a princely income from a property which he had never seen.[1] Unhappily it was a custom which was not only too common in Ireland, but it had even had its origin there.[2] The old leaven still worked. Irish landlords lived anywhere but in Ireland.

[1] Froude, *History of England*, Vol. II, P. 127.

[2] In charging Cecilius with neglect of duty we must not overlook the fact that there were periods in his administration of Maryland when he was "under bonds not to leave the kingdom." See Page 122.

But in another respect Cecilius Calvert was the very man Maryland then needed, for he was a clear-headed man of business, "who had understanding of the times to know what Israel ought to do."[3] He resembled his father in giving his chief attention to business rather than religion, not that he was an irreligious man. But apparently he was not very much under religious influences, never even contributing a shilling, as far as the public records show, towards the building of a church or school house in his colony.[4]

Still, notwithstanding this characteristic, he was unquestionably a really great man, who more largely than any other gave Maryland her bent, and he rightly finds a place among the makers of America. He was pre-eminently Maryland's lord in a broader sense than even ownership would imply, for he framed her form of government, supervised her planting, settled her local disputes, and kept her on good terms with the mother country throughout all the troubles of the parliamentary period, alternately enjoying the friendship of King Charles the First, then of Oliver Cromwell—the Lord Protector—and finally of King Charles the

---

[3] 1 Chronicles, xii, 32.
[4] Neill, *Terra Mariæ*, P. 132.

Second. Handicapped though he was by his absenteeism, by local prejudice, and above all by the profession of a proscribed religion he was ever a power in Maryland.

Such, then, being the second Lord Baltimore, we shall not marvel at the promptness and vigor he displayed in at once turning to account his magnificent domain. The task before him was stupendous, and bearing in mind how unfitted he was by temperament to be an adventurer at all, we should readily have pardoned him had he altogether delegated its burdens to others. With a province of eight million acres—an empire in extent—his responsibilities were well-nigh those of a king. For it was not as if his province was under an orderly and settled government, with its industrious people already dwelling in flourishing towns and villages; its farm houses dotting the landscape in all directions, its mines in full operation, and the fisheries of its bays and rivers affording ample employment to its fishermen; over all of which he had but to exercise the purely formal, and perfunctory office of governor, and draw therefrom his royalties and rents. Such a stewardship would have been no sinecure, as our modern capitalists well know. The proprietary's task was however a far greater one than that ; for it was not that of mere administration, but of creation and organization. He was called upon to people his land with industrious settlers who should themselves create towns and villages, and turn the solitudes of rivers and woods into centres of commercial activity, to the end that there might be built up in those parts "of America not yet cultivated, though inhabited by a barbarous people," a strong and active colonial life. Grand was the vision which shaped itself before his eyes. Not less was it than the making of another England, and transplanting of all her aristocratic forms and ancient customs to the virgin soil of Maryland ; where there should be Courts Leet and Courts Baron, and where he, the first Lord Proprietary, should be the acknowledged founder and first lord of a line of trans atlantic gentry which might, in years to come, rival in the splendor of territorial aggrandizement, and in weight of office and dignity, even the earlier nobility of England herself. It was thus for him to add a jewel of surpassing beauty and lustre to the English Crown, and thereby earn both the gratitude of the mother country, and a distinguished place among her most illustrious sons.

Of all this there was no sign as yet. Maryland

was the stretched canvas upon which, as with the hand of genius, he must paint a goodly picture; the rough block of marble from which he must release an angel. But until this was done the canvas and marble were canvas and marble only. Those rivers teeming with fish, those forests full of game, that soil, fertile, rich and deep, those mines yet untouched, abounding in coal and iron; were all valueless to him and to the children of his people, until the vision was fulfilled. The proprietary had need of divine guidance. And the prayer of the youthful King Solomon might well have served him for a model:—"O Lord, my God, thou hast made thy servant king instead of David my father, and I am like a little child: I know not how to go out or come in. . . . . Give therefore thy servant an understanding heart."[5]

Whatever were his feelings on succeeding to his inheritance, Cecilius Calvert lost no time in formulating his plans. All England must know of Maryland. Public attention must be drawn to her golden opportunities. He needed emigrants for his plantation. Able-bodied men only were desired; especially such as could handle well the tools of the artisan and the mechanic, and the implements

---

[5] 1 Kings, iii, 7 and 9.

of husbandry. But for all acceptable candidates, abundant were the rewards. Were they poor he would see that they were afforded the means of going to the new country. Had they money to invest, this was the time. The profits were absolutely sure, and they were so large that every man who did not embrace this chance of investing would be losing the opportunity of his life.

Concerning the special inducements offered we know all on the reliable authority of the lord proprietary himself, for there is in existence an "account of Cecil Calvert, Baron of Baltimore, which he himself faithfully compiled, from the reports scattered through England by travelers, who had sought their fortunes in the new world," in which the character, quality and state of the country, and its numerous advantages and sources of wealth were amply set forth.[6] This tract or prospectus printed to influence public opinion, declared it to be the intention of "the Most Illustrious Baron" to sail for his province about the middle of the following September, and to lead

---

[6] The curious tract published in 1666 by George Alsop, "A character of the province of Maryland," from its style and from its dedication to Lord Baltimore and the merchant adventurers, we may infer that it was paid for by them in order to encourage emigration.

thither a colony. There was no risk of loss, the tract continued, for having studied the advantages and disadvantages of other colonies, the baron was convinced that his own promised "the most prosperous success." His authorities for this roseate view were, first and foremost, certain writings which his own father had left behind him—"an eye witness reliable and worthy of all credit;[7]—and, in the next place, the reports of other eye witnesses constantly coming from that country or places not far from it. Besides, in confirmation, there were the published statements of Captain John Smith, who first discovered the country.[8] And in addition to this testimony he might add the unanimous reports, in agreement therewith, of very many then living in London, who formerly came from these countries, and intended to return there.

Now to all those who should "accompany and assist him in so glorious an undertaking, the Baron offered many inducements, in the most generous and liberal spirit."[9] Although at the same time

---
[7] Cecilius Calvert, "*An Account of the Colony of the Lord Baron of Baltimore.* P. 45.
[8] *The True Travels, Adventures and Observations of Captain John Smith in Europe, Asia, Africa and America.*
[9] *Account*, P. 46. New conditions were issued in 1635. See *Archives*, Pp. 47, 49. These conditions assigned to every emigrant from England, bringing in five men, one thousand acres of land,

he would not have his countrymen suppose that his principal object was the raising of crops and the planting of fruit trees; for his first and most important design was to spread the knowledge of the true God—a design worthy of Christians, yea, of angels. Let them think, therefore, most of all, of the spiritual fields whitening to harvest. Men then in London were telling how they had seen ambassadors at Jamestown in Virginia, sent by the Indian kings to beg for religious teachers who should instruct their people in the doctrines of Christianity, and regenerate them in the saving waters of baptism. And those Indians were still crying, "Come over and help us." Surely no better work could engage their attention than to respond to such a pathetic appeal, "for it was the work of Christ, the King of Glory."[10]

Coming back to mundane considerations, let them note the climate. It was like the "best parts of Arabia Felix * * * serene and mild, not op-

---

with manorial privileges—subject to an annual quit rent of twenty shillings; if he brought in a less number, he should have assigned to him one hundred acres for himself, one hundred for each servant, and if he had a wife and children, one hundred for his wife, and fifty for each child under sixteen years of age, subject to an annual quit rent of two shillings for every hundred acres.

[10] *Account*, P. 46.

pressively hot like that of Florida and old Virginia, nor bitter cold like that of New England." On the contrary " preserving a middle temperature between the two, it enjoyed the advantages and escaped the evils of each." The country was rich in rivers and bays navigable for large ships and abounding in fish. On one of the rivers, the Potomac, there was such a lucrative trade with the Indians that a certain merchant in the last year exported beaver skins to the value of forty thousand gold crowns. Oaks grew there so straight and tall that beams sixty feet long, and two and a half feet wide, could be cut from them, while cypress trees of immense girth grew to a height of eighty feet before they had any branches. There were plenty of mulberry trees to feed silk-worms. Chestnut trees large as in Spain, and cedars equaling those of which Libanus boasts. Vines of wonderful fruitfulness; gooseberries like their own; three kinds of plums; deer and swine so abundant as to be an annoyance. Herds of cows and wild oxen, fit for beasts of burden and good to eat. The woods were full of horses; wild goats abounded; so did muskrats, beavers, martens, weasels, which did not destroy hens as theirs did. Wild turkeys were there twice as large as the domestic turkey.

Peaches were so abundant that an honorable and reliable man actually declared that last year he gave one hundred bushels to his pigs. All kinds of beans and roots were common there, besides peas, which grew ten inches in ten days. It was, moreover, such a good grain country, that, in the worst years, the seed yielded two hundred fold; at other times generally for one grain five or six hundred; but in the best years fifteen hundred to sixteen hundred was the usual yield, and this in one harvest!! Moreover, the soil was so rich that it afforded three harvests a year!! It surely only needed the concluding statement, that gold and pearls were to be found there, to make Maryland the El Dorado of the nations."[11]

The advertisement was skillfully worded. All good things were combined. To a missionary, the sight of pagan Indians holding out their babes for baptism was an irresistible temptation; the capitalist was as irresistibly lured by the prospect of a fortune in beaver skins; while before the eyes of

[11] What a satire on all this puffing was the letter of the king to the governor of Virginia, in which, bespeaking a kindly welcome and ready help for the adventurers, he requests the Virginians to permit them to buy and transport into Maryland such cattle and other commodities as they needed. Surely Maryland needed no such assistance. She was rich and increased in goods and in need of nothing. See, Alsop, P. 43.

the poor, illiterate peasant, long before the days of forty acres and a mule, was dangled the prize of independent land ownership, combined with large shares in the profits of the very latest colonial venture.

Thus there were two classes of motives, the spiritual and the commercial, to which the lord proprietary appealed in seeking the settlers he needed. The first was the very common-place one of self-interest and self-aggrandizement. Emigrants to Maryland would gain sometimes fifteen hundred fold or sixteen hundred, and that three times a year! The second, less common, but to some minds equally attractive, was the evangelization of the heathen. Priests who taught the Christian religion to the children sitting in darkness would not go without their reward—a reward not less real because only to be reaped when at the final judgment "they that be wise shall shine as the brightness of the firmament; and they that turn many to righteousness as the stars for ever and ever."

One would naturally have supposed that this appeal would have been attended with very disastrous consequences to England herself; at any rate that the Roman Catholic portion of the population "hounded from every hundred in the three kingdoms,"[12] would have immediately answered it. For less than religious liberty—man's dearest possession on earth—cities have been depopulated.[13] But on the present occasion, strangely enough, there was no such fever; no hasty mortgaging of estates; no rushing to the markets by property holders desirous of realizing on their property; no ruinous selling of ploughs and agricultural implements by the farmers, nor of tools by the artisans. And as with the men, so with the women. None were found disposing of their trinkets to secure a passage to that new world where they would gain liberty of conscience for themselves and for their children. Apparently, strange as it seems, that world had no charms for them, and in consequence this public appeal fell so flat that two sorry ships, one of three hundred and fifty tons, the other of fifty, were amply sufficient to carry the true Israelites, some two hundred and odd persons in all,—"out of the house of bondage to the land flowing with milk and honey."

Very different in its successful issue was the beginning of the Puritan colony at Massachusetts

---

[12] *Md. Hist. Soc., F. P., No. 18.* P. 9.
[13] Quoted by Prescott, *Peru.* P. 193, Vol. I.

Bay. No touting for emigrants was required then, nor any painting of rose-colored pictures of the American land. Nevertheless it required not less than eleven ships to transport the seven hundred men, women and children, who forthwith offered to leave forever their native soil. And this was but a beginning. So great was the exodus at one time that even royal authority was invoked to put a stop to it.[14]

But this is not all. A still more remarkable feature of the expedition organized with so much energy remains to be noted. A religious census of the passengers makes it abundantly clear that even out of those who did respond to the appeal only an insignificant proportion were members of the Roman Catholic Church.[15] Beginning with the first name upon the list, that of Leonard Calvert, brother of Cecilius, and leader of the expedition, as was to be expected from his family connections, he was a member of the Roman Catholic Church. The next name to his, however, was that of a member of the English Church, Jerome Hawley,[16]

---

[14] *Old Times in the Colonies.* P. 165 and 184.
[15] *Md. Hist. Soc.*, F. P., No. 18. Pp. 32 and 176.
[16] William Hawley, brother of Jerome Hawley, was a Protestant. Jerome was a Treasurer of Virginia. No Roman Catholic could have held that office.

who accompanied the expedition as councillor of the new province. Thomas Cornwaleys, whose name stands third on the list, also a councillor of the province, like Hawley, was a member of the English Church.[17] Then as we proceed the strange fact is revealed that at least three-fourths of the emigrants were not members of the Roman Church at all, but of the English. We have this on authority which cannot be impugned.[18] "By far the

[17] Cornwaleys is by some authors regarded as a Romanist. See Browne, *George and Cecilius Calvert*. P. 45. An interesting contribution to the settlement of the question of his religious opinions is found in his use of the language of King James' Bible. In his letter to Lord Baltimore of April 6th, 1638, see Chapter xiv—he says : " My lord, I may properly use the language of the Gospel, I cannot dig and to beg I am ashamed." The Douay version of the scriptures does not have this particular rendering of the original, its language being as follows: "And the steward said within himself, what shall I do? because my Lord taketh away from me the stewardship? To dig I am not able ; to beg I am ashamed." Had Thomas Cornwaleys been a Roman Catholic, he would scarcely have been found using the language of the Protestant Bible. As additional evidence on the same question all Cornwaleys' relatives were English Church people. "A brother was Rector of a Suffolk Parish. In the graveyard there is a stone in memory of Frances, wife of Samuel Richardson, clerk, daughter of Thomas Cornwaleys, Esquire, died June 24, 1684." who was probably the aunt of the Maryland Commissioner. See Neill, *Founders of Maryland*. P. 69. Moreover, Cornwaleys' second son, Thomas, born in 1662, just after his mother's return from Maryland, was a clergyman of the Church of England, and died in 1731. See Neill, P. 81.

[18] Quoted, *Md. Hist. Soc., F. P.*, No. 18, P. 32. See also " *Records of the English Province of the Society of Jesus*," Vol. iii, 7th series, Pp. 362 and 364. London, 1877.

greater part were heretics," wrote one of two Jesuit missionaries on board the Ark; and again, more explicitly, "three-fourths were heretics." [19]

Mirabile dictu. Eighteen months have elapsed since the charter was granted, and now, after all England has been thoroughly canvassed less than fifty Roman Catholics have been pursuaded to leave England in response to this opportunity of worshipping God according to their consciences,[20] notwithstanding, too, the unparalleled prosperity thrown in as a make weight.[21] Yet it is said that "the Catholics flocked to Maryland." [22]

[19] Yet Mr. McSherry writes of these emigrants: "Nearly all of whom were Catholics and gentlemen of fortune and respectability." P. 25. As to their Catholicity, Mr. McSherry is right. They called themselves Protestant Catholics. As to their being gentlemen of fortune and respectability, it is a pity that being such they did not see fit to pay their very moderate boards bills before they left England.

[20] Cecilius himself attributed the delay in gathering his company to the opposition which the expedition had aroused. See *Strafford's Letters*, I., P. 178. The real difficulty seems to have been to get men who were willing to leave England.

[21] Of this very time we are told, *Md. Hist. Soc., F. P., No. 18.,* P. 17, "It seems as if England was no longer a place where men could be free, and while the Protestants were preparing to seek new homes for themselves in the wilderness, the Roman Catholics, impelled by the same necessity, and driven by even more cruel laws, began to concert among themselves measures by which a sanctuary for their religion and liberties could be provided on the same continent where so many other Englishmen were finding refuge."

[22] Quoted by Polk. Pamphlet in Epis. Lib., Balto. P. 15.

But even more remains to be told. Lord Baltimore himself, the Moses who was to lead these children of Israel out of Egypt found at the last moment that he could not go to Maryland with them. Surely "the pious pilgrims who placed their ships under the protection of God, raised their hearts in prayer for the success of the great enterprise which they had undertaken," and sailed away from the homes in which they had been born, "in order to plant the seed of freedom and religious liberty to secure to themselves and their children the inestimable privilege of worshipping God according to the dictates of their consciences"[23] deserved better treatment than this. How forlorn they must have felt having go to without their rightful leader. But he tried to console them. It was, he said, his own sorrowful misfortune, "but, by reasons of some unexpected accidents" he found it more necessary for their good to stay in England some time longer, for the better establishment of his and their rights, than it was fit the ship should stay for him, but by the grace of God he fully intended next year to be with them.

These adventurers pilgrims for conscience sake! They themselves forsooth would have been as-

[23] McSherry, *History of Maryland*, P. 26.

tounded could they have foreseen their appearance on the stage of history in any such sensational role. They certainly were the oddest set of "pilgrims" ever known. Young men wanting to see the world were there. Peasants too, desirous of bettering their condition. Jesuit priests, eager to do missionary work among the Indians, and hopeful of regaining some of the vanished prestige and lost influence of their society. Even the scapegrace class with ruined reputation and broken by licentiousness, was represented there.

But even had they been for the most part Romanists and not Anglicans to obtain religious liberty was beyond their power. Look at their patron's charter. They could not go beyond that. Carrying that instrument with them, their journey was a fruitless one. Better, far better, in such a case would it have been for them to do as the pilgrim fathers of New England had done, and, on the vessel which bore them, draw up their own constitution which every man should sign, and every man obey. An Irish peasant believing his cabin haunted, had made up his mind to leave it. But he was loath to go. Poor though it was, it had sheltered him and his family. But at last he was unable longer to endure the presence of the spirit. So there came a time when outside of the wretched shanty a little cart stood, and on it all his household goods were stored. He had cast the die, and he was going away. A passing neighbor inquired if he was flitting. Before he could answer a voice out of the midst of the stuff replied, "Aye, we're fiittin'." It was the voice of the spirit. "Oh," groaned the poor peasant, "if he is going we might as well stay where we are." So in good faith might the adventurers as well have said, "If that charter is going we may as well stay where we are."[21]

The expedition was to have left England about the middle of September. But it was not actually ready to leave Gravesend, its first port of departure, till October 19th; nor its final port in the Isle of Wight till November 22d, 1633. It had doubtless many embarrassing obstacles to contend with ere it finally started; but two difficulties beset it of such

[21] Something like this was actually done by the first Lord Baltimore. His grant of lands in Longford County, Ireland, dated February 18th, 1621, was made subject to the condition that he should not sell the land to Roman Catholics. He had also to require all settlers to take the oath of supremacy and be conformable in point of religion. As soon as he professed himself a Roman Catholic, he could not rightly hold the land thus granted, and so on February 12th, 1625, he surrendered his patent, which he received again on March 11th, with the religious clause struck out. See Wilhelm, P. 117.

a character as to afford a perfectly satisfactory explanation of all the delays which occurred.

The first difficulty was of the nature of an attachment which had been served on the vessels because several of the adventurers had not paid their board bill. A certain Mr. Gabriel Hawley had contracted with a Mr. James Clements, and other citizens of Gravesend, for the boarding of some of the men at one shilling a day, while they awaited the ships' departure.[25] Before the time for settlement came, Hawley had been cast into prison for debt, the prison being the supposed remedy in that day for failure to pay one's debts our enlightened fathers not possessing the appreciation of the situation belonging to the untutored Indian, who, when confronted with a like condition, laconically said, "Ugh! In prison no catch beaver." Yet, as Hawley was merely Baltimore's agent, Clements and his fellow-sufferers forthwith brought suit against Lord Baltimore himself.[26] The case eventually went before the Privy Council, with what result, however, is not known.

The second difficulty was a more serious one. After the ships had left Gravesend it became

[25] *Md. Hist. Soc., F. P.*, No. 9. Streeter, Pp. 106, 107.
[26] *Archives of Maryland, Council*, 1636–1667, P. 24.

rumored [27] that they were going, not to America at all, but to Spain, and that they were carrying arms and soldiers. In great haste a government vessel was dispatched after them to bring them back again. Upon being overtaken and brought back to Gravesend, a thorough and satisfactory examination was made, and the oaths of allegiance and supremacy were administered to all.[28] Released at last, the vessels again started but all the emigrants were not yet on board. The rest were taken on at the Isle of Wight, where opportunity was seized to smuggle the two Jesuit priests on board.

Mindful of the fact that some of the adventurers were Roman Catholics, and that Protestants are sometimes unreasonably afraid of Romanism, and apt to take offence where none is intended, Lord Baltimore, as the very first of his parting injunctions to his deputies in charge of the expedition, bade them "cause all acts of Roman Catholic religion to be done as privately as may be, and that they instruct all Roman Catholics to be silent on all occasions of discourse on Religion * * * and this to be observed at land as well as at sea."[29] The Lord Proprietary would not have his colonial

[27] Neill, *Terra Mariæ*, P. 58.
[28] Neill, *Founders of Maryland*, p. 87.
[29] *Calvert Papers* I, P. 133.

enterprise wrecked through its being identified with Romanism. He acted wisely.

Of course such an injunction would have been an impossibility under the religious pilgrimage theory. True pilgrims glory in their religion. There is for them no bowing down in the house of Rimmon. They come out of the midst of their unsanctified brethren shaking the dust off their feet, losing their homes but maintaining their convictions and their independence. They practice no rites in secret for wherefore but to practice them boldly do they become pilgrims at all.[30]

[30] McMahon, P. 198, note. Mr. McMahon, while wishing to "avoid all invidious contrasts turns with exultation to the pilgrims of Maryland."

CHAPTER IX.

THE JOURNEY OF THE ADVENTURERS TO MARYLAND, AND THEIR ARRIVAL.

1633-34.

> You sail and you seek for the fortunate Isles
> The old Greek Isles of the yellow birds' song?
> Then steer straight on through the watery miles—
> Straight on, straight on, and you can't go wrong;
> Nay, not to the left—nay, not to the right—
> But on, straight on, and the Isles are in sight.—
> The fortunate Isles where the yellow birds sing
> And life lies girt with a golden ring.
> —JOACHIM MILLER.

Nothing so abundantly proves the practical wisdom of the lord proprietary as his combined appeal for farmers and missionaries. Without the goodwill of the Indians the colony could not hope to prosper. It would ever be apprehensive of the fate which had overtaken earlier colonies. At any minute the dreaded Indian war-whoop might ring through the dense forests, and, after a life and death struggle, the homes of the settlers be given to the flames, and their mutilated corpses left unburied upon the field. The missionary even now is often an indispensable factor in the progress of trade and commerce. A shrewd business man upon being urged by a missionary to open a trading station in New Guinea replied : " Your mission has not been long enough established there to make it worth while for us to go at present." But no practical business man of today sees the missionary's usefulness any more clearly than did Lord Baltimore, two hundred and fifty years ago, as he advertised for men of Christlike zeal whose work it should be to lead even the wild Indians to contribute to the success of the province he had inherited. It was doubtless this consideration which prompted the sole reference to religion in the advertisement, wherein he so pathetically appealed for Christian teachers to relieve the minds of the poor Indians of Maryland of their painful suspense with regard to the future welfare of their unbaptized infants.

To one of the missionaries, Father White, we are indebted for a very full account of the voyage of the adventurers to Maryland, and of the events immediately following upon their arrival, he having left us a narrative, or rather two narratives, giving a full description of the same, one written in English, the other in Latin. The English narrative, written at the suggestion of Leonard Calvert, was at once forwarded by him to England, enclosed in a letter of his own to a certain Sir Richard Lechford, whom he addresses as "kinde partner." We should naturally have expected that anything of the nature of a report, or description of the country, would have been sent first and foremost to his own brother the lord proprietary. But "Articles of Agreement made 7th October, 1633, between Leonard Calvert of London, Esquire, and Sir Richard Lechford of Shellwood, in the County of Surrey, Knight,"[2] followed by a "Bond from Leonard Calvert to Sir Richard Lechford, dated 19th October, 1633"[3] sufficiently explains Leonard's action. Accordingly the governor sends the narrative to his partner, thus speaking of it: "I have herewith sent you * * * a more exact journal of all our voyage than I could find time to deliver you in this letter * * * This I have sent you was writ by a most honest and discreet gentleman, wherefore you may be confident of the truth of it"[4]— the "honest and discreet gentleman" being none

---

[1] *The Calvert Papers*, No. 3, *Md. Hist. Soc., F. P., No. 35*, P. 19.
[2] *Ibid.* P. 13.
[3] *Ibid.* P. 17.
[4] *Ibid.* P. 23.

other than Father White himself. The Latin narrative entitled, Relatio Itineris in Marylandiam,[5] was evidently the Jesuit priest's official report to his Superior, the Very Reverend Father, General Mutius Vitellesetis, the English head of the Jesuit Society. When we come to study these two narratives side by side it is at once evident why one account

[5] *Relatio Itineris.* P. 10.

(a) The "*Briefe Relation of the Voyage unto Maryland*" is one of eight papers received from Mr. Phillips. See Preface, Pp. viii and ix. It was circulated *in printed form* in the year 1634. See copy in Whittingham Episcopal Library—a library invaluable to the student.—Baltimore.

(b) The Latin MS. is practically the same account with certain changes and additions. It has had a mysterious history. Generally quoted as if it were the original authority, it was probably not published till 1832. The original, it is said, was discovered in the Archives of the Jesuit Society at Rome, by an American priest of the Society, who made a copy of it, which he placed in Georgetown College, D. C. On the *Md. Hist. Soc.* asking permission to copy the manuscript it was discovered that it had "unaccountably disappeared from the Archives of the Society." Subsequent search revealed it in fragmentary form in Loyola College, Baltimore.

"The acquisition of the English version has naturally led to an inquiry as to which version, the English or the Latin, is to be regarded as the original, and to whom the authorship is to be accredited." *Md. Hist. Soc. F. P., No. 35,* P. 6. *The Calvert Papers,* No. 3.

"The English version is an original letter, and not a translation from the Latin." *Calvert Papers, No. 3,* Pp. 7 and 8. From internal evidence both versions are evidently the work of an ecclesiastic, and as Father White was the senior priest of the Maryland mission, both accounts doubtless are from his hand.

would not have been satisfactory. The English narrative was for the information of British investors, and others interested in the financial success of the colony, generally Protestants; the Latin account was for the eye of the reverend gentleman's ecclesiastical superiors. Consequently in the English text all descriptions of peculiarly Roman ceremonial are studiously omitted, as not being likely to impress the readers favorably; while accounts of the nature of the soil and the character of the products, are enlarged upon: in the Latin text the Roman ecclesiastic feels that he can speak his mind freely.

The Latin narrative begins thus:—"On the twenty-second of the month of November, in the year 1633, being St. Cecilia's day, we set sail from Cowes, in the Isle of Wight, with a gentle east wind blowing. And after committing the principal parts of the ship to the protection of God especially, and of his most Holy Mother and St. Ignatius, and all the guardian angels of Maryland, we sailed on a little way between the two shores." There, as the breeze failed them, they lay becalmed until night, when a favorable and strong wind arose. Next morning, aided by the breeze, they sailed past the pointed rocks near the Isle of Wight, which from their appearance are named the Needles. On account of the double tide at this point, which ofttimes whirls away the strongest ships, and either dashes them against the rocks on the one side, or on the neighboring shore on the other, the Needles "are a perfect terror to sailors."[6]

The English account omits all notice of this peculiar religious ceremony, and with very good cause. Not twenty-four hours previously the lord proprietary had given the voyagers written instructions that all acts of Roman Catholic religion were to be done privately, and yet here, at the very outset, there is celebrated a ceremony of a distinctly Roman Catholic character. Surely this was conduct not easily to be excused, for it was disobedience on the part of men who as ministers of religion should have been the first to set an example of faithful obedience to properly constituted authority, indeed it was even more than disobedience. It was the first of a long series of deliberate acts of disloyalty, which more than anything else contributed to the discrediting of the Jesuit Society in Maryland, and to the overwhelming it with disaster. Neither did the evil done end with the suffering of the Jesuits. The punishment of the guilty involved

[6] *Relatio*, Pp. 10, 11.

troubles for the innocent, as so often it is seen to do in every sphere of human life and conduct—resulting as it did on three separate occasions in the Lord Proprietary of Maryland losing his province.[7] For the three revolutions which shook Maryland to her foundations were all Protestant revolutions which depended for their success on the emphasizing of religious differences, and especially upon the accentuation of the fact, that the lord proprietary himself was of the same unpopular church with the Jesuits. The Protestant party in Maryland, powerful in numbers, and upheld by the laws of England, hated to see a Roman Catholic at their head, and hence turbulent times.

Some justification of the doings of the Jesuit missionaries may, perchance, be attempted on the ground that the servants of Christ ought to obey God rather than man. We ought, indeed, always to obey God come what may: but there was no divine command that the Jesuits should be among the Maryland adventurers at all. Surely if the proprietary's rules were such that they could not honestly carry them out they had small right to be aboard his ships. That they only did what their

---

[7] The first occasion being in 1644, for two years; the second in 1655, for six years; and the third in 1689, for exactly a quarter of a century.

consciences directed them to do can readily be admitted. Nevertheless it would have been better if their consciences had been more enlightened, since such a ceremony at the beginning of their voyage was well calculated to provoke religious strife and dissension. To say nothing of prayers to the Blessed Virgin for her protection, what did the average British Protestant know of St. Ignatius? Or what, if he knew anything, would he be apt to think of him? Then as to the guardian angels of Maryland, Who were they? It is a pious opinion, founded on Christ's words, that each soul has a guardian angel, but where have we any authority for the idea that countries, and especially countries inhabited as Maryland then was by pagan Indians, are similarly favored?

Surely it was neither wise nor charitable to hold such a religious service as this in an expedition of which "three-fourths were heretics," an expedition sailing under the flag of Anglican England to establish a colony where Englishmen, so far as regards all their ecclesiastical relations, were to live under the very same laws which they had been living under in the old country. Moreover such action was not just to Lord Baltimore himself, as tending at the outset to jeopardize his venture.

For he was the real head of the expedition, as he was its sole organizer, and the bearer of a large portion of the expense incurred by it. Were this thing to become known in England it might even cost him the forfeiture of his patent.

I suspect that to this very act of disobedience the Protestants on board ascribed the troubles that followed, when shortly afterward a mighty storm arose. Hardly, in fact, were they out of sight of land when high winds springing up caused a great tempest to break upon the ships. Almost instantly the sea was as a wild beast seeking in its blind rage their utter destruction. Huge waves rolled over their vessel, and the blackness of the night added to the terror of the adventurers. The Dove was soon seen by those on board the Ark showing a light at her masthead. It was the signal agreed upon when danger was imminent. All at once this light disappeared from the sight of the men on the larger vessel. The Dove without doubt had gone down that instant with all on board, and gloomy thoughts filled the hearts of the voyagers in the Ark. But they had to look to themselves, for although they had a ship of four hundred tons burden—than which "a better could not be built of wood and iron"—they were in the greatest danger. A brief lull brought only a temporary respite. With the return of the storm, redoubled in its fury, the hopes that had quickly risen as quickly vanished away, for it really seemed as if "all the malicious spirits of the storm and all the evil genii of Maryland had come forth to battle against them."[8] Evidently Maryland's guardian angels were not doing their duty. It was now the last day of November, and many of them feared it would be their own last day. Clouds blacker than ever were rapidly accumulating. To increase their terror a sunfish appeared swimming with great efforts against the course of the sun."[9] A fearful omen this. Nor did they think it proved a false one. For the rising gale, with which the night closed in, had ere morning become a furious hurricane, striking terror into the hearts of the bravest. Nothing doubting but that the fate of their fellow-adventurers on the Dove was only too surely awaiting them also, they committed themselves unto prayer. But as the ship, of which they had now lost all control, with its solitary mainsail torn from top to bottom, "drifted about like a dish in the water, at the mercy of the winds and the

[8] *Relatio*, P. 15.
[9] *Ibid*, P. 15.

waves," [10] they patiently awaited the end. The Roman Catholics sought comfort in offering "prayers and vows in honor of the Blessed Virgin and her Immaculate Conception, of St. Ignatius, the Patron Saint of Maryland, St. Michael and all the guardian angels of the same country." The Protestants contented themselves with calling directly upon God, for they had learned from Holy Scripture that it is at His word that the "stormy wind arises which lifteth up the waves thereof." [11]

But "the night is long that never finds the day." The wildest storm spends its force at length, and dies away in peace. So this one. Presently came one of those perfect calms at sea when it is hard to realize that the depths could have been so troubled, or that the waves were ever as the strong mountains engaged in mortal combat. Then hope revived once more, and although the voyagers were now mourning the loss of brave companions, their hearts grew lighter as all immediate danger to themselves passed away.

Personally we have much reason to be thankful for that storm, since it is due to it that we have the unimpeachable authority of Father White himself [12]

[10] *Ibid*, P. 16.
[11] Psalm 107, v. 25.
[12] *Relatio*, P. 16.

for saying that the object of the voyage, so far as he and his brethren were concerned, was to preach to the heathen. For when "praying more fervently than was his usual custom," he set forth to Christ the Lord, to the Blessed Virgin, St. Ignatius and the angels of Maryland, that the purpose of the journey was to glorify the blood of the Redeemer in the salvation of barbarians, and also to raise up a kingdom for the Saviour. The storm abating upon the offering up of this prayer, he "understood much more clearly the greatness of God's love towards the people of Maryland,"[13] to whom he had been sent to minister.

Favorable winds blowing steadily towards the south and southeast took the adventurers along the shores of Spain, past the straits of Gibraltar and the Madeiras, and on to the Canaries, then called the Fortunate Isles. Sailing thence they came to anchor in a large bay, where there was nothing to be feared except the calms which, with dry humor, they remarked were "exhausting to the supplies of navigators."

It was now the Festival of the Nativity of our Lord, and in order "that that day might be better kept wine was given out; and those who drank of it

[13] *Ibid*, P. 17.

too freely were seized next day with a fever; and of these not long afterwards about twelve died, among whom were two Catholics." "The loss of Nicholas Fairfax and James Bearfoot" continues the writer "was deeply felt among us."[14] Had the day been properly kept this sad loss of twelve men of the company would never have occurred. Yet observe how this very incident indirectly confirms the truth of the historian's statement, that there was a very large preponderance of Protestants in this expedition. Twelve died, of whom only two were Roman Catholics.

The cup of the adventurers was not, however, to be one of unmixed bitterness. Judge of their unutterable joy, as they presently saw the little Dove, which for six weeks they had regarded as lost, sailing gallantly into the harbor. There was then a happy reunion of parted friends, and the company on the Ark soon heard how on that eventful night, when they supposed the little pinnace had gone down with all on board, that she had simply run before the driving storm back to the Scilly Islands, there to remain until the ocean grew calm again.

After the reappearance of the Dove no further mishaps occurred, and the reverend historian chats

[14] *Ibid*, P. 21.

JOURNEY OF THE ADVENTURERS. 163

pleasantly about the various places they stopped at after leaving Barbadoes, with its corner prices for provisions, its excessively warm climate and its wonderful cabbage with a stalk two hundred and eighty feet high; its pine-apple—"the queen of fruits"—with its spicy taste "like that of strawberries mixed with wine and sugar;" and Metalina, with its savages fat and shining with red paint, who knew not God, and devoured human flesh, having not long before disposed of several English interpreters in that way. Soon they sighted the Carribee Islands of Guadaloupe, and Montserrat, so called from the shape of its rough mountains, with its colony of Irishmen. Refugees were these Irishmen from ecclesiastical tyranny, for they had been banished from Virginia on account of professing the Roman Catholic faith. Special charms must Montserrat have possessed for their co-religionists on the Ark and the Dove. Yet on they went until they reached Moevius, with its pestilential air and fevers; then on to St. Christopher's, where they spent ten days. Here they saw land for the last time till, on the twenty-seventh of February, 1634, they reached Point Comfort in Virginia, " full of apprehension, lest the English inhabitants should be plotting against them."[15] Evidently the adven-

[15] *Ibid*, P. 30.

turers had heard of the first Lord Baltimore's treatment of the Virginians, and feared that condign punishment might be visited on them.

> "Suspicion always haunts the guilty mind;
> The thief doth fear each bush an officer."

Their apprehensions were groundless. The colonists of Virginia had been most arbitrarily deprived of a part of their land by the king. Nevertheless, if not genuinely loyal to their sovereign lord, they were at least politic enough to follow his instructions to the letter. And the new arrivals had no need to complain of any lack of warmth in their welcome. Indeed after being kindly entertained for eight or nine days "by the Virginians they parted from them with regret." So kindly were they treated that George Calvert, a brother of Lord Baltimore, and one of the gentlemen adventurers decided to remain there. Here, too, they saw Clayborne, back from his unsuccessful visit to England. With little tact Leonard Calvert seized the opportunity of reminding him that he, with the people of Kent Island, were now subjects of the Lord Proprietary of Maryland, and should acknowledge his jurisdiction. Clayborne, contending that Cecilius Calvert's charter did not give him any rights on Kent Island, whose inhabitants had even been represented in the Virginia legislature, declined obedience. Leonard Calvert replied by forbidding Clayborne to trade on the Chesapeake without a license from himself.[16] Clayborne retorted by drawing a lively picture of Indians waiting for Leonard's scalp, and the scalps of his companions.[17] Undeterred, however, by the dangers thus described on the third of March the travelers set sail for the Potomac River, to which a favorable breeze rapidly bore them, having been over three months on the voyage.

As they coasted along the Maryland shore, their first view of the country went far to confirm the marvellous statements of the *Account*. With the Potomac they were delighted. Never had they beheld a larger or more beautiful river. They had always thought of the Thames as a royal river. Other rivers might perchance be grander, even, as Abana and Pharpar were grander to the Syrian Captain than the rushing stream of Jordan. But the Thames was without a rival. Flowing steadily from its home in the Cotswold Hills through the meadows, and beside the country towns of the Midlands, till at length it bears on its stately

---
[16] Neill's *Founders of Maryland*, P. 49.
[17] Anderson, Vol. II, P, 121.

waters the shipping of mighty London, it is emphatically England's river; her historic river, her ideal river, as dear to her sons as the Jordan to the Hebrews, or Father Tiber to the Romans: But now its glory had departed. "The Thames" sadly confesses the historian, "seems a mere rivulet in comparison with the Potomac." Then, too, the Potomac was not disfigured with swamps, but had firm land on each side. Moreover, fine groves of trees appeared, not choked with briars and bushes and undergrowth, but growing at intervals as if planted by the hand of man, so that one might drive a four-horse carriage through the trees.

The arrival of the adventurers had not been unobserved by the natives, who fully aroused now began to line the shores. At night fires blazed through the whole country, while messengers were dispatched in all directions to report that "a canoe, like an island, had sailed up the Potomac with as many men as there were trees in the woods." Yet despite the troops of Indians in their war-paint and feathers the adventurers, sailing up the Potomac about forty miles, brought their ships to anchor off St. Clement's Island,[18] and forthwith landed.

[18] This Island does not now appear on the maps.

On the same day, being the Day of the Annunciation of the Blessed Virgin Mary—the 25th of March—in the year 1634, the priests celebrated mass on the island after the Roman ritual, "a thing which had never been done before in that part of the world." "After we had completed the sacrifice," continues the historian, "we took upon our shoulders a great cross, which we had hewn out of a tree, and advancing in order to the appointed place, with the assistance of the governor and his associates, and the other Catholics, we erected a trophy to Christ the Saviour, humbly reciting, on bended knees, the Litanies of the Sacred Cross with great emotion."[19] This is the Latin version. The tone of the narration forbids the charitable assumption that all this was done "as privately as may be." And thus, as the voyage had begun with an act of disobedience, so it ended. The version for

[19] This is the Latin account, *Relatio*, P. 33. The English account runs as follows: "We went to a place where a large tree was made into a cross and taking it on our shoulders we carried it to the place appointed for it. The Governor and commissioners putting their hands first unto it, then the rest of the chiefest Adventurers. At the place prepared, we all kneeled down and said certain prayers; taking possession of the country for our Saviour: and for our sovereign Lord the King of England." The entire absence of any mention of the mass in this service is noteworthy, as also is any special mention of the Roman Catholics, and their Litany of the Holy Cross.

the investors contains no mention of the Roman ceremonial.

There is in existence a picture illustrative of a scene at the close of this first celebration of mass by the Jesuits, and I cannot forbear quoting from a description of it:— "Here, on the side of a hill that slopes to the waters of the bay the colonists and the Indians are assembled. At the left of the picture is erected an altar, appropriately draped and ornamented with various holy symbols, and on which the just-used sacramental vessels are placed. A rude cross of wood, freshly hewn, surmounts the altar. Father White, in the robes of his order, stands upon the upper step of the altar with arms upraised and hands outstretched, as if invoking the blessing of heaven on all present. A little lower and on one side of the altar, an attendant swings the sacred censer, from which the faint smoke of incense ascends. In the centre of the picture stands Governor Calvert and the chief of the Indians, pledging friendship to each other." In connection with this picture it might be well to recall Lord Baltimore's express instructions to the Roman members of the expedition: "All acts of Roman Catholic religion to be done as privately as may be, and this by land as well as by sea."

In the fact of the adventurers having a simple religious service there was nothing calling for special notice. It was a proceeding in entire harmony with the pious and simple-hearted ways of those times. Sir Humphrey Gilbert had followed precisely the same course in Newfoundland. Sir Francis Drake did the same in California, and the magnificent stone cross on the spot stands today for a witness of the fact. So, too, had other Englishmen acted on that same coast nearly thirty years before. On the day after Newport, the commander of the first expedition for the settlement of Virginia, landed near the Falls of James River, the Holy Communion was celebrated and the erection of a Church was immediately begun.[20] Had the Maryland adventurers been influenced by even less worthy motives these religious services would not have been wanting. Religion entered more or less largely, in theory at all events, into all the doings of those times. Whether they were merchants seeking trade, or soldiers bent on conquest, it was all the same. "In the name of the Prince of Peace" said the gifted Robertson speaking of the conquerors of Peru, "they ratified a contract of which plunder and bloodshed were the objects."[21]

[20] Wilberforce, Page 122.
[21] *Peru*, Vol. I, Page 237. *America*, Vol. III, Page 5.

It was thus in a religious spirit, and in accordance with the example of all who had preceded them to America, that the Maryland adventurers said their prayers, and took possession of the country for their Saviour and for the English king.

This claim on behalf of the King of England seems strange when we remember that the king had claimed that land already, and of "his special grace, certain knowledge of and mere motion had given, granted and confirmed" it to Cecilius Calvert as Lord Proprietary. Apparently this was a necessary legal requirement for the proper conveyance of the property, and not therefore to be regarded as either unreasonable or superfluous. But there was no need to claim the land for the Saviour. Maryland had been already claimed for Christ when she was part of Virginia. But that nothing might be wanting to make the land a Christian land, no great way to the northward from where the adventurers stood lay Kent Island, with its English Church, where Sunday by Sunday the Gospel had been faithfully preached by a priest of the English Church.

CHAPTER X.

FOUNDING A CITY TO DWELL IN.

1634.

> Say, strangers, for what cause
> Explore you ways unknown? Or whither tends
> Your voyage here? Whence came you? From what race
> Derived? And bring you hither peace or war?
> —TRAPP. "VIRGIL."

According to the *Instructions* which the lord proprietary had given the adventurers, the time had now arrived for them to seek out "a fit place in his lordship's country " where they might settle down, —a fit place being defined as first, healthful and fruitful ; next, easily fortified ; and, thirdly, convenient to trade both with the English and the savages.[1]

Upon finding such a place the people were to be forthwith assembled together, and his majesty's letters patent publicly read by the secretary. This being done, the proprietary's commission to the governor and councillors was next to be read; followed by a short declaration to the people as to

[1] *Calvert Papers*, II, P. 123.

the intention of the proprietary towards his plantation. From this declaration the emigrants learned, apparently for the first time, that in undertaking to plant Maryland Lord Baltimore was seeking "first, the honor of God, by endeavoring the conversion of the savages to Christianity, secondly, the augmenting of his majesty's empire and dominions in those parts of the world by reducing them under the subjection of the Crown, and thirdly, the good of such of his countrymen as were willing to adventure their fortunes and themselves in it.[2] How singularly disinterested this lord proprietary is! Perhaps, however, we ought not to take too literally the somewhat inflated language of a courtly document of the seventeenth century, especially as our doing so will make it very difficult to acquit Lord Baltimore of professing a pious disinterestedness, which he certainly did not possess. He was as far as possible from giving himself any serious concern about the Indians and their salvation. Except in so far as he depended on them for his supply of beaver skins and other commodities, he hardly seemed to be aware of their existence. Indeed, so conspicuously was this the case that no great while afterwards one of the

[2] *Calvert Papers*, I, P. 136.

Jesuit fathers somewhat sneeringly commented on the manifest lack of all that pious interest in the infidels, "heretofore so much pretended,"[3] "there being no care taken at all to promote their conversion."[4] Having selected a place "to settle the plantation," the governor and councillors were next to choose an ample space for the building of a fort within which, or near to it, they were to build, for the seat of his lordship, or his representative, a convenient house, with a church or chapel adjacent. Near unto these buildings they were also to make choice of a place " to seat a town."[5]

To successfully carry out these instructions Leonard Calvert at once entered into communication with the Indians. Leaving the larger vessel at St. Clement's, he sailed in the smaller one up the Potomac as far as the Indian village of Piscataway, about eighty miles from the bay, a little above, but nearly opposite Mount Vernon. In this village he found a Captain Henry Fleet from Virginia, engaged in trade with the Indians.[6] Fleet from

[3] *Calvert Papers*, I, P. 166.
[4] *Calvert Papers*, I, P. 162.
[5] *Calvert Papers*, I, P. 138.
[6] Fleet had lived so long among the Indians, first as a captive and then as a freeman, that he had learned to speak their language better than his own. Fleet's *Journal*, Neill, *Founders of Maryland*, P. 37.

the first seems to have been very favorably impressed by the Englishmen, who had so suddenly appeared upon the scene, and to have been very anxious to serve them in any way. It was fortunate that he was so kindly disposed, for the chief of the Piscataway Indians had assembled five hundred warriors to oppose their landing. Under Fleet's influence, however, the hostile chief was so far conciliated as to say, that he would neither bid them go nor bid them stay. This done, Fleet at once led the governor and his party to the St. Mary's River, which flows into the Potomac about twelve miles from its mouth, assuring them that they would find there an ideal site for a city. He had spoken well. Sailing up the St. Mary's about six or seven miles, they came to a village of the Yaocomico Indians, so charmingly situated that in all Europe they could scarcely have found one to surpass it for beauty of position. The site looked over "a harbor where five hundred ships might ride securely at anchor."[7] It was Fleet's old trading post and, in former years, the scene of his captivity among the Indians.[8] Delighted beyond measure with the place they immediately decided to settle

---

[7] McMahon, P. 253.
[8] Neill, *Founders of Maryland*, P. 11 and 12.

down. Purchasing the village from the Indians, together with thirty square miles of territory, to which they gave the name of Augusta Carolina—the present St. Mary's County—the adventurers "tooke possession of the place and named the town St. Maries." Forthwith they began to build their fort, their church and their city, according to their instructions. In the meantime the priests fitted up one of the wigwams to serve as a chapel for themselves and their co-religionists. This wigwam was the first place of Christian worship in St. Mary's, although not the first in Maryland, that honor belonging to the English Church on Kent Island.[9]

Thus was founded, on the 27th of March, 1634, the city of St. Mary's, which for sixty years was

[9] It is very difficult to understand why our Roman Catholic brethren so persistently claim to have been first in Maryland. Because even had the Calvert expedition been Roman Catholic it would not have given them this honor, either politically or ecclesiastically. Yet in an address by Rev. Dr. Conaty, Rector of their University in Washington, D. C., delivered in Baltimore on "Pilgrims' Day," March 31, 1897—described by the press as a scholarly effort—these words are reported to have been said: "We hear much to-day about the Catholics and their plots to run America. Have men forgotten history, or do they read it? Catholics discovered and first colonized America. A hundred cities and a thousand lakes and streams bear Catholic names. They were first in Maryland." The orator's own question here occurs to the mind :—"Have men forgotten history, or do they read it?"

the seat of the government of Maryland, and the headquarters of a rival commonwealth in the new world to the commonwealths of Virginia and Massachusetts.

Their beautiful dwelling place charmed the emigrants. That little tract of country which they had secured from the Yacomicoes was theirs as no other land was in all America. It was home. Previous to their purchase of it from the Indians it had been but as the rest of the country, just earth and water, where perchance they might settle down and find a means of subsistence. Any other spot the day before would perhaps have suited them just as well, but now that they had chosen it no other place was so sacred to their eyes; their hearts went out to it, their thoughts were centred upon it. There patriotism had already kindled its fire, which now burned steadily and brightly in every man's heart. For in Augusta Carolina, after weary months of voyaging across the broad Atlantic, they had at last found their hearth stone. No longer were they homeless men. They had a place on earth which they could call their own.

Fleet did not go unrewarded. On May 9th, a few weeks after the colonists landed, there was assigned to him two thousand acres on St. George's River in return for his good offices.[10]

As soon as the adventurers were installed in their new home, the Governor of Virginia, Sir John Harvey, came to pay them a state visit. There came also about the same time the King of the Patuxents. The King of the Yaocomicoes was already on the spot. In honor of the occasion "the Ark's great guns spoke aloud." The Indians were filled with wonder and admiration. With such auspicious beginnings was the birth of the infant settlement attended. Soon work began in earnest. The land was surveyed, and the surrounding country carefully mapped out, and divided into hundreds. Trees were felled, fields planted, homes built, streets laid out, and soundings taken of the rivers and bays. Everything was done in the most practical and business-like manner. Soon the settlers were able to abandon the ships which had so long sheltered them, and to take up their dwelling on the land. Social courtesies with the Indians were exchanged and good feelings engendered. The Indian warriors showed the strangers how to hunt the game with which the woods abounded, while the women taught them how to cook the

[10] Neill, *Founders of Maryland*, P. 17.

maize which their fields produced so luxuriantly. Trade commenced, and all things promised success. No clouds darkened the sky in those first days of colonial life as the Marylanders went forth to their work and to their labor, until the evening.

And yet, if one could have taken a bird's eye view of Maryland, it would have been evident that other problems than those of the choice of a site for immediate settlement, of present support and future trade, would soon press upon the settlers for a solution. To say nothing of the probability of internal dissensions arising out of the peculiar composition of the colony, certain external difficulties were looming ahead very threateningly. Throughout the entire country were scattered the villages of many Indian nations with whom they could not always hope to keep the peace. Then there were besides settlements of other Old World adventurers who, like themselves, had come to try their fortunes in the New World. With the growth of the colony these various settlements would be brought into competition with them, and perhaps into bitter antagonism. Much evidently depended on the attitude which the new arrivals would adopt, both towards the Indian tribes and the earlier settlers.

As to the Indians, the problem was of course no new one. It had been before every colony which had ever settled in America from the days of Cabot down. But the presence of other white men, earlier in the field than they, was a new feature. Manifestly in dealing with these first comers exceptional tact would be needed on the part of the Marylanders, and especially of Lord Baltimore himself. Unhappily, not only Lord Baltimore, but even the Marylanders, failed to appreciate the gravity of the situation. Looking upon those early settlers as mere intruders, they so acted that strife was at once stirred up between them.

These earlier settlements were at some distance from the home of Baltimore's followers. The first[11] in importance, though perhaps not in priority of foundation, was Clayborne's settlement on Kent Island. When the Marylanders were at Jamestown, Leonard Calvert, as we have seen, had taken the opportunity of notifying Clayborne that he was

[11] In 1629 one Godyn, a Hollander, had purchased a territory on the western bank of the Delaware River, about the present sites of Wilmington and Newcastle. Six years previously this region had been occupied by Hollanders, who had built a fort called Fort Nassau, and were preparing to maintain their position against all comers. Then too, earlier perhaps than all, was the settlement on Palmer's Island at the mouth of the Susquehanna.

now a member of the Maryland colony, and must relinquish all relations with, and dependence upon, Virginia. The result might have been fore-seen. This was the letting in of strife. Upon receiving Leonard's report of the interview Baltimore failed to exhibit his usual good sense. Writing out to his brother he ordered him to seize Clayborne, and keep him in close confinement at St. Mary's, and forthwith "to take possession of his plantation on the Isle of Kent."[12] Baltimore's haste was the more unnecessary, and even inexcusable, because just previously to the setting out of his expedition it had been decided that the matters in dispute between himself and Clayborne should be settled by a court of law.[13]

In the meantime, probably at Clayborne's request, a meeting of the Virginia Council had been held, at which Clayborne had inquired how he should demean himself in respect to Lord Baltimore's patent, and his deputies then seated in the bay. It was answered by the board that "they wondered why any such question was made; they knew no reason why they should render up the right of that place, the Isle of Kent, more than any other

---

[12] Neill, *Founders of Maryland*, P. 51.
[13] *Ibid*, P. 59.

place formerly given to this colony by his majesty's patent, and that the right of my lord's grant in England being yet undetermined, we are bound in duty and by our oaths to maintain the rights and privileges of this colony." [14]

This was in March, 1634. In July of that year the king told Lord Baltimore that it was contrary to justice and his own intentions to dispossess Clayborne and his colonists of their lands.[15] Again on October 8th the king wrote to the Virginia Council, and all Lieutenants of Provinces in America requiring them to assist "the planters in Keetish Island, that they may peaceably enjoy the fruits of their labors, and forbidding Lord Baltimore, or his agents, to do them any violence." [16]

It was not denied by the Virginians that the little island lay within the limits of Lord Baltimore's grant, but as the Maryland charter only covered places "hitherto uncultivated" they asserted that Kent Island was untouched by the grant. The proprietary, however, contended that as Clayborne had nothing more than a license to trade on

---

[14] *Ibid*, P. 49. Sparks, P. 107.
[15] Allen, *History of Maryland*, P. 17.
[16] Neill, *Founders of Maryland*, P. 51. On April 4th, 1638, the Commissioners of Plantations reported the right and title to the Isle of Kent to be absolutely with him, P. 55.

Kent Island, granted under the seal of Scotland, he could not claim proprietary rights on the island. It was therefore a case of disputed ownership. But Baltimore made the mistake of resorting to arms instead of waiting for the judgment of the courts.[17] All this was the more to be regretted because, however well founded his claim to the possession of Kent Island might have been, the first settlers there could hardly fail to regard him, armed though he was with a royal charter as a man who had stolen away their birthright. Unfortunately Lord Baltimore throughout displayed the spirit and temper of those old barons who followed.

> The good old rule,
> the simple plan,
> That they should take who have the power,
> And they should keep who can.

Perhaps in addition he was animated by personal feeling against Clayborne, and of this unhappily there appears too much evidence to leave it a mere supposition. In fact the existence of a personal enmity on the part of Lord Baltimore was only too apparent, due of course to his knowledge of the strained relations which existed between Clayborne and his father owing, in the

---

[17] Allen, *History of Maryland*, P. 17; Neill, *Founders of Maryland*, P. 51.

first place, to Clayborne's attitude over the oath question, and in the next place to his unceasing opposition to his father's petition for a portion of Virginia. It was at all events acting under his orders, dated September 4th, 1634, that the Marylanders proceeded to extremities, the immediate effect being a battle on the Pocomoke River—" the first naval battle in America "—between two pinnaces, the St. Helen and the St. Margaret, under the command of Cornwaleys, and a shallop from Kent Island under Lieutenant Warren. In the fight one of the St. Mary's men was killed. Among the Kent Islanders Lieutenant Warren himself was killed and two of his men. Later on another battle took place which also ended disastrously for Clayborne, one of the men taken being subsequently hanged "for felony and piracy." Thus was the Maryland colony, in the infancy of its existence, hurried into the commission of acts of such a high-handed character as were well calculated to cost Lord Baltimore his province. This result seems to have been feared, for immediately afterwards Jerome Hawley sailed to England to defend these doings as best he could. He arrived in London in June and appeared without delay before the Privy Council.

But far more disastrous was the final result of the policy of violence. By it Clayborne became the bitter and lifelong enemy of Lord Baltimore, whose mistake cost him many times more than all Kent Island was worth.

Eventually, at a meeting of the Lord Commissioners for Plantations held at Whitehall, 4th of April, 1638, the Archbishop of Canterbury being in the chair, the disputed territory was declared to be the property of Lord Baltimore. As an illustration, however, of the uncertainty of the law's judgments, the very same plea which Clayborne now put forth ineffectively, was put forth very effectively by William Penn some years later. The cases were exactly parallel, and the judgments exactly reversed.[19]

It is a relief to turn away from scenes of strife and contention among brethren to witness the conduct of the Maryland adventurers towards the Indians. Here a scene is presented which it is a pleasure to contemplate. There was peace, at any rate at first, and for some time afterwards, between the red men and the strangers, and an intercourse mutually beneficial. Later on came war, but no sign of that could have been detected in the kindly relations which at first existed. The meeting of the two races was all that could be desired. If the white men received a generous welcome to the land broad enough for all, the Indians in return were recipients of even a greater blessing. From the white men they heard the story of the Gospel—of how Jesus had died to save them from their sins. True, the Christian teacher had much to encourage him, for the heathen were very willing to be taught, having learned by earlier dealings with Englishmen to love and trust them. And if they were not exactly holding out their babies for baptism it was only charitable to suppose that this was because they had not fully perceived the necessity of the new birth by water and the Spirit, where it might be had.

These Indian nations have all utterly disappeared from Maryland, and scarce a trace of them remains; little more than the names, strange to our Anglo-Saxon ears, of rivers and places which one meets with everywhere. For had it not been for the Indians we should not now be speaking of Potomac and Patuxent; Pocomoke and Pomonkey, of Wicomico and Nan je moy. What these, and many other similar Indian names, mean is too often a secret buried in the graves of a vanished race. Yet it is a satisfaction to know that while they tarried with us they were not spiritually neglected. Unfortunately few records remain to tell us what was done, and as the records we have are derived mainly from Jesuit sources, it is entirely unreasonable to expect any graphic account of Anglican missionary work from such a quarter. The Jesuits have not failed to give us, as was natural, somewhat lengthy accounts of their own earnest, evangelistic labors. But as their accounts are so mixed up with legends of the miraculous, it is hard to say how much is to be believed—a circumstance which makes the whole unreliable. But although the Church which first preached Christ, made the first Indian convert, baptized the first Indian chief, and claimed as a son the first Apostle of the Indians, all in the country of which Maryland once formed a part, has no tale to tell of splendid heroism and apostolic zeal on the part of her children who followed the leadership of Leonard Calvert, yet we cannot believe that she altogether failed in her duty towards the red men of Maryland.

These Maryland Indians were not of one tribe or nation only, but of many tribes. Yaocomicoes, Susquehannas, Choptanks, with many others—their names seemed legion. Of various dispositions towards the adventurers, it was with the peaceable and well disposed Indians of southern Maryland—who were of the southern branch of the Algonquin family, which had its villages from Canada to South Carolina and from the Atlantic to the Rocky Mountains—that the colonists first came into contact. Fortunate indeed was it for the infant colony that it had its early dealings with these tribes and not with the wild and warlike Susquehannas, who belonged to the fierce Iroquois nation of the north and west, as in that case the meeting between the white men and the red men, when the former were but a feeble folk, would not have terminated in the gift of a few beads and trinkets, hatchets and yards of cloth, in exchange for thirty square miles of territory, and the making of a convenient peace between them. Thrice happy in their immediate neighbors were the first colonists of Maryland.

The contrast has often been pointed out between the way in which the settlers in New England dealt with the natives with whom they came in contact, and the way in which Marylanders dealt with them. To the New Englanders the Indians were Canaanites to be rooted out of the land. Joshua, the leader of the armies of Israel, was their model. There was much truth in the quaint distich,

> "At first they fell on their knees,
> Then they fell on the aborigines."

And this notwithstanding the Christian purpose of their colonization enterprise, the first seal of Massachusetts representing an Indian giving utterance to the words, "Come over and help us."

Now not Joshua, in his fierce extirpating zeal, as carrying fire and sword he spread desolation far and wide through the enemies' country, but Abraham in his commercial dealings with the Hittites, when he bought the field of Machpelah, was the model of the Marylanders. In a like spirit with that of Abraham, they bought from the Indians, wigwams, corn and land, for all of which they paid in such things as the natives valued most. No wrong was done. No blood was shed. It has been insinuated that the white men were getting the best of the bargain. Perhaps they were, but there is no proof of it. Migratory bands of Indians have not much use for land, and the axes and cloth and ornaments meant much to them. Besides, it is on record that, owing to the incursions of the Susquehannas, the Yaocomicoes were glad to get rid of their land at any price. In fact at the time when the Maryland adventurers suddenly appeared in their village, they were on the point of leaving it forever.

We may willingly admit that the conduct of the Marylanders was dictated as much by prudence as by a sense of justice, and the teaching of religion. Their interest lay in conciliating the Indians, not in alienating them. War meant ruin to both, and the white men knew it. It was not, therefore the Indians' land they were buying with those hatchets and trinkets, but their favor and good will. We commend their course. Peace, if it be peace with honor, is to be sought at any price.

It is also true that the tribes were so disunited that a combination of their forces against the newcomers was never even possible, although had they been united they would, in the event of war, have been more than a match for the colonists. In this respect there is a remarkable parallel between the state of things which existed in Maryland then, and the state of things which exists in India now. The English could not hold India for a day were the millions of Hindustans united. But disunited, speaking different languages, of different religious beliefs, having, in fact, nothing in common save residence in the same country, a handful of Englishmen control Hindustan. So it was in Maryland. Before a solid foe the Maryland settlements would have gone down in a moment; but there was no union among the Indians, and the little settlement on the Potomac grew and flourished.

CHAPTER XI.

SHEEP WITHOUT A SHEPHERD: THE BEGINNINGS OF THE MARYLAND CHURCH.

1635.

> Thou art ever present, Power supreme!
> Not circumscribed by time, nor fix'd to space,
> Confined to altars, nor to temples bound
> In wealth, in want, in freedom or in chains,
> In dungeons or on thrones, the faithful find Thee!
> —HANNAH MOORE.

The parting *Instructions* of Lord Baltimore betray the existence among the adventurers of diverse interests, the presence of the

> " little rift within the lute
> Which, widening more and more,
> Makes all the music mute."

The adventurers were as a house divided against itself; part crying, "I am of Paul," and part, "And I of Cephas." In modern phraseology: "I am of Canterbury;" "And I of Rome."[1]

For a time, however, there was far less friction than might have been looked for. This was due

[1] I Cor., iii, 4.

to several causes. In the first place there was evidently the kindest feeling on the part of the Anglican Churchmen towards their Roman Catholic fellow-adventurers. This was entirely natural. Men who had spent months together on an ocean voyage—an experience which always brings people closely together—would not be apt to be extreme to mark what was done amiss where no personal loss or injury was inflicted. It is true that in committing the expedition at the outset to the guardianship of Roman Catholic saints and unknown angels, a wrong key-note had been struck by the priests, and one which made it easier for them, when they sighted land, to pursue a similar course in giving to the headlands they passed, and to the waters over which they sailed, Roman Catholic names. Not that this was in itself any very important matter, but it certainly was a significant one. The strong tower does not show the direction of the wind, but the bending reed does. It was therefore, entirely in a natural way that the Jesuits passed on to celebrating mass in that "ample manner" which had once stirred to its depths the protestantism of the Rev. Erasmus Stourton, in the elder Baltimore's time. Still, though acting entirely contrary to the commands of the lord proprietary, no offence was probably taken by the Protestants. To them their fellow-voyagers' penchant for naming the various headlands, and points of interest along the coast, after defunct bishops and mythical personages would seem nothing more than an odd fancy, at which there was nothing that even zealous Protestants could be justly scandalized.

An evidence of kindly feeling on the part of the Protestants is to be seen in the way in which Captain Fleet showed how absolutely free he was from all sectarian bias and narrow-minded prejudice, for it was by his aid that the missionaries were enabled to preach the Gospel to the Indians. He was their interpreter at a time when they were as powerless to influence for good or for evil the red men of Maryland, as they would have been had they remained in Europe. Witnessing that neighborly act one naturally exclaims: "Behold how good and joyful a thing it is for brethren to dwell together in unity." It sounds somewhat unkind to read shortly afterwards: "We do not put much confidence in the protestant interpreters."[2] Mistrust begets mistrust, as love begets love. Whether they trusted this particular Protestant interpreter or not,

[2] *Relatio Itineris.* P. 41. *Md. Hist. Soc., F. P., No. 7.*

he was the one man who had made all their communications with the Indians possible, and to whom alone they owed the beautiful site of their city. Unhappily this was not the only indication of the Jesuits' real sentiments towards their Protestant fellow-countrymen. A little later on they describe one of them, an Anglican named Snow, as an obstinate heretic, his offence being that he was a consistent Churchman, who did all in his power to keep his brethren firm in the faith of their fathers.[3] But as these opinions about their Protestant neighbors were not made public, no ill-will resulted.

Another cause for the absence of friction was to be found in the character of the first missionaries themselves. They were not men of intemperate zeal, utterly lacking in tact and judgment. Indeed, if all who went out with the first expeditions had been like Fathers White and Altham, there might have been, apart from their antagonism to the instructions of Lord Baltimore, and the inability they labored under, incidental to the Jesuit position, to recognize the Catholicity of their Anglican brethren, little or nothing whatever to find fault with. In their willingness to live and let live; in

---

[3] Neill, *Founders of Maryland*, P. 99.

the sweetness of their lives; and in the constancy of their faith, these first missionaries were an example unto their brethren, who followed them into Maryland. Had the later arrivals been like them, Lord Baltimore would probably never have had occasion to regret their presence in his colony. Good, honest men, according to their light, were those fathers, and full of missionary zeal. To be sure, their zeal sometimes led them into errors of judgment, but nevertheless, even on the part of those who differed from them, it would have been strange if there had not been a feeling of respect towards men so self-denying and self-sacrificing as they were. Alone of all men in Maryland they were not seeking riches for themselves, and they deserve a very high place in Maryland history. When not an English clergyman was found to go out to the colony, although the greater part of the adventurers were members of the English Church, to their honor be it spoken, these men volunteered and went. It would therefore ill become Churchmen to condemn them. Embarking on the same enterprise together, their future was singularly unlike. One was taken, and the other left. On Kent Island Father Altham had soon run his course, and was laid to rest in his grave beside the

Chesapeake, while Father White lived on to see himself, after strange vicissitudes and some painful sufferings, an old man among men, awaiting the Master's call in the England of his birth, rather than in the Maryland of his adoption, to which he all in vain had longingly hoped to return, and where he hoped also, like his brother Jesuit, that he might find his last resting place.[4] With the Puritan Eliot in New England, and the Anglican Whitaker in Virginia, he, too, deserved the title of "The Apostle of the Indians."

Let me now invite attention to the actual condition of the religious life of the unshepherded Church of England settlers during the first years of the colony's existence. I think we shall see that, bad as things were, they might easily have been very much worse; at least if we may venture to judge from the few materials at our command. For in the paucity of our information the description Canon Bright has given us of the early Church in Britain may almost verbatim be given of the early Church in the Province of Maryland: "During the Roman period the Church of Britain shows like a valley wrapped in mists, across which some fitful lights irregularly gleam. We know nothing

[4] *Ibid*, P. 104.

of its episcopal succession, very little of its internal life, or of its efforts at self-extension. We read of some of its buildings as having been known to exist at Canterbury, Caerleon, Verulam, and we may add, on that most interesting spot, then girdled in by waters and known as Ynys-vitryn, or Avalon, 'the glassy isle' or the Isle of Apples, our present Glastonbury, where the tall green peak of the tor of St. Michael looks down on the stately ruins of the great Abbey which succeeded to the 'old church,' made originally of twisted wands, and ranking among the oldest sanctuaries in Britian." [5]

So too in Maryland, during its "Roman period," or to speak more correctly its Jesuit period, under the irregular gleaming of the fitful lights we read something of its buildings, and something also of its internal life. Much more we could hardly expect to find, since religious observances could not form a large feature in the daily life of people who were struggling for a foothold and a livelihood. And yet the Churchmen at St. Mary's soon had their church in which they worshipped God and in which from time to time ordained clergymen, or in their absence qualified laymen, led their devotions. It has been suggested that this was a union church,

[5] *Early English Church History*, Bright, Chapter 1, P. 10.

which the Protestants and Romanists had joined forces to build, and in which they alternately worshipped.[6] Given a strong imagination the suggestion is quite a reasonable one. A vivid imagination is a convenient thing to have on hand. Those who have it will see no improbability in the suggestion. Most Churchmen, however, will continue to believe that this was the church which had been built in accordance with the instructions of the lord proprietary, its erection having been determined upon by him as much, we may presume, to satisfy the law, as out of regard for the spiritual needs of the settlers. It was probably this same church which a few years afterwards Leonard Calvert, the governor, and Mr. Lewger, the secretary, determined to purchase, with other buildings and land adjoining, in the name and for the use of the lord proprietary.[7] The purchase was not consummated for good and wise reasons which we shall see hereafter.

Shortly after the erection of this building for the benefit of the St. Mary's church people, other churches began to be built across the river, as the settlers, moving farther west, covered with their

---

[6] Davis, *Day Star*, Pp. 33, 34.
[7] *Md. Hist. Soc. F. P.*, No. 9, Streeter, P. 183.

homesteads the whole of the peninsula now known as St. Mary's and Charles Counties, so that within five years of their first landing there was a church at Poplar Hill, in what was known as St. George's Hundred.[9]

But who ministered in those churches? Were there any Anglican clergy in Maryland? On Kent Island, there certainly was one clergyman—the Rev. Richard James—at the time of the arrival of the adventurers. It may be that there had been more than one on the island, even before Mr. James' pastorship, for the records speak of "allowances for ministers."[10] But, alas, nowhere else in the St. Mary's colony was there one to be found. Truly those shepherdless adventurers, more in number than the parishioners of many an English Rector, presented an affecting spectacle, exposed on the one hand to the various temptations incidental to early colonial life, when men are apt to act as if God had been left behind, and on the other hand to the seductions of Romanism. For these unshepherded men were of the same flesh and blood as the people of Christian England. They had

---

[8] Ethan Allen, *History of Maryland*, P. 22.
[9] The term 'hundred' indicates the growth of population—it describes a territory whereon a hundred families were settled.
[10] Ridgely, *The Old Brick Churches of Maryland*, P. 6.

come forth from quiet English villages to seek their fortune in the new world. No doubt many an entrancing vision had floated before their eyes. They had pictured themselves, ere they had left old England's shores, gaining wealth and station in the new country, and they had even had visions of how they would spend the eventide of life. Some day they would come home again to the old village, to the old home, to sleep in the old churchyard—God's acre—where their parents, and their kinsfolk and acquaintance lay. It was all very well, but there was another side to the picture, one little thought of then. It was not all gain. Some things they could not carry away with them. In the years to come it might be different, but at first, and for long, they would sadly miss

> "the grey Church-tower
> And the sound of the Sabbath bell."

To be sure, they did not leave religion itself behind. God was everywhere. That thought would comfort them in their loneliness and in their exile. They could still pray to Him, still feel His presence and His power, still say with truth:

> I know not where His islands lift
> Their fronded palms in air;
> I only know I cannot drift
> Beyond His love and care.

It speaks well for these expatriated children of the English Church that, notwithstanding their shepherdless condition they, did not allow their churches to stand unused from month to month, as so many mere sad and silent memorials of their spiritual mother's neglect. They themselves held services in them as best they could; some of the more devoutly inclined, and better educated of their number, regularly conducting these services.[11] There is something really inspiring in the sight of these self-exiled Churchmen cut off from the means of grace, bravely endeavoring to supply their pastorless condition, doubtless buoyed up with the hope that, at no distant day, some godly minister would come and settle in their midst.

But although the adventurers neither at the beginning, nor for many years afterwards, had any resident clergyman to minister unto them, it would be entirely unreasonable to suppose that none ever visited the settlement. Indeed, remembering that the colony stood about mid-way between the Kent Island and the Jamestown settlements, it

[11] We know from the account of the dispute over the volume of sermons in Mr. Lewis' house, that the Churchmen gathered regularly at their place of worship in St. Mary's. Moreover, by an early proclamation of the Governor, the inhabitants were required to provide themselves with guns, powder and shot, before going around to the church or chapel.

would be impossible to conceive of the clergy settled in those places as never visiting the Marylanders. On the contrary we doubt not that as often as opportunity offered they would be found among the shepherdless flock of St. Mary's. We may pretty safely infer that one such visit was made on or about the twenty-sixth of March, 1638. On that day a license was granted to William Edwin to marry Mary Whitehead.[12] But fortunately we are not left to surmises. The records tell of the visit to St. Mary's of the Rev. Thomas White of Virginia, who, on the occasion of his visit,[13] made William and Mary man and wife. Perhaps on the whole the colony might easily have been in a yet worse position.

Then, too, the absence of any appearance of persecution of these shepherdless ones is a pleasing feature of these early days, contrasting as it does most favorably with the doings of those in authority, not very long afterwards, when evil counsels prevailed. Clearly at first there was no ill-will between the two parties, but each attended to its own business. The main body of the colonists building their church, and securing clergymen

---

[12] *Md. Hist. Soc.*, *F. P.*, *No. 9*, Streeter, P. 278.
[13] Ridgely, *The Old Brick Churches*, P. 42.

wherever they could, from Kent Island or Virginia; and the Jesuit missionaries ministering to the small handful of their co-religionists at St. Mary's, and making preparations by learning the language, and otherwise, to prosecute their missionary work among the Indians. But notwithstanding the lack of ordained teachers, these were the halcyon days of the colony, and like the halcyon days of the primitive Church they were not to endure for long. With the next batch of adventurers came the evil genius of the colony. This was none other than "Mr. Thomas Copley, Esq,"[14] a Jesuit who is credited with having fallen from grace by marrying a nursery maid, but who, never-

[14] Thomas Copley "Esquire," arrived in the province on the 8th of August, 1637. Notwithstanding his title of Esquire, Mr. Copley was a Jesuit priest. He seems to have been much engaged in business, and did not neglect the worldly interests of himself and his companions. In presenting claims for lands, according to the Conditions of Plantation, in proportion to the number of persons brought over by him, he includes the names of "Mr. Andrew White" and "Mr. John Altham," who were also Jesuit priests, and who had come over with the first colonists. According to the specifications of his claims, there came with White and Altham in 1634, twenty-eight servants, for whom he was entitled to six thousand acres of land; and with himself nineteen, for whom he claimed four thousand acres more, making ten thousand in all. He was also engaged in sending out goods for trade with the Indians. See Streeter, *Md. Hist. Soc.*, F. P., No. 9. P. 98.

theless, notwithstanding this mesalliance, acquired a potent voice in Maryland affairs.[15]

Of Thomas Copley, and his influence in Maryland, it might be well for me here to say a word or two. The actual part that this man played in Maryland affairs has never been properly understood. It has been customary with some historians to regard Clayborne as Maryland's "evil genius."[16] With far more propriety and justice that bad pre-eminence may be claimed for Father Copley. If he had started on his career in Maryland with the avowed intention of doing as much evil as he could to the cause he represented he could scarcely have succeeded better than he did. It was a most unfortunate circumstance for his co-religionists that he should have acquired the control which he did of Maryland affairs. Had he never seen Maryland it is more probable that his brother Jesuits could have done a lasting work among the earlier settlers. Never had they had a fairer opportunity of carrying out their ideas than they possessed at the foundation of Maryland. Everything was in their favor. The Anglican Churchmen, without a priest of their own, were an unshepherded flock,

---

[15] Neill, *Terra Mariæ*, P. 70.
[16] Hawks, P. 25, and others.

who might in time be confidently expected to join the Roman Church if the Jesuits in their dealings with them should prove wise as serpents and harmless as doves. It was to be sure a strangely anomalous position for the English Churchmen in the Maryland colony to be put into, a position so anomalous indeed as to attract the attention of the most casual observer. By law they were still members of the English Church, and the Bishop of London was still their diocesan. But the Bishop of London was three thousand miles away, and at that time the English Court had no conception of the rise of a Greater Britain beyond the seas, of which such expeditions as that of Lord Baltimore was but one of unconscious beginnings. Consequently, the adventurers in leaving England had cut themselves off from communion with the faithful. This, unhappily, was not an unheard of position for Englishmen to find themselves in; its counterpart existing in other infant colonies. But in Maryland there was in the presence of the Jesuit priests a new and unique element of danger, with its future possibilities of endless complications. Altogether it was an unfortunate state of affairs, and one which no doubt encouraged Copley to enter upon that policy of aggression which ultimately brought nothing but ruin and disaster to the Jesuits themselves, and the cause they represented.

A thorough-going ultramontane in spirit, yet carefully hiding his priestly status so that for a time it does not even seem to have been suspected by the colonists, without tact or judgment, lacking both the wisdom of the serpent and the harmlessness of the dove, but ever the power behind the throne, Father Copley entered upon a policy of violence where gentleness and sweet persuasiveness would have wrought untold wonders. He was the worst enemy to his own order that Maryland saw in the early years of the Barons of Baltimore. To him the old fable of the relative power of the northern blast and the genial influence of the southern sun might have taught an invaluable lesson. But that lesson he never learned. And so he went on his way, trusting to the arm of strength, and sledge-hammer blows to accomplish results for the souls of men. But it was then as ever:— "Not by might, nor by strength, but by My spirit, saith the Lord of Hosts."

It was chiefly due, no doubt, to Copley's efforts that the few Roman Catholics who were on board the Ark and the Dove had accompanied the expedition. It is evident that when Lord Baltimore advertised for emigrants the Jesuit Society considered that it had in his new plantation a favorable opportunity of extending its influence in America under the English flag. Maryland, to be sure, did offer them opportunities in this direction denied them elsewhere. New England was forbidden territory to them; so was Virginia. But the Lord Proprietary of Maryland was a Roman Catholic, and with him, or rather with his relatives, they had great influence. What might not, then, his appeal for emigrants augur for them and for their Church? Why should they not accept the Lord Baltimore's terms and furnish him with just the settlers his province needed? The terms were good.[17] Two hundred acres for every man sent out went to the successful agent. The society became one of Lord Baltimore's recruiting agencies; its

[17] McSherry, P. 42. "The first Conditions were issued in 1633. For every five persons between the ages of fifteen and sixty, two thousand acres of land, at a rent of four hundred pounds of wheat—for less than five persons, at the rate of one hundred acres for each man, one hundred for his wife and each servant, and fifty acres for each child under sixteen, at a rent of ten pounds of wheat for every fifty acres. In 1635, for every man brought in, a grant was made for one thousand acres, at a rent of twenty shillings. Grants of one, two, and three thousand acres were erected into manors, with the right, to their owners, of holding Courts Leet and Courts Baron."

executive officer for this purpose being this same Thomas Copley, whose first venture as an emigration agent resulted in the sending to Maryland of not less than twenty-eight persons. But "doth Job serve God for naught?" Father Copley subsequently presented on behalf of the Jesuit Society a claim against Lord Baltimore for six thousand acres of Maryland land. Successful, however, as it was, this process of acquiring land was too slow for Copley's energetic soul. He himself, with nineteen more emigrants under his charge, for whom he was looking for four thousand more acres of land, soon afterwards went to the new colony, where he inaugurated so specious a scheme of securing land from the Indians, that had it eventually succeeded, Baltimore would soon have had no land to call his own in all the Province of Maryland. But even Copley was not a match for Lord Baltimore.

CHAPTER XII.

"WHILE THE GOVERNMENT IS CATHOLIQUE."[1]

1637.

> Sure 'tis an orthodox opinion
> That grace is founded in dominion.
>   —BUTLER, "Hudibras."

With Mr. Copley's advent in 1637 the relations existing between the Anglicans and their Roman Catholic brethren were at once changed. Copley was of an energetic nature and matters were not moving fast enough. Putting ships in charge of angels, naming places after dead men, was all very well in its way, but it did not gain converts. The times demanded a more active and practical propaganda. Consequently, a new era of work had to be inaugurated. Aggressive work must be undertaken; the enemy's country invaded; sea and land

---

[1] See *Md. His. Soc., No. 28, Calvert Papers No. 1, Page 166.*
 It is curious how jealously the Roman Catholics in common usage appropriate this title 'Catholic', because in their own official documents they style their Church "the Roman Catholic", or "Holy Roman Church." Lord Baltimore did not hesitate to speak of it as Romish, (*See Maryland Archives, Council* 1, P. 1676,)

compassed to make a proselyte. Too long had the sword remained in the scabbard, and the standard of the Church been kept out of sight. Immediately the lot of the unshepherded flock became far from enviable.

To be sure, Mr. Copley was not the superior of the Jesuit order in Maryland. With his matrimonial record against him, that was out of the question. He was just one of those strong, masterful men who, without official position, simply by force of character wield a wide influence, and who have been known at times to rule even the holders of sceptres. Therefore it was that, following upon his arrival the policy of the Roman Catholics suddenly became one of aggression. And for this the time was opportune. Kent Island was shortly afterwards subdued by order of Lord Baltimore, and its Protestant settlement broken up. Among the sufferers was Gertrude James, widow of the English Rector of Kent Island, who had recently died while on a visit to England in company with Clayborne.[2] Mrs. James still lived on the island, and although justly entitled to some special consideration on account of her husband's position and work, her cattle and all she had were sold away from her[3]

[2] Allen, *Md. Toleration*, P. 29.
[3] *Ibid*, P. 30.

without the slightest compunction. It was a cruel wrong. But a worse wrong was to follow. Although tried, almost beyond endurance, by temporal misfortunes, and recent bereavement, she had now to bear, in the uprooting of her husband's work, what was probably even a greater trial than the loss of her earthly goods. On the spot where the English priest had so lately preached and taught, a priest of the Roman Church was forcibly settled. It was a high-handed proceeding on the part of its authors, and one likely to bring its nemesis. By Copley it was no doubt regarded as a mere incident in the plan of campaign.[4]

Other incidents of a somewhat similar nature now began to follow with startling rapidity, all breathing the intolerant spirit of the new regime and pointing to the deliberate attempt on the part of the Jesuits to clear the colony of the numerous "heretics" with which it was infested. Their methods of accomplishing this were various; chiefly, however, they sought succees by vigorous efforts of proselytising, by rigidly excluding Angli-

---

[4] "The records have been carefully searched. No case of persecution occurred during the administration of Governor Leonard Calvert from the foundation of the settlement of St. Mary's to the year 1647." See Davis, *The Day Star*, P. 38. Is not this a case of persecution, and a very bad one too. ?

cans from political office, and by working the legislature in their own interests. It is evident that they had begun to regard Maryland as their domain. A rude awakening was in store for them.

The Jesuit priests would have been more than mortal if they could have refrained from proselytising amongst those who were spiritually in so forlorn and helpless a condition. And at this no just cause of offence can be taken. Their methods may have been open to objection, and even to serious censure; but there can be no question as to its being the duty of every priest, and even of every layman, to use all lawful means to save his neighbor's imperiled soul. And when so fair an opportunity of doing good presented itself to these Jesuit priests, as was now offered in Maryland, they could only have been men lacking in all vital belief in their own creed, had they been content to settle down upon their lees without making an effort to use it. To win the Protestants should not have been difficult, and had the priests only been men of tact and good judgment, presenting their views with calmness and moderation, maintaining a kindly respect for Anglican prejudices, carefully abstaining from saying or doing anything likely to wound the feelings of their neighbors, ready at any time to minister in the spirit of meekness to the sick and suffering, above all showing forth the beauty of the religion they professed by holy self-denying lives, they might have won all. And this at first seemed to have been their plan of work. But Copley ruined all. He could not wait. He was like a man who digs up the seed sown to satisfy himself that it is growing.

No censure, therefore, can justly be passed upon the priests, if in obedience to their convictions they compassed sea and land to make one proselyte. Whether their efforts were always well advised in this respect, there will be no need for me to express an opinion since we have their own voluntary statements describing the methods they pursued. These statements are to be found in their annual letters to England, the first of which is dated in the year 1635. In that letter the writer merely informs his superior that there are "three priests and two assistants who in the hope of future results endure their present toils with great cheerfulness."[5] Next year's letter states that "four priests are at work in the Mission with one lay assistant." In 1638, however, we first come across evidence of direct and systematic proselytising on

[5] *Letters*, *Md. His. Soc.*, *F. P.*, *No. 7*, P. 54.

the part of the missionaries. "Meanwhile," the letter for that year relates, "we devote ourselves more zealously to the English; and since there are Protestants as well as Catholics in the Colony, we labor for both, and God has blessed our labors. For among the Protestants nearly all who have come from England, in this year 1638, and many others, have been converted to the Faith, together with four servants[6] whom we purchased in Virginia (another Colony of our kingdom) for necessary services, and five mechanics, whom we hired for a month and have, in the meantime, won to God." These servants in reality were negro slaves, of whom the missionaries had several. For one of them, a mulatto named Francisco brought in by Father White, Copley claimed an emigrant's share of land. He was the first slave in the colony of which there is any notice.[7] The Jesuits have therefore the honor of having introduced slavery into Maryland. It has been attempted to pass this distinction on to the Puritans, but justice requires us to refuse to deprive the Jesuits of whatever

[6] Slaves are mentioned in the records of this same year being especially exempted from the operation of the Act for the Liberties of the People, *Archives of Maryland, Assembly*, 1637-8-1664. P. 41.

[7] Neill, *Terra Mariae*, P. 69.

praise they may be entitled to for their services in this matter.

The Roman campaign was now in full cry. The colony had been four years in existence, yet the Jesuits had not apparently any remarkable returns to show as the result of their efforts, and of their unparalleled opportunities. The evangelization of the heathen Indians had not gone forward as rapidly as they had expected it would have done;* while they had had comparatively little success among their white neighbors. In fact, beyond attending to the spiritual interests of their own people, they had scarcely been able to accomplish anything at all. It was perhaps due to this failure that they had entered upon a more active propaganda which could not fail to be exasperating. One account, taken from the same letter of 1638, exhibits them as forcing their way into houses against the opposition of their occupants; and however creditable to their perseverance and indomitable energy that method of making converts was, it did not reflect favorably upon their good judgment, since it was exceedingly well calculated to defeat its own objects. Here is the story related by the writer describing the occurrence as one

* *Letters*, P. 55.

for which much praise is due:— "A certain man, entirely unknown to us, but a zealous disciple of the Protestant religion, was staying with a friend who was still more zealous; and having been bitten by one of the snakes which abound in these parts, was expecting death. One of our company, finding this out, took with him a surgeon, and hurried to the sick man, who, it was reported, had already lost his senses, with the intention of ministering to his soul in any way that he could. But the host, divining his intention, tried to thwart his pious efforts. And the priest, as he could find no other opportunity, determined to stay all night with the sick man. But the host prevented this too, and, lest the father should be admitted at night, he appointed a guard to sleep on a bed, laid across the door of the chamber occupied by his friend. Nevertheless, the priest kept on the watch for every opportunity of approach; and going at midnight, when he supposed the guard would be especially overcome by sleep, contrived, without disturbing him, to pass in to the sick man, and, at his own desire, received him into the Church."[9]

[9] *Ibid*, P. 57.

Again, the following incident:—" Another man, when one of us tried to bring him to the orthodox faith, repulsed him with the answer, 'that he had vowed he would never embrace that faith.' A short time afterwards, this wretched man was attacked by disease, and brought to the last extremity, before the father was advised of his sickness. He, however, hastens to the sick man with all speed, and finds him insensible, yet still breathing. . . . The father, therefore, determined to make use of the present opportunity, inasmuch as he could not hope for another one afterwards. And when by various communications he had obtained (as he judged) the consent of the sick man, understanding from him that he wished to be made a Catholic, because he was sorry for his sins, and anxious to be absolved from them, he absolved him from his sins and anointed him with the sacred oil. After this had been done the sick man, in a day or two, was perfectly restored to his senses."

Again: "Another man, who was of noble birth, had been reduced to such poverty, by his own unrestrained licentiousness, that he sold himself into this colony. Here he had been recalled by one of us to the right faith and the fruit of good living. This man being brought to the last extremity by a severe disease, and taking all the sacraments, about an hour before his death, asked his Catholic attendant to pray for him. It is probable that an evil angel presented itself to his sight; for almost at the very point of death, he called the same attendant and said, with a cheerful voice: "Don't you see my good angel? Behold him standing near to carry me away, and I must depart;" and thus happily, (as we are permitted to hope) he breathed his last. Since his burial a very bright light has often been seen at night around his tomb, even by Protestants."

The next year's report ends thus:—"To the hope of the Indian harvest are to be added also no mean fruits to be reaped in the colony and its inhabitants, to whom, on the principal festival days of the year, sermons are preached, and the catechetical exposition given on the Lord's day. Not only Catholics come in crowds, but also very many heretics—not without the reward of our labors; for this year, twelve in all, wearied of former errors, have returned to favor with God and the Church."[10] Apparently the missionaries were beginning to feel encouraged. That twelve persons

[10] *Ibid*, P. 73.

had been gathered into their Church does not indeed seem a great return, but they were thankful that a beginning had been made. Next year they deemed that they had even greater encouragement still. In the language of the report "everywhere the hope of harvest has dawned." [11]

But the missionaries claimed the power of working miracles. Witness the following very remarkable account: "It has also pleased the divine goodness," runs the annual letter, "by the virtue of His cross, to effect something beyond mere human power." "The circumstances are these: A certain Indian, called Anacostan, from his country, but now a Christian, whilst he was making his way through a wood, fell behind his companions a little ahead, when some savages of the tribe of Susquehannoes, which I have mentioned before, attacked him suddenly from an ambuscade, and with a strong and light spear of locust wood (from which they make their bows) with an iron point oblong at the sides, pierced him through from the right side to the left, at a hand's breadth below the armpit, near the heart itself, with a wound two fingers broad at each side. From the effect of this, when the man had fallen, his enemies fly with the utmost

[11] *Ibid.* P. P. 77.

precipitation, but his friends, who had gone on before, recalled by the sudden noise and shout, return and carry the man from the land to the boat, which was not very far distant, and thence to his home at Pascataway, and leave him speechless and out of his senses. The thing being reported to Father White, who by chance was but a short distance off, he hastened to him the following morning, and found the man before the doors, lying on a mat before the fire, and enclosed by a circle of his tribe—not indeed altogether speechless, or out of his senses, as the day before, but expecting the most certain death almost any moment; and with a mournful voice joining in the song with his friends which stood around, as is the custom in the case of the more distinguished of these men when they are thought to be certainly about to die. But some of the friends were Christians, and their song, which, musically indeed, but with plaintive inflection of tone was, ' May he live, O, God ! if it so please thee ; " and they repeated it again and again, until the father attempted to address the dying man, who immediately knew the father and showed him his wound. The father pitied him exceedingly, but when he saw the danger to be most imminent, the other things being omitted, he briefly runs over the principal articles of faith; and repentance of his sins being excited, he received his confession; then, elevating his soul with hope and confidence in God, he recited the Gospel which is appointed to be read for the sick, as also the Litany of the Blessed Virgin, and told him to commend himself to her most holy intercessions, and to call unceasingly upon the most sacred name of Jesus. Then the Father, applying the most sacred relics of the most holy cross, which he carried in a casket hung to his neck, but had now taken off, to the wound on each side, before his departure directed the bystanders, when he should breathe his last, to carry him to the chapel for the purpose of burial.

It was now noon when the father departed; and the following day, at the same hour, when by chance he was borne along in his boat, he saw two Indians propelling a boat with oars toward him; and when they had come alongside, one of them put his foot into the boat, in which the father was sitting. Whilst he gazed on the man with fixed eyes, being in doubt, for in a measure he recognized him by his features who he was, but in part recollecting in what state he had left him the day before, when the man, on a sudden, having thrown open his cloak, and having disclosed the cicatrices of the wounds, or rather a red spot on each side, as a trace of the wound, immediately removed all doubts from him. Moreover, in language with great exultation he exclaims, 'that he is entirely well, nor from that hour at which the father had left yesterday, had he ceased to invoke the most holy name of Jesus, to whom he attributed his recovered health.'"[12]

But side by side with these efforts, not always tactful, to persuade men to accept the dogmas of the Roman Church, coupled with their remarkable claims to the possession of divine power, went overt deeds of persecution by the Jesuits. As early as 1638 there was an instance of the kind in St. Mary's. This was the act[13] of William Lewis, who forbade two of his servants to read in his house a book of sermons written by an English clergyman.[14] It was a particularly bad feature of the case that Lewis was Father Copley's, agent and we may therefore see Copley's hand in this piece of intolerance. Lewis' language about the book and its author, and indeed the Anglican clergy generally, was such that all the Churchmen in the colony were up in arms about it. In their eyes Lewis was

[12] *Ibid*, P. 87-88.
[13] *Md. Hist. Soc., F. P., No. 9*, Streeter, P. 232.
[14] Rev. Henry Smith, *Sermons*, (published in 1592.)

a traitor, who should be severely dealt with. There was even some talk of appealing for redress to the Governor of Virginia. This, however, was not necessary; a crisis had arisen, but it was not a greater one than the Government of Maryland was able to settle. It was just an unfortunate dispute of this sort which Lord Baltimore had feared as dangerous to his province, and Governor Calvert knew his brother's mind. A lenient sentence would have been mis-timed clemency. Accordingly Lewis was fined five hundred pounds of tobacco, and was bound over to good behaviour, giving security therefor in three thousand pounds sterling.

It was not until 1642 that any similar act of intolerance is met with. In that year, Mr. Thomas Gerard, the lord of St. Clement's Manor, took away the keys and books of the Church at St. Mary's.[15] Mr. Gerard was heard in his own defence, but he also was mulcted in a fine of five hundred pounds of tobacco—the same to be paid towards the support of the first minister who should arrive. Again the fine was out of proportion to the offense in ordinary times, but in the Maryland colony the times were not ordinary by any means. At any

---

[15] *Md. Toleration*, Allen, P. 44 ; also Neill, *Founders of Maryland*, P. 100.

moment a conflagration might occur, and those who under such circumstances were found playing with fire deserved punishment.[16]

---

[16] Commenting on these cases a Roman Catholic author says: 'Faithfully did Cecilius, the Proprietary, execute the pledge he had given to the members of the English Church. How intoxicating is the taste of power! How apt are we to forget the obligation we owe to those whom we command! How easy was it for the Proprietary, in an obscure and remote part of the world, beyond the immediate eye of the Crown, to commit acts of petty cruelty and oppression towards those who differed with him on points of faith, not only by excluding them from civil offices, but also in many other respects. The singular fidelity with which the second Baron of Baltimore kept his pledge, presents one of the best examples upon record, one of the purest lessons of history, one of the strongest claims to the gratitude of Maryland and to the admiration of the world." Davis, *The Day Star*, P. 34. Indeed! With Virginia, watching with lynx-like eyes the course of the Maryland government, ready to accuse it of the least unfaithfulness to its Charter, and he himself, detained in England as a pledge of his government's good behaviour, he was not apt to become intoxicated with the taste of power, nor to be found starting on a crusade of persecution. His own co-religionists accused Cecilius Calvert of being inimical to their interests, and indifferent to the claims of his Church. But no one ever accused him of lacking a proper regard for his emporal welfare.

CHAPTER XIII.

WORKING THE LEGISLATURE.

1637.

> Keep leets and law days.
> —SHAKESPEARE.

The first Legislative Assembly ever held in Maryland, of which we have any record, began its sessions at St. Mary's on the 25th of January, 1637, under the presidency of Leonard Calvert. All the freemen of the province had been summoned to appear, and a complete list is extant of those who were present and of those who were absent. Absentees, represented by proxy, were excused; the others, with three notable exceptions, were amerced for non-appearance. These exceptions were the three Jesuit priests, "Mr. Thomas Copley, Esq., Mr. Andrew White, Gent., Mr. John Altham, Gent,"[1] all residents in St. Mary's hundred. Like the laymen, they had been summoned to take their places as legislators. On the assembling of the House, however, Robert Clarke, described as 'gent'

[1] *Archives of Maryland, Assembly,* Page 63.

on the records, but who was in reality servant to Mr. Copley, appeared for them and excused their absence by reason of sickness. That all the reverend gentlemen were laid low at one time could not fail to be a subject of much comment. Probably the circumstance occasioned many surmises as to the character of the epidemic which had thus incapacitated the clerical gentlemen. Eventually however they were permanently exempted from attendance, it being found that it was not sickness, but an unwillingness to fill the part assigned them, which was the cause of their absence.

The objection of the priests to appear as legislators was due no doubt to the assumption involved in the summons that they were laymen. For it will be observed that it was as such that they were summoned; their clerical status being ignored. Their attitude on this occasion was probably suggested by the fact that the clergy of the English Church are forbidden to sit in the House of Commons. Mindful, therefore, of this the Jesuits refused to appear in the legislative assembly of Maryland. Were they not clergymen too? Why this invidious distinction? What justification was there now for it? It was bad enough to have to submit to such discrimination in England. But they would have none of it in Maryland. They would not come. They would compel the House to recognize their priestly status, and in this they succeeded.

Now for a mere sentimental objection of this kind we may be inclined to marvel that the Jesuits should have been willing to forego such an opportunity as membership in the House afforded them of personally influencing legislation in their favor. And we shall be inclined to do this the more when we remember on what ground it was that the English clergy were excluded from the Lower House of Parliament. For it was not as clergymen that they were excluded, but as members of a class or order already represented by their bishops in the Upper House. Regarding them as quite sufficiently represented in Parliament already, and considering furthermore that they possessed an exceptionally influential position in the country generally by virtue of their official status, the law refused them any additional representation. Still, the reasons for this action were not always remembered, and the public had become familiar with the idea that it was by virtue of their priestly office that the clergy were ineligible for election to Parliament. Hence the law forbidding them to sit in the House of Commons had come to be regarded as equivalent to a recognition on the part of the government of their clerical office, as in fact, a sort of hall-mark stamped upon their spiritual claims. And this impression was deepened and confirmed by the different treatment accorded to the various non-conformist sects, not excluding the Roman. Unlike the Church clergy the various ministers of these dissenting bodies might be legally elected as members of the House of Commons, and there sit without a penalty. The refusal of the Jesuits in Maryland appears to show that they also were under the popular delusion as to the origin of the restriction.

The suggestion,[2] gravely made, that this refusal of the Jesuits to sit in the first Maryland Assembly was due to a commendable unwillingness to become involved in disputes attending the transaction of merely mundane affairs is provocative of a smile. When was a Jesuit known to be averse to the fascinations of wire pulling and to the profits of successful politics? Indeed, so far were the Jesuits from refusing to have anything to do with legislative affairs, that Mr. Copley boasted that his overseer, Mr. Lewis, had more proxies in

[2] *De Courcy*, Pp. 28, 29.

the House than anyone else, he having not less than seven—and this in a House of only seventy members![3]

This will be a convenient place to explain the organization of the early legislative Assemblies of Maryland; for unless we have some general idea of their constitution, much that would otherwise be quite simple and intelligible, will be impossible to understand. Every freeman in Maryland, was regarded as a member ex-officio—freemen being such citizens as were over twenty-one years of age, and not held by indenture or otherwise in personal service. After a time, as the colonists increased in numbers, the principle of representation had to be resorted to, but at first each freeman possessed the right of speaking and voting, either in person or by proxy, upon the laws by which he was to be governed. Slaves and indentured servants,[4] so long as they remained in service, were

---
[3] *Calvert Papers* No. 1, *Md. Hist. Soc.*, Page 158.
[4] These indentured servants were practically slaves, for the indenture that bound them to their master during the period of servitude gave the master complete control over them with the right to punish them severely for any offense, or to hunt them down should they attempt to escape from bondage. An announcement like that which follows, which appeared in the Pennsylvania Gazette as late as July 28, 1784, was at one time very common :— " Just arrived from Londonderry, on brig

naturally denied this privilege. The restriction was a reasonable one, although for a few years it operated prejudicially against the Anglican Churchmen. These, as we have seen, numerically considered, were greatly in the majority throughout the province, but politically they were weak, a very large number of them being of the unfranchised, indentured class. It is true that among the "gentlemen" who came in the Ark there were some good, staunch Churchmen, but of this class the Roman Catholics for a short while had the majority, and hence, also, political power. Accordingly, when the first Assembly was gathered together on a basis of freeman suffrage, although Churchmen on actual ballot were in an overwhelming majority, the Romanists were in a position to materially influence proceedings in their favor. "The Government" was "Catholique." Thus the first Maryland Assembly presented the singular spectacle of a considerable community of Englishmen subject to Roman Catholic influence at a time when the celebration of the Mass was a capi-

Peggy, Captain Stewart, a number of fine healthy men and women servants and some small boys, whose times are to be disposed of to the best bidders by the Captain on board, or by Campbell and Kingston on the wharf." These 'servants' were whites.

tal felony in England. For the first time since Mary's reign, English supporters of the papacy found themselves able to dominate a legislative assembly in their own interests. And they were not slow in taking advantage of the situation.

With these facts in mind let us try to see what the first Assembly of Maryland attempted to do. After the necessary preliminaries had been settled, a draft of certain laws transmitted to them for their assent by the lord proprietary was debated and rejected. At once the question necessarily arose: What laws was the colony under? This being not quite clear it was suggested that the House would do well to agree upon some laws till they could hear from England. Whereupon the governor denied that such power existed in the House. A dead-lock seemed imminent, but Captain Cornwaleys helped the House out of its difficulty, by reminding its members that they were under the laws of England. Admitting this generally, the governor thought there were circumstances under which these laws could not be operative. What, for example, he asked, would be done with enormous offenders, there being no power to punish offences against loss of life or member? To this the Captain replied that such offences could scarcely be committed without mutiny, and in that case they could be dealt with by martial law.[5] The House then settled down to business and, the governor's objections being disposed of, the assembly next proceeded to take the initiative itself. Fourteen bills were then read for the first time. Other bills soon followed, among them an "Act for the Liberties of the People." Unfortunately while we have a list of the titles of the various acts passed by this assembly, together with a list of those which were rejected, we have not the text of the acts themselves. This is the more to be regretted, inasmuch as there is reason to believe that one of the acts which passed the Assembly was afterwards bitterly opposed by the Protestants. At any rate a letter of complaint from Captain Cornwaleys was sent to the lord proprietary predicting that the action of the House would bring disaster upon the whole province.[6] To judge by the tone of the let-

[5] *Archives of Maryland, Assembly,* Page 17.
[6] *Calvert Papers No. 1,* Pages 169-181.
 The letter was dated 6th of April and really seems at first sight to have been written not merely after the first but also after the second Assembly held March, 1638. This change of dates, caused by the change from the Old to the New Style of reckoning, is often very confusing. Let me make the matter clear at once, so far as the dates of the letter and the assemblies

ter, the objectionable measure could only have been
one which closely touched, even if it did not seriously jeopardize, their rights as English Churchmen.

We are not left, however, entirely without any
clue to the character of the legislation which only
awaited the signature of the proprietary to make it
the law of the colony. In the Assembly of 1638
there was an act passed which plainly touched the
rights of that branch of Christ's Holy Catholic
Church of which the writer was a most loyal member. This was the "Act for Church Liberties,"
and a more lawless proceeding carried out under
the forms of law, than this particular measure it
would be difficult to find. In direct violation of
English statutes, its immediate, but hidden effect
was to place the clergy of the Roman Church

are concerned. The Assembly of 1637 met in January : by
modern reckoning this would be January 1638. The Assembly of
1638 met in February and March, closing March 24th, the last
day of the year O. S. This in our modern chronology would be
1638 also, for the new year began March 25th. Now Cornwaleys' letter criticising the doings of the Assembly was dated
April 6th, 1638, a date untouched by our modern style of
reckoning. Consequently it will be seen that his letter was
written after the holding of the first, and before the holding of
the second Assembly.

For a fuller explanation of the change from Old to New
Style, see Bozman, Vol. I, Page 347, appendix A.

beyond control of the civil power, exempting them from taxation and many of the duties of citizenship, and enabling their Church, among other things, to hold property independent of the state, which by the statute of mortmain even the English Church herself could not do. " Be it enacted," ran this remarkable act, "by the Lord Proprietary of the Province, by and with the advice and approbation of the free men of the same, that Holy Church, within this Province, shall have all her rights, liberties and immunities safe, whole and inviolable, in all things."[7] Its very vagueness rendered it additionally dangerous, for what were these rights and liberties which the state could not touch?[8] As commonly understood they were the rights of the Church to hold property free from taxation, and to have the clergy exempt from civil authority. Considering that even in England the clergy had no such privileges as were here conferred upon the Roman clergy in Maryland, it was hardly a wise proceeding to force through the infant legislature

[7] *Archives of Maryland, Assembly*, Vol. I, Page 40.
[8] Bancroft, Vol. I, Page 251, says: "Those rights and liberties, it is plain from the Charter, could be no more than the tranquil exercise of the Roman worship." Father Copley soon made it clear that he had more in view. See *Calvert Papers*, No. 1, Page 157 and following.

of the province such a radical measure as this. Time had been when the English Church possessed all these so-called rights, liberties and immunities; but after centuries of strife and contention she had been gradually dispossessed of them, until now her clergy were as amenable to law as the long suffering laity themselves, and England was free from a body of grasping ecclesiastics, by a strange misconception regarded as the Church—as if the Church were the clergy only—fattening on the good of the land while repudiating the authority of the very laws which made their possessions secure to them.

Some such act as this it was which no doubt caused Thomas Cornwaleys to write as he did. It may have been that the legislation complained of formed a part of the "Act for the liberties of the people." Or it may even have been that the legislation was as yet only proposed, and that the Protestants seeing its nature, protested so strongly against it that it never was enacted. At any rate, whatever it was, the ire of the chief Protestant of the colony was profoundly stirred by it, and hence the letter in question.

Assuming that the protest was directed against the "Act for Church Liberties," or one like it, we cannot wonder at its fiery character. The burnt child dreads the fire: England had had enough of Rome. We have indeed been assured that that Act could not have contemplated the establishment of the Roman Church, inasmuch as the declaration of its first section, "Holy Church within this Province shall have all her rights and liberties," is but a re-iteration of the first clauses of Magna Charta which declares "that the Church of England shall have all her rights aud liberties inviolate."[9] It was nothing of the sort. The Roman Catholics had not the slightest

---

[9] *Md. Hist. Soc.*, F. P., No. *18*, Johnon, Page 51. See also *Day Star*, notes, page 30.

It is commonly forgotten that this was in its origin a distinctly anti-papal document, its very first clause asserting the freedom of the English Church from the dominion of the Papal. A very remarkable proof of this forgetfulness was afforded in a sermon preached by Cardinal Gibbons, on the 22nd March, 1885. Preaching on civil and religious liberty, the scholarly and liberal Cardinal claimed that the (Roman) Catholics had always defended and upheld the religions and civil rights of the people. This was to many quite a new idea, but the preacher was prepared to prove his statement, and he proceeded to instance the giving of Magna Charta. "The measure," he said, "which is probably the measure of greatest benefit to the civil rights of mankind in modern times, is the Magna Charta of England. It is the foundation not only of English but also of American Constitutional liberty. Who were its authors? The (Roman) Catholic Archbishop of Canterbury and the (Roman) Catholic Barons of England." Thus the Cardinal; but Pope Innocent III, the head of the Roman Church, and *speaking as such*, actually declared the Charter null and void, ex-communicated the barons for their share in passing it, and further more pro-

intention of doing so foolish a thing as re-iterating the statement that the English Church should be free from papal interference. What they really did was this: Having deliberately substituted the the term 'Holy Church' for 'Anglicana Ecclesia' they declared, not that the Christian Church in Maryland should be free from unlawful interference, on the part of the temporal power, but that the Roman Church should be free from all interference of any kind whatever, whether previously lawful or not. Of this there can be no reasonable doubt. It must be admitted, says Burnap, that they established the (Roman) Catholic Church as the religion of the state.[10] Burnap even goes further, and says that "it was the intention of this Act to put the Catholic religion in the same position with regard to the government in Maryland, as it had occupied with regard to the government of England before the Reformation." Burnap is here laboring under the common, but happily disappear-

---

ceeded to excommunicate the Archbishop of Canterbury himself unless he would consent to undo his own work, and put the ban of the Church upon the noble barons who had supported him.

See also the Cardinal's book, *The Faith of our Fathers*, P. 229 for the same erroneous views.

[10] Burnap's *Calvert*, Page 171.

ing delusion, that it was not the old English Church, but the Roman, which existed in England before the Reformation. The word 'Reformation' might have helped him to a better understanding. But, passing this error by, he is a good witness as to what the Jesuits meant to do, and what they actually did.

We may rest assured that the Roman Catholic legislators deliberately adopted the somewhat indefinite term 'Holy Church' as the one which would best suit their purposes. For to them there is but one Holy Church, and they would certainly never have admitted that what they affect to regard as Henry the Eighth's Parliamentary Church was part of it. The term was therefore by no means indefinite to them. In their minds Holy Church and Roman Church were interchangeable terms. But it would never have done to use the term 'Roman Church.' Hence they fell back upon this indefinite term as being all they required. Their worldly wisdom in this respect was abundantly justified later on, when the Rev. Francis Fitzherbert, a Jesuit priest on trial for breaking the law, defended his course saying, that by "the true intent of the 'Act concerning Religion' every Church pro-

fessing belief in God the Father, Son and Holy
Ghost, is accounted Holy Church here." [11]

But the "Act for Church Liberties" was hopelessly at variance not only with the Magna Charter of
England but even with the Maryland Charter,
since it was a direct repudiation of the clause of
that charter which required that nothing should
be done contrary to God's Holy and True religion—
a phrase which in the mouth of King Charles who
gave it meant the Church of England and no other.
Yet even if the king had not meant this, or had
been remiss in his duty towards the Church, at the
head of the committee which passed its judgment
upon all such grants, stood the Lord Archbishop
of Canterbury, none other at that time than
William Laud, in whose hands the interests of the
Church were well guarded. Happily, however, the
good offices of the Archbishop were not required.

We have no certain means of knowing how the
Churchmen of Maryland came to vote for so dangerous a measure as the "Act for Church Liberties." Probably at first they did not suspect the
true character of the innocent looking act, which
was only intended to give the foreign Church her
"rights and liberties." Surely only a bigot would

[11] Davis, *Day Star*, Pages 55-60, notes.

object to that, and in Maryland, Churchmen have always been singularly free from bigotry. But they soon saw that they had committed a mistake, a piece of culpable folly, which could bring nothing but ruin and disaster. The Protestants had voted for the establishment of Rome : their act was suicide. As such it was the beginning of the end —an intimation to them to put their houses in order and abandon the colony. Naturally their eyes were soon found turning longingly to the neighboring colony of Virginia. Of course it may have been that the Protestants, in voting for the Act, supposed it was their own Church for which they were legislating. In this case, bitter but unavailing like that of Esau, must their repentance have been. They had sold their birthright, nay, they had given it away.[12]

It will here help us to understand better the exact position of the two parties into which the colonists were now divided if we recall the state of things which existed in England a few years after-

[12] Eventually the Protestants got over their fears and permitted the Act to pass in a modified form. See *Archives of Maryland, Assembly*, P. 83. A subsequent Assembly in 1640 re-approved the Act in a somewhat fuller manner. Probably by this time the government being no longer Roman Catholic all fear of Rome had fled, and these English Churchmen were now establishing their own Church.

wards when James II was king. James was a Roman Catholic whose courtiers endeavored to persuade him that his mission in life was to overthrow the ancient National Church and to substitute for it the Church of Rome. King James, with his feeble intellect, was to succeed, where Philip of Spain, Queen Mary and Cardinal Pole, all united, had ignominously failed! He overthrow the Church of England? He might as well have attempted to roll back the tides of the ocean, or alter the courses of the stars. He, the saviour of the Church? A second Edward the Confessor? Well, in another it was a splendid ambition, not unworthy even of a great man. But for him it was folly. Yet vainly confident of success, he entered upon the struggle which was to terminate in the undoing of himself and his house; seeing not, at any rate heeding not, his people's growing exasperation at every new act of injustice against the Church of England which was rapidly bringing the end nearer. At last the storm broke, and it swept him from his throne. Without a blow the Protestant William of Orange became king in his stead, while all that remained of the mighty James' brilliant effort on behalf of the Italian Church was summed up in Article IX of the Bill of Rights of 1689.—" It hath been found by experience that it is inconsistent with the safety and welfare of this Protestant Kingdom to be governed by a Popish Prince, or by any King or Queen marrying a Papist." A more complete and crushing defeat it would be difficult to find. It fulfils our Lord's warning: " Whomsoever shall fall on this stone shall be broken; but on whomsoever it shall fall it will grind him to powder."

The Maryland case was not as tragic as the English in its final issue. But in its earlier stages, and even in its later developments, it bore quite a strong resemblance to it. In Maryland there was a Roman Catholic head of the government, who, like James, was subjected to Jesuit influence, which was being used to forward precisely the same ends. So, too, its immediate result was the same, for it caused such dissatisfaction among the Anglican members, that when in 1643 the authority of the King of England was superseded, and the government changed, almost as a matter of course an insurrection immediately followed in Maryland, when the Roman priests were expelled, and Lord Baltimore's authority repudiated.

Fortunately for the Lord Proprietary of Maryland he was able truthfully to say what the English king could not say, that he was in no way concerned with the doings of his co-religionists. They only were to be blamed.

CHAPTER XIV.

THE APPEAL TO THE LORD PROPRIETARY.

1638.

Poise the cause in justice equal scales,
Whose beam stands sure, whose rightful cause prevails.
—SHAKESPEARE.

The letter of Captain Cornwaleys[1] shows how bitter was the feeling against the measures which had been agitated in the colony. Beginning with a reference to the damages he had personally sustained from William Clayborne, Cornwaleys informs Lord Baltimore that an Act for Clayborne's attainture was on its way for his confirmation. That Act, however, was but one among others "of which if there were none more unjust, he would be as confident to see Maryland a happy commonwealth as he was then of the contrary, if his lordship should not be more wary in confirming than they had been in proposing." Earnestly therefore does he beg Lord Baltimore not to

[1] *Calvert Papers*, Vol. I, P. 169.

sanction the least clause of the proposed legislation until "it had been thoroughly scanned and resolved by wise, learned and religious divines, to be nowise prejudicial to the immunities and privileges of that Church which is the only guide to all eternal happiness, and of which they would show themselves the most ungrateful members that ever she nourished if they attempted to deprive her of them." What those grievances were, and how they were to be remedied, the lord proprietary can ascertain from those who are far more knowing in the rights of the Church than he is. His duty is done when he has importuned his "lordship, who alone now can mend what has been done amiss, to be careful to preserve the honor of God Almighty, who only can preserve both him and Maryland." This done, in the spirit of David, when he said, "I have been young and now I am old, and yet saw I never the righteous forsaken, nor his seed begging their bread," he tells Lord Baltimore that "he never yet heard of anyone who suffered loss by being bountiful to God or His church, and he would not have him fear to be the first. He acknowledges that these are matters not properly falling within his cognizance, but he cannot willingly consent to anything that may not stand with the conscience of a 'real Catholic.'[2] In the event of this protest meeting with no success he will withdraw himself, and what is left of his property beyond the reach of approaching evils. Not that the alarming outlook was a condition of affairs entirely unforeseen by him, as his lordship might remember, for the first requisite that he had insisted upon being guaranteed to him ere he was willing to sail to Maryland, was his liberty of conscience, notwithstanding that his lordship had laughed at his fears as utterly groundless and chimerical. Plainly Cornwaleys is of the opinion that the promises made had not been kept, his religious rights being now seriously threatened by the proposed legislation. Other troubles he has, which affect him greatly. Trade conditions are not satisfactory, and the lord proprietary's promises

[2] Our Roman Catholic brethren are so accustomed to claim the exclusive use of the word Catholic as descriptive of themselves, that it is as well to draw special attention to this description of himself given by the foremost Churchman of the colony. Churchmen are Catholics, even more than they are Protestants. The National Church of England has never even called herself Protestant, and it is only by an accident that our own Church has done so. "I am a Catholic" once wrote William Penn, "but not a Roman Catholic." (Neill, *Terra Mariæ*, P. 73.) This is the position of every Churchman. Thomas Cornwaleys seems to have thought that as a member of the Catholic Church of England he was more of a Catholic than he would have been if he had been a member of the Italian Mission.

to the first adventurers are still unfulfilled; and discontent, in consequence, is rife in the colony. But the religious difficulty is the most serious one.

Such is the opposition taken by the foremost Protestant Catholic in the colony. His letter is a temperate, yet earnest protest against any breach of faith, on the part of the proprietary, in matters connected either with religion or commerce, but especially against his allowing the Roman Catholic Church to profit by the foolish mistakes of inexperienced legislators. It was practically a confession that the Protestants were either helpless to protect themselves, or had been hoodwinked into passing laws which had imperilled their liberties as Churchmen, and their rights as Englishmen. The real object of that legislation was now obvious. It was for the benefit of the Roman Church in Maryland. On no other hypothesis can we understand the writer's despairing feelings, allied with bitterness. No other explanation of his letter is possible.

The vessel which bore the the letter of the Protestants' champion also bore one from Thomas Copley,[3] written three days before it,[4] and dealing

[3] *Calvert Papers, Vol. I*, P. 157.
[4] In endorsing the letter he had received from Captain Cornwaleys, Lord Baltimore made a mistake of ten days, describing it as written April 16th. Cornwaleys himself dated it April 6th.

with precisely the same subjects. Father Copley's relations with his lordship were not as easy as were those of the captain. Reports were abroad that he and his colleagues were not quite as loyal as they might be. After attempting an explanation of this, a somewhat labored one to be sure, and not very convincing, the Jesuit priest entered upon the real business of his communication. He, too, writes about the laws for ratification, but "tell it not in Gath, publish it not in the streets of Askelon," he meddles so little with political matters that he has only just for the first time hastily read the laws in question! However, if he might venture to judge by so brief an acquaintance, he must confess they contained some things he was not at all satisfied with. Unhappily he had had to make the same confession with respect to the laws sent to them by his lordship. These were even more objectionable still, especially the new Conditions of Plantations. But Church affairs distress him more, for he is of the opinion that God's blessing cannot be given to much which had been proposed. In this respect he and Thomas Cornwaleys agreed well together. But they soon part company. That which Cornwaleys complained of so bitterly was most acceptable to Copley, who naturally says nothing whatever about it on the present occasion. That Roman Catholicism had just received a very sub-substantial concession went for nothing. He thinks nothing of it as he forwards a statement concerning the privileges and immunities that he desires his Church shall receive. But first, he has some very serious complaints to make. Not only is no care taken to promote the conversion of the Indians [5]—although just in what way this reflected upon Lord Baltimore, and not upon himself and his brother ecclesiastics, the Jesuit priest does not say—but there is no attempt to provide for, or to show any favor, to ecclesiastical persons. It was actually bruited about that privileges were not due to them *jure divino*, nor until the Commonwealth had granted them.

Still more galling was it that a converted Indian king might not give his converter so much land as would suffice for the building of a church. From this statement, in conjunction with Mr. Copley's dealings with the Indians, I infer that, in his judgment, at least several thousand acres were required to accommodate a suitable building. Meanwhile about his own very extensive transactions in land

---

[5] Davis, *The Day Star*, P. 165, speaks of Lord Baltimore as "the patron of the early Roman Catholic Missions!"

with the Indians he is judiciously silent. He even assures Lord Baltimore that he will take no land but under his lordship's title.

His next grievance was the provision that every manor must have an hundred acres in glebe land. To Mr. Copley this was naturally a most humiliating condition, besides being a very inconvenient one, for the Roman priests in Maryland had blossomed into extensive landowners since their arrival. Could it indeed be that Lord Baltimore meant that they should set apart so much of their land for the support of the Protestant clergy? This was really too dreadful to contemplate. Perish the thought! Yet Lord Baltimore's injunctions on this point were but the following out of the old English plan of providing each parish church with an adequate endowment in the form of glebe lands, so that it could be worthily supported. Obviously his aim was to act towards his distant colony in precisely the same way that other landlords were accustomed to act on their English estates. For this purpose we shall do well to praise Lord Baltimore.

But now comes the worst blunder of all. Oh, the pain and grief it causes Mr. Copley's righteous soul. In a catalogue of enormous crimes, perjury and the like, was numbered the "exercising jurisdiction and authority without lawful power and commission derived from the lord proprietary." Thus "even by Catholics" a law had been passed under which any Catholic bishop or priest might be hanged for no other crime than exercising his functions in Maryland, without having first obtained the consent of the secular authority.

Having now made his complaints known to Lord Baltimore, Copley, fearing his lordship may not do the right thing, proceeds with fatherly care to make certain suggestions for his guidance. These are:

First; that before doing anything about the laws proposed he would read over and ponder well the Bulla Coenæ. This document is a great favorite with Mr. Copley. He has that strong faith in its efficacy that some people have in certain cure-all remedies, which have positively never been known to fail. Remembering its anti-protestant character, I cannot help believing that if Maryland had ever sought the services of a grand inquisitor general, a man on whom Torquemada's mantle had visibly fallen, Mr. Copley would have been the very man for the post, he having the making of an ideal inquisitor.

Secondly; that in things concerning the Church

his lordship should take good advice of the Church —that is, of course, of that part which is of the Roman obedience.

Thirdly; that his lordship would send him a a private order that, while the government is Catholic, they may enjoy the following privileges: That the Church and their houses may be sanctuary; that they themselves, their domestics, and half, at least, of their planting servants, may be free from public taxes and services, and that the rest of their servants and their tenants, though outwardly they do as others do, yet privately, the custom of other Catholic countries may be observed, so that Catholics, out of bad practice, come not to forget those respects which they owe to God and His Church; that though in public they suffer their course to be heard and tried by public magistrates, yet in private they know this is permitted only for a time, because ecclesiastical jurisdiction was not settled, and, finally, that though they relinquished the use of many ecclesiastical privileges yet that it should be left to their discretion to determine when it was requisite to do so.

At length Mr. Copley brings his letter to a close. It is an exquisite production. The writer's style is inimitable. By turns defiant and humble; it is all for Lord Baltimore's good. He hopes everything will be well, but he is not over sanguine. He is a busy man, and an old proverb hath it that a "busy man never wants woe," and so with a sad heart and gloomy forebodings, he makes an end. He has stated the case for the Roman party in Maryland, and he can do no more.

Lord Baltimore was aghast. His indorsement of the letter shows this, that indorsement reading thus: "Mr. Thomas Copley to me, from St. Mary's, herein are demands of very extravagant privileges."[6] There is, in addition, a side-note to one of the foregoing clauses to this effect: "All the attendants as well as servants, he here intimates, ought to be exempted from the temporal government."[7] Roman Catholic though he was, Lord Baltimore might well stand aghast when he received Copley's letter and read therein his "very extravagant demands." Probably as an honest man, abhorring hypocrisy, the suggestion that he should make a secret treaty with the Romanists under which they would publicly appear to be subservient to the laws like other men, but in

[6] *Calvert Papers, Vol. I*, P. 157.
[7] *Calvert Papers, Vol. I*, 166.

reality free from them, only tendered to further embitter his relations with a society which numbered such a shining ornament as Mr. Copley among its honored members.

When these two letters reached Lord Baltimore affairs in England were casting dark shadows before them. We do not know how Lord Baltimore gave his judgment at the time. One would suppose that his mind was quickly made up. As between the captain and the priest there could be no question who was the wiser counsellor. It was no time to be establishing Romanism in an English colony. He would act wisely in having no legislation in his province not in harmony with English statutes. The Protestant Catholic layman, and not the Jesuit priest, had spoken best for Maryland. Indeed Lord Baltimore had every reason for following the advice of Captain Cornwaleys, since in so doing he was as much forwarding his own interests as he was maintaining the rights of the Protestants. For it was not for his welfare or peace of mind, that there should be any *imperium in imperio* in that province, of which he was absolute lord proprietary under the English Crown. To a man of his disposition a power over which he had no control must have been personally very distasteful, and as dangerous as it was distasteful, since it was sure to bring him into conflict with English public opinion. So that however good a Romanist he was, and however anxious he may have been to further the interest of his Church, he could not prudently have followed Copley's advice. He knew the law and he was without excuse if he broke it, and he had no intention of being pilloried as an example of disobedience to it,[8] nor of giving hostages to fortune. Neither would he imperil his property by any ill-timed generosity. Indeed, so impartially did he act, that one would scarcely have suspected him of being a Roman Catholic at all, much to the chagrin of the Jesuits who had reckoned upon manipulating him as a son of "the Church." Their extreme disappointment, and the depth of their resentment, may be accurately gauged from Mr. Copley's warning that Baltimore was liable to bring upon himself the terrible censures of Bulla Coenæ. Was he aware of this? Or had he no fear of it? Even among heretics "the Church" enjoyed greater privileges than it did under his rule.

Such was the man with whom the Jesuits had to

[8] Neill, *Terra Mariæ* P. 132.

deal. He was not, it must be allowed, promising material on which to work, and recognizing this they groaned under the yoke. They might as well, aye better, have stayed in England, as live under the absolute lordship of one who seemed to put beaver-skins and corn before the Kingdom of God and His righteousness. Yet, had they known it, their safety lay only in obedience. The storm which swept them away from Maryland would never have broken had they listened to the advice of the proprietary and followed his injunctions.[9] But this was the one thing they did not intend to do. In Maryland at any rate they had the upper hand. It was all very well for the lord proprietary to lay down plans but it was another thing to enforce them. Communication between him and his distant province was often slow and uncertain, and always irregular. Much might be done of which the absent lord would never hear at all, and at any rate months must elapse before any course of action entered upon by them could be repudiated. And advantage was not seldom taken of this. Then, too, they controlled the young Governor of Maryland and as long as they could do this they had little to fear. And so it speedily became evident that it is one thing to give laws,

[9] *Calvert Papers, Vol. I*, P. 132.

and another to enforce them, even although you have right, justice and sweet reasonableness on your side, when dealing with men who have their own purposes to serve ; and yet upon whose co-operation you depend for success. The precautions of Lord Baltimore were excellent, but

> The best-laid plans o' mice an' men
> Gang aft a-gley.

And so, consequently, notwithstanding the law and the voice of authority, the Jesuits entered upon a course which only an enemy would have desired them to take. Ignoring alike the dictates of prudence and the injunctions of the lord proprietary, they had began a contest for supremacy in Maryland which was to end in their own undoing ; for supremacy was just what they could not have in any English colony. Had they been satisfied to contend for liberty, to practice their religion in peace and quietness, to minister unostentatiously to their own people and to carry the tidings of the Gospel to the heathen Indians, they would not merely have been left unmolested, but they would have gone far towards realising the dreams of their superiors in making Maryland a Roman Catholic province. But they were not wise in their generation, and as they chose to pursue a policy of aggression they were overwhelmed by disaster.

CHAPTER XV.

BATTLES WITH THE JESUITS—THE DEFEAT OF LORD BALTIMORE. 1638—1641.

> " 'Twas blow for blow, disputing inch by inch,
> For one would not retreat, nor t'other flinch."
> —BYRON: "Don Juan."

The letters of Captain Cornwaleys and Father Copley, must have been anything but pleasant reading to Lord Baltimore. At a time when he had practically made himself bankrupt through having put all his available assets into his Maryland venture, and just at the moment when he was beginning to expect a rich return from that investment, he is confronted with the spectacle of a religious quarrel, parting his settlers into two rival religious factions, and dividing Maryland herself into two hostile camps. It was as if a chasm had suddenly yawned at his feet, into which at any moment might be irretrievably precipitated all his expenditure in the past; all his brilliant prospects for the future; and even his very tenure of the province itself.

Other information which came to Lord Baltimore about the same time tended still further to increase his anxiety. This was concerning the conduct of Father Copley. Notwithstanding Copley's professions of loyalty, and his assurance that under no circumstances would he receive land from the Indians, except under Baltimore's seal, it now transpired that at the very time he was making this statement he was secretly acquiring from King Pathuen the valuable estate of Mattapany, near the mouth of the Patuxent River.[1] This alone was bad enough, but what lent the affair an importance out of all proportion to itself, and caused to the lord proprietary infinite anxiety and alarm was the action of the Jesuit Society which, far from disclaiming responsibility for its agent's misdoings, boldly took his part and justified his conduct. Moreover, not content with doing this, for the sake we may presume, of consistency, the society openly disputed Lord Baltimore's title to any lands not ceded to him by the Indians. It even went on to deny the right of the English Crown to grant Maryland, and scoffed at his lordship's claims as againt the Indian kings.[2]

Fortunately, there was now one man in the colony upon whose activity, ability and loyalty Baltimore

[1] *Md. Hist. Soc., F. P. No. 18.* Pp. 56, 63.
[2] *Md. Hist. Soc., F. P., No. 9.* P. 249

could confidently rely to cope with the crisis which had so unexpectedly arisen, and to avert the serious dangers which thus threatened the very existence of his colony. This man was John Lewger, the secretary, who had arrived in the province on Nov. 28th, 1637. Lewger was a Roman Catholic, but of that moderate and conservative type which found no favor with such men as Copley. He had formerly been a clergyman of the English Church, but, unlike the majority of converts, had not thought it necessary on joining the Roman Church to become more ultramontane than the ultramontanes themselves. They do Rome an injustice who assert that she crushes out of her children all individuality. Cardinal Manning did not see eye to eye with Cardinal Vaughan. Even Leo XIII does not walk in the footsteps of Pius IX. Neither was Lewger a Romanist after the Copley type. He was of course always a *persona non grata* to the Jesuits. Acceptable to the more conservative Romanists, who were for the most part like himself scholars, and gentlemen, the Jesuits, in Maryland conventional phrase, "had no use for him." To them he was only an ex-minister who "yet retained much of the leaven of heresy." [3] But none perceived more clearly than

[3] *Md. Hist. Soc., F. P., No. 18.* P. 80.

he did the dangerous tendency of their position, and it is his hand that we see in the law which provided that Roman ecclesiastics who presumed to exercise their office in Maryland without a license should be liable to be put to death. No wonder the Jesuits did not love him. Evidently he was "a man who had understanding of the times to know what Israel ought to do."

Lord Baltimore, confidently relying on the co-operation of this able, learned and clear-sighted secretary, devoted to his interests, and having the advantage of being on the spot, lost no time in instructing him to take up the gauge of battle which the Jesuit priests had thrown down. Thus instructed, Lewger at once opened an anti-Jesuit campaign, on the points at issue, in the House of Assembly, which met on the 25th of October, 1640.[4] The account of the beginning of hostilities is best given in the words of the Jesuits themselves: "Therefore this Secretary having summoned the Parliament in Maryland, *composed with few exceptions of heretics*, and presided over by himself, in the name of the Lord Baltimore himself, he attempted to pass the following laws repugnant to the Catholic faith and ecclesiastical immunities:

[4] *Md. Hist. Soc., F. P., No. 18.* P. 63.

That no virgin can inherit, unless she marries before twenty-nine years of age; that no ecclesiastic shall enjoy any privilege, except such as he is able to show *ex Scriptura*, nor to gain anything for the Church, except by gift of a Prince, nor to accept any site for a church, or cemetery, nor any foundation from a convert Indian King, nor shall anyone depart from the province even to preach the Gospel to the Infidels by authority of the See Apostolic, without a license from the lay magistrate; nor shall anyone exercise jurisdiction within the province which is not derived from the Baron, and such like." [5]

From the Jesuit point of view this legislation was sufficiently drastic for all purposes. But Lord Baltimore's own measures at headquarters were even more drastic still. Without waiting for the result of Maryland legislation, Baltimore had determined to cut the gordian knot by demanding the immediate and complete removal from his province of the Jesuit missionaries. We find him therefore soon after the adjournment of the General Assembly of 1640, petitioning the Sacred Congregation of the Propagation of the Faith to remove the refractory priests. In August 1641 this petition

[5] *Ibid.* P. 81.

was favorably acted upon, and Dom Rosetti, titular Archbishop of Tarsus, with a body of secular priests, was appointed to take charge of the Maryland Mission.[6] But the fathers had yet to be heard from. They not unnaturally objected to such a summary dismissal. They were not conscious of having done wrong to any man. Rather did they feel that a grievous wrong had been done *them*. Contending that they had been misrepresented and misunderstood, and asserting that they were suffering at the hands of an autocratic, and not over orthodox secretary, whose enmity they had unjustly incurred, they offered a respectful but firm protest against thus being ignominiously sent back to England. " The Fathers," they said, concluding a somewhat lengthy protest which went over the whole ground, "do not refuse to make way for other laborers, but they humbly submit for consideration whether it is expedient to remove those who first entered into that vineyard, at their own expense, who for seven years have endured want and sufferings, etc., who have lost four of their own confreres, laboring faithfully

---

[6] "*Records of the English Province of the Society of Jesus,*" edited by the Jesuit Father Foley, and published in London, in five volumes, in 1877, 1878 and 1879, Vol. III, 7th series. P. 365. See also *M. H. S., F. P., No. 18.* P. 64.

unto death; who have defended sound doctrine and the liberty of the Church, with odium and temporal loss to themselves, and *who are learned in the language of the Savages*,[7] of which the priests to be substituted by the Baron Baltimore are entirely ignorant, and which priests either allow or defend that doctrine from which it must needs be that contentions and scandals should arise, and the spark of faith be extinguished, which begins to be kindled in the breast of the infidels.[8]

It was doubtless due to this appeal that Dom Rosetti never saw Maryland, and that the Jesuit priests went on their way without interference from their superiors, with the result that Baltimore was obliged to give his attention to the devising of other means of getting rid of these troublesome ecclesiastics. His failure to accomplish his aims in other ways at any rate satisfactorily accounts for the issuing, on November 10th, 1641, of new Conditions

---

[7] *Md. Hist. Soc., F. P.*, No. 7. *Excerpta Ex Diversis Litteris Missionariorum.* Pp. 84 and 85.

The claim that the missionaries were learned in the languages of the savages hardly agrees with the statements of the next year's report. "For the difficulty of this language is so great, that none of us can yet converse with the Indians without an interpreter—a statement which is in strict accordance with their practice of always being accompanied by an interpreter.

[8] *Md. Hist. Soc., F. P.*, No. 18. P. 82.

of Plantation, to take effect on the Festival of the Annunciation of the Blessed Virgin Mary, 1642. In these conditions were two sections aimed directly and exclusively at the Jesuits. By these sections all fraternities and associations, spiritual or temporal, were prohibited from holding land without the assent of the civil magistrate.[9] These anti-clerical prohibitions, which were in agreement with English Statute Law, rendered null and void the Assembly Act of 1639 which had given to "Holy Church" her privileges and immunities. But they did far

[9] (5) "Moreover, that no Corporation, Society, Fraternity, Municipality, Political Body (whether it be Ecclesiastical or temporal), shall be capable of or shall have the benefit, in virtue of the preceding conditions of plantation, of receiving for itself, of inheriting, of possessing or enjoying any lands in the said Province, either in right of their own or of any other person or persons, for their own use, interest or benefit, or in trust for them without farther particular and special license first had and obtained for this end under the hand and seal of his Lordship. And if perchance any such grant should happen to be given to or obtained by any Corporation, Society, Fraternity, Municipality, Political body (whether this be Ecclesiastical or temporal), or any person or persons whatsoever for their use, interest or benefit, or in trust for them without such farther particular and special license, as above, first had and obtained, that then all such grants of whatsoever land within the Province so made or to be made, as above, shall be by the very fact void of all intent and purpose."

(6) "Moreover, that no person or persons, whatsoever be their condition or state, nor their heirs nor assigns, shall give, concede, alienate any lands or tenements within the said

more than that. In Lord Baltimore's anxiety to annihilate Jesuit influence these new Conditions pressed far more severely upon the Society than even English law did. It really seemed as if the one subject of now all absorbing interest to Baltimore was how to destroy Jesuit influence in Maryland, let the cost be what it might.

The fate of these Conditions when they reached the province is very suggestive. Their crux was undoubtedly the anti-Jesuit sections. Yet apparently these very sections alone were never published in Maryland. Even to the secretary, to say nothing of the governor, they seemed too radical. Although these officials well knew what obedience required they actually went to the priests for a conference. Nothing can show more conclusively than this the nature of the control which the Jesuits exercised in the province, nor more clearly demonstrates the precise meaning of

Province, assigned or conceded, or to be assigned or to be conceded to him or them to any Corporation, Society, Congregation, Fraternity, Municipality or body, Politic (whether this be Ecclesiastical or temporal), or to any person or persons whatsoever in trust or to such use or uses, or to any use or uses contained, mentioned or prohibited in any Statute of Mortmain made before in the Kingdom of England without particular and special license before had and obtained for this end under the hand and seal of his Lordship." See *Md. His. Soc., F. P., No. 9.* P. 250, Streeter.

Father Copley's phrase: "While the Government is Catholique." The account of the interview is preserved in the handwriting of the secretary,[10] and very painful reading it is, as we read of how he and the governor went to the "good men about difficulties," and how, entrenching themselves behind the terrific thunders of the bull, *In Coena Domini*, the priests declined obedience, with the result that the obnoxious sections were not published, even Mr. Lewger deeming it best not to push matters to extreme by publishing them.

The Jesuits had triumphed. Poor Captain Cornwaleys must have been in despair. But all Maryland knew that it was not with Lord Baltimore's consent. And the people hastened to show their confidence in him. In the Assembly which met March 21st, 1642, the members "out of their desire to return his Lordship some testimony of their gratitude for his great charge and solicitude in maintaining the government and protecting the inhabitants in their persons, rights and liberties, and to contribute some support to it, so far as the young and poor estate of the colony will yet bear," passed "an act for granting a subsidy of fifteen pounds of tobacco for every

[10] *Ibid*, P. 251.

taxable inhabitant of the Colony, the first yet imposed on the settlers."[11] This act must have been peculiarly grateful to Lord Baltimore, entirely dependent as he was at this time upon the hospitality of his wife's relations."[12]

After this victory of the Jesuits there was a temporary cessation of hostilities. It was as if peace had been established. Possibly the priests thought that Lord Baltimore had accepted the situation and was about to make the best of it. But they did not know the man with whom they were dealing if they thought this. Between himself and them, at all events between his aims and theirs, a gulf was fixed which could not be bridged over. For Lord Baltimore, Roman Catholic though he was, was no Jesuit, and he would have no Jesuit priests interfering with his cherished project of making his colonial venture a brilliant success. That they had so far successfully opposed him, and maintained their independence, was no real gain to them, for it only left him more determined than ever to curtail their zeal, to restrict their aims and to prove to

[11] *Md. Hist. Soc., F. P., No. 9.* P. 255.
[12] Cecilius Calvert, after his marriage with the daughter of the first Lord Arundel, of Wardour, lived at Hook House, the dower-house of Lord Arundel. See Neill, *Founders of Maryland.* P. 101.

them more effectually that he, and not they, was the master of Maryland. It surely shows how little the society understood the depth of Lord Baltimore's resentment, and the nature of his antagonism, when, no long time after they had refused his request for the withdrawal of the priests, they actually sought his permission for the sailing of two additional missionaries. Naturally the request was instantly refused. Already there were more of their order in Maryland than he wanted, as he thought he had made quite plain. If he could not get rid of those already there he could at least prevent others going. The refusal caused consternation in the Jesuit camp. Finding him resolute the Jesuits hastened to make terms with him, and they agreed to abide by the following concordat: "Considering the dependence of the government of Maryland on the state of England, unto which it must (as near as may be) be conformable, no ecclesiastical person whatever, inhabiting or being within the said province, ought to pretend or expect, nor is Lord Baltimore or any of his officers, (although they be Roman Catholics) obliged in conscience to allow to said ecclesiastics, in said province, any more or other privileges, exemptions, or immunities for their persons, lands or goods, than is allowed by his majesty or his officers or magistrates to like persons in England. And any magistrate may proceed against the person, goods, etc., of such ecclesiastic, for the doing of right and justice to another, or for maintaining his proprietary prerogative and jurisdictions, just as against any other person, residing in said province. These things to be done, without incurring the censure of *bullæ coenæ*, or committing a sin for so doing.[13] The society even went on to admit that it had no right to the lands given to its agents by the King of the Patuxents, or other Indian chieftains, and it promised to execute an instrument placing it out of the power of its agents to offend in the future, as they had done in the past. It even consented to withdraw its claims for exemption from temporal jurisdiction.

On this understanding the missionaries were allowed to depart. Alas for the trustfulness of Lord Baltimore! As soon as these new missionaries arrived in Maryland they repudiated the agreement, and became one with their rebellious brethren. In the Jesuit letter of 1642 the writer thus glosses over this discreditable breach of trust: "One thing, however, remains not altogether to be

[13] *Md. Hist. Soc., F. P., No. 9.* P. 254.

omitted, though to be touched on lightly, to wit: this thing, that occasion of suffering has not been wanting from those, from whom rather it was proper to expect aid and protection; who, too intent upon their own affairs, have not feared to violate the immunities of the Church, by using their endeavors, that laws of this kind formerly passed in England and unjustly observed there, may attain like force here, to wit: that it shall not be lawful for any person or community, even ecclesiastical, in any wise, even by gift, to acquire or possess any land, unless the permission of the civil magistrate first be obtained. Which thing, when our people declared it to be repugnant to the laws of the church, two priests were sent from England who might teach the contrary. But the reverse of what was expected happened; for our reasons being heard, and the thing itself being more clearly understood, they easily fell in with our opinion, and the laity in like manner generally." [14] So the solemn agreement having served its purpose was flung aside as the hunter flings aside the burnt cartridge which has brought down his game. But as we have seen, these "good men" did not number a love of truth among the virtues with which

[14] *Excerpta Ex Diversis Litteris Missionariorum.* P. 88.

they were equipped. They were not of those who swear unto their neighbor and disappoint him not, though it were to their own hindrance. With the continued submission and subservience to the priests of his own brother, and the unwillingness of even the devoted, and thoroughly sympathetic Lewger to follow out his directions to the end; above all with the broken pledges of the priests before him, one almost hears Lord Baltimore exclaim: Ye disciples of Ignatius Loyola, ye are too hard for me, "and I am this day weak, though anointed king."[15]

After all, we need not wonder at the difficulties of Lord Baltimore with the "good men." It was a very old fight which was being renewed on Maryland soil. Should the Church be independent of all civil authority, rendering it no allegiance, and discharging no duties towards it? The Jesuits boldly claim that it should. And for a time they triumphed. But their victory meant utter ruin for Baltimore. There can be only one supreme power in any land.

Lord Baltimore was exceedingly unfortunate in having to fight this question out so far from the

---

[15] II Sam. 2 : 39.

base of operations, but he was more unfortunate still in having the Jesuit Society as his opponent. For that society has always been a thorn in the side even of the strongest and best settled governments. It has a well deserved reputation of shrinking from nothing that will advance either its own interests or the interests of its Church. Indeed, its never ceasing efforts since its inception in 1534 until now to control for its own purposes the governments of the world, has again and again caused even Roman Catholic countries to prohibit its existence within their borders, so exceedingly mischievous and harmful has its influence always been, wherever its principles have had time to bring forth their fruit. That these governments were justified in their action we have evidence of a very remarkable character. By one of the infallible Pontiffs, Clement XIV., in the celebrated bull, "*Dominus ac Redemptor Noster,*" the society was suppressed in all the states of Christendom "for the peace of the Church." It was therefore with a strange want of foresight, and an utterly unaccountable lack of appreciation of the gravity of the step he was taking that Lord Baltimore ever permitted the Jesuits to get a foothold in his province. For once removed from the restraints imposed upon them in England, their conduct had soon alienated the best men in his province, spread sectarian bitterness, stirred up religious strife, arrayed men in two parties and speedily, as the result of it all, brought their patron into conflict with the authorities in England, creating an impression there, never wholly removed, that the Roman Church had an undue and dangerous influence in Maryland.

We may perhaps assume that Lord Baltimore, with a large-hearted charity, which always does a man infinite credit, though it is not always to his financial advantage, had believed better things of his Maryland priests, as he remembered the splendid work done in other lands by the order. It was, indeed, easy to think of the Jesuits as pioneers of missionary enterprise, for they had often been the first to enter upon unknown fields, and claim them for Christ and the Church, especially in America. "The history of their labors," writes Bancroft, "is connected with the origin of every celebrated town in the annals of French America, not a cape was turned, not a river entered, but a Jesuit led the way!" Moreover, obedience was the rule of their life. They were emphatically "the men who obey orders." So he might have hoped that all would go well. But then it was not his orders they were pledged to obey, even though he was Lord Proprietary of Maryland.

If he had forgotten this he paid dearly for his error. He had sown the wind and he was to reap the whirlwind. Thrice that mistake cost him, or his family, the loss of the province. On the third occasion the only condition on which it could be restored was that his descendant abandon the Roman Church and become an Anglican, a condition which Benedict Leonard Calvert, in the spirit of Henry of Navarre, who thought Paris "worth a mass" found it not difficult to comply with. And in his days the Calvert family returned permanently to the old Church of the land, the Church of their forefathers.

CHAPTER XVI.

GATHERING CLOUDS.

1642—1648.

> The sky
> Is overcast, and musters muttering thunder,
> In clouds that seem approaching fast, and show,
> In forked flashes a commanding tempest.
> —BYRON.

Tidings of the Jesuits' doings and of the trouble occasioned thereby soon reached England, and there, like seeds falling on a rich and fertile soil, they forthwith produced an abundant harvest. At once Baltimore's enemies seized upon the reports as a pretext for efforts to deprive him of his province. The experiment, it was claimed, of giving to a Roman Catholic ample and generous powers over the fortunes of English subjects had been tried and had been proved a dismal failure. From the first it had been regarded as but another of those many tactless performances by which the Stuart kings were continually demonstrating to the nation their utter incapacity to level up to the measure and the standard of their opportunities and responsibilities.

In consequence of this agitation on March 26th, 1642, Lord Baltimore was summoned to appear before the House of Lords to answer for the alleged misconduct of his officers in Maryland, as if he had been conniving at the realization of their schemes, and abetting them in their lawlessness. Was ever an absolute lord in a more pitiable plight? Fighting Romanism abroad, and at the same time accused of advancing its interests at home. Unhappy Lord Baltimore! He was between the upper and the nether mill-stones. We have nothing, but the most meagre details of the inquiry before the Upper House. But that the lords did not take any very serious view of the situation is evident from the fact that, apparently, they took no action beyond placing Baltimore under bonds not to leave the kingdom, his previous disability in this respect having been removed.

But if we may judge of the character and nature of the whole charge from one portion of it, we shall not be surprised at the indifference of the lords. He had, so it was said, actually inserted a provision into the laws of the colony, protecting the Virgin Mary from reproach[1]—an accusation which indi-

---

[1] Ethan Allen, Manuscript book in Episcopal Library, Baltimore, P. 28.

cates that his opponents were not very familiar with the teaching of Scripture on the subject of the honor due to our Blessed Lord's mother. It is painfully evident from this incident alone that Lord Baltimore was face to face with extremely unreasoning partizan malice, and that he would have to walk warily if he would retain possession of his proprietary rights. Happily he could say that the troubles in Maryland were none of his making, and that he was even then engaged in a life and death struggle with the Jesuits there, for the very purpose of bringing about their final and complete submission to his authority.

Lord Baltimore's justification of himself on this occasion did not however end his difficulties, nor remove serious ground of apprehension for the future. The political sky was black with clouds, and he had soon far more urgent reasons for being anxious about his tenure of Maryland, than anything which might reasonably be expected to result from an impartial judicial inquiry. Events were moving rapidly in England. Every day the king was becoming more unpopular. Threats of civil war began to be heard on all sides. Finally it came, and on the twenty third of October, 1642, the first battle took place in that terrible fratricidal strife which was to witness the death of King Charles I upon the scaffold by the hands of the common executioner. For some time previous to that tragedy Lord Baltimore could scarcely have had much hope of ultimate tranquility. But after it had occurred, and England had received an object lesson in such a policy of 'Thorough' as even Strafford had never dreamed of, all hope must have effectually died out of his heart, for only by King Charles' personal favor was he Lord Proprietary of Maryland. The royal favor itself had now become a serious disadvantage. But as a Roman Catholic recipient of the king's bounty he labored under a more serious disadvantage still. Even the likelihood of his being involved in whatever hard fate threatened the unfortunate king was not nearly so remote as Baltimore could have wished it to be. He had even begun to fear for his life.[2] In the new turn of events which was lifting up Cromwell and the saints to supreme power in England it was a dangerous thing for a man to be suspected of encouraging Romanism. Better far to be a Mohammedan seeking proselytes than to be charged with advancing the cause of the dark idolatries of the modern Babylon, as all good Puritans held they had Scrip-

[2] *The Calvert Papers*, No. 1, P. 220.

tural authority for so describing Rome. Next to the work of destroying the erroneous opinions and practices which had found place in the National Church the Puritans turned with holy exultation to extirpating Romanism out of the land. Jehu destroying Baal out of Israel was their ideal saint and governor.

It was thus becoming increasingly evident that the only course which held out for Lord Baltimore a bare prospect of safety was for him to speedily rout the Jesuits. Nothing must be allowed to interfere with that one grand object. Even his relations to his Church must be subservient to it. He must burn all his bridges behind him. To be sure, even this might prove of no avail, it being only a forlorn hope at the best. But it was the only course which held out any possible prospect of success, and he determined to follow it. Having this in view, Baltimore undertook the work in a way so thoroughly characteristic and eminently practical as could not fail to compel the admiration of his enemies. Across the seas on the New England shore, where the Pilgrim Fathers had landed, there was rising a splendid commonwealth. The men of that commonwealth were in religious faith one with the party now coming to the front in England—Puritans every one of them and consistent haters both of prelacy and papistry.[3] Why should he not offer Maryland acres to some of these? It would propitiate the new power in England, and also bring into his colony settlers, who, with a little encouragement from him, would keep the Jesuits in order. Better soldiers he could never hope to find, for the Puritan is ever ready for war; a member he of the true Church Militant. Writing forthwith to Massachusetts, he made gracious offers to all who would migrate to Maryland, but without success, as an entry in the journal of Governor Winthrop under date October thirteenth, 1643, clearly

---

[3] The rise of the Puritans is generally referred to the reign of Queen Elizabeth (1558-1603); but their opinions are to be traced back a few years further. During the reign of Edward VI., one section of Church reformers whose opinions were modeled on those which obtained in Switzerland, the name of "Sacramentaries," and were practically the founders of the Puritan movement. These disaffected Churchmen who objected to the sign of the cross in baptism, to "all curious singing and playing at the organs," to copes, surplices, saints' days, and the like received about the year 1566, the name of Puritans or Precisians.

The Puritan movement went on as a movement within the Church for many years; it produced sects made up of those who would not remain in the Church except on their own terms; and it was placed supreme over the Church under Cromwell. The Puritans were Churchmen who had no idea of leaving the Church. Indeed, their leading men poured out their wrath upon those who separated from the Church and stirred up religious divisions in the country.

shows, Maryland at that time having no attraction for the New Englanders.[4] The idea, however, once conceived was never lost sight of, and later on, undeterred by the terrors of excommunication, he eventually filled his province with Puritans, who so far as clearing it of Jesuits was concerned, certainly did not disappoint his expectations.

To return, however, to the point. About the time Lord Baltimore was feeling most keenly the difficulties of his position as proprietary he wrote a letter to his brother in Maryland which is a perfect revelation in itself. In this letter, which is so important that, lengthy as it is, I venture to give it almost in extenso, we can see not only the determination of the Jesuits to win their cause at all costs and hazards, but the increasing bitterness of Lord Baltimore towards the Jesuit Society itself, and towards the Roman Church, of which

---

[4] Neill, *Founders of Maryland*, P. 109. "The Lord Baltimore being owner of much land near Virginia, being himself a Papist and his brother Mr. Calvert, the Governor there, a Papist also, but the colony consisting of both Protestant and Papist, he wrote a letter to Captain Gibbons of Boston and sent him a commission wherein he made a tender of land in Maryland to any of ours that would transport themselves thither with free liberty of religion, and all other privileges which the place affords, paying such annual rent as should be agreed upon, but our Captain had no mind to further his desire, nor had any of our people temptation that way."

it formed so influential a part. He is drifting from his theological moorings, and this by the act of the Romanists themselves. His words have almost the ring of one of Luther's fiery denunciations. He does not hesitate even to bring the name of the Pope into the discussion, and to affirm by a reference to contemporary events that there were circumstances under which opposition to him would be just and lawful. The letter[5] is written to his brother Leonard Calvert, and is dated, London, 23rd November, 1642. It was written immediately after one dated 21st November, in which he had given his brother sundry directions for the conduct of his affairs. This one, written upon the spur of the moment, dealt with a matter of which, we infer, he was two days before entirely ignorant. "Good Brother," he begins, "just now I understand, that notwithstanding my prohibition to the contarie, another member of those of the Hill there,[6] hath by a slight, got aboard Mr. Ingle's ship in the Downs to take his passage for Maryland

---

[5] *The Calvert Papers*, No. 1, P. 216. This letter was lost for two and a half centuries.

[6] The "Hill" referred to was the Hill of St. Inigoes, (evidently a corruption of St. Ignatius) on which the Jesuits dwelt, and where they owned considerable property. Lord Baltimore constantly refers to the Jesuits in this contemptuous way.

which for divers respects I have reason to resent as a high affront unto me. . . . This gentleman, the bearer hereof, Mr. Territt, will acquaint you more particularly with my mind herein, and with the opinion and sense which divers pious and learned men here have to this odious and impudent injury offered unto me, and with what is lawful and most necessary to be done in it, as well for the vindication of my honor as in time to prevent a growing mischief upon me, unto whom wherefore I pray give credit. Mr. Gilmet will, I know, concur in opinion with him, for upon divers consults had here (before he went) he was well satisfied what might and ought to be done upon such an occasion. In case the man above mentioned who, goes thither in contempt of my prohibition, should be disposed of in some place out of my province before you can lay hold of him; for they are so full of shifts and devices as I believe they may perhaps send him to Potomac Town, thinking by that means to avoid your power of sending him back into these parts; and yet the affront to me remain, and the danger of prejudice also be the same, for (whatsoever you may conceive of them who have no reason upon my knowledge to love them very much if you knew as much as I do concerning their speeches and actions here towards you) I am (upon very good reasons) satisfied in my judgment that they do design my destruction; and I have too good cause to suspect that if they cannot make or maintain a party by degrees among the English to bring their ends about, they will endeavor to do it by the Indians, by arming them against all those that shall oppose them, and all under pretence of God's honor and the propagation of the Christian faith, which shall be the mask and vizard to hide their other designs withal. If all things that clergymen should do upon these pretences should be accounted just, and to proceed from God, laymen were the basest slaves and most wretched creatures upon the earth. And if the greatest saint upon earth should intrude himself into my house against my will, and in despite of me with the intention to save the souls of all my family, but withal give me just cause to suspect that he likewise designs my temporal destruction, or that being already in my house doth actually practice it, although withal he does perhaps many spiritual goods, yet certainly I may and ought to preserve myself by the expulsion of such an enemy, and by providing others to perform the spiritual good he did, who shall not have any intention of mischief towards me, for the law of nature teacheth this, that it is lawful for every man, in his own just defence, vim vi repellere, those that will be impudent must be impudently dealt withal. In case, I say, that the party above mentioned should escape your hands by the means aforesaid, (which by all means prevent if possibly you can) then I pray do not fail to send Mr. Copley away from thence by the next shipping to those parts."

"The Princes of Italy who are now up in arms against the Pope, (although they be Roman Catholics) do not make any scruple of conscience by force of arms to vindicate the injury which they conceive he would have done unto the Duke of Parma: by wresting a brave palace, not far from Rome, called Capreroly, with a little territory about it, from the said Duke for one of the Pope's nephews: nor do they much esteem his excommunications or Bulls in that business for they believe them to be unjustly grounded, and therefore of no validity; although they continue, notwithstanding, Roman Catholics, and these are the Duke of Florence, the State of Venice, the Duke of Parma and the Duke of Modena Reggio: who are now joined in league and have an army of about forty thousand men raised up against the

Pope, and he near as many against them upon the quarrel above mentioned, in so much as it is generally conceived here that Rome is sacked by this time, or else that the Pope hath given full satisfaction to the aforesaid Princes, for he is thought too weak for them."

" In fine if you do not with a constant resolution and faithful affection to me, execute what I have here directed, (whatsoever inconvenience may come of it) and according to what you shall understand to be my mind herein more particularly by word of mouth from the said Mr. Territt, you will, as I said, betray me to the greatest dishonor and prejudice that ever one brother did another. . . . I understand that notwithstanding my prohibition the last year you did pass grants under my seal here to those of the Hill of St. Inigoes, and other lands at St. Mary's, and also of one hundred acres of land at Pascataway, some of which as I am informed you conceived in justice due unto them, and therefore thought yourself obliged to grant them, although it were contrary to my directions, which to me seems very strange, for certainly I have power to revoke any authority I have given you there either in whole or in part, and if I had thought fit to have totally revoked your power of granting any lands there at all in my name, certainly no man that is disinterested could think that you were bound nevertheless in conscience to usurp such an authority against my will, because in justice divers planters ought to have grants from me; for when I have revoked the power I gave you for that purpose any man else may as well as you undertake to pass grants in my name, and have as much obligation also in conscience to do it. I leave it to you to judge when I did give directions to you not to grant any more lands to those of the Hill there upon any pretence whatsoever, I did so far as concerned them revoke that power I formerly gave you of granting lands there, and it was a great breach of trust in you to do the contrary. And for aught you know some accident might have happened here that was no injustice in me, to have refused them grants of any land at all, and that by reason of some act of this state it might have endangered my life and fortune to have permitted them to have any grants at all which I do not (I assure) mention without good ground. I shall earnestly therefore desire you to be more observant hereafter of my directions, and not expect that I should satisfy your judgment by acquainting you still with my reasons why I direct anything; for then my power there were no more than any man's else, who may with reasons persuade you to do or forbear anything as well as I. And I do once strictly require you not to suffer any grants of any lands for the future to pass my seal here to any member of the Hill there, nor to any other person in trust for them upon any pretence or claim whatsoever without especial warrant under my hand and seal, to be hereafter obtained from me for that purpose. So I rest.

Your most affectionate loving brother,

London, 23d November, 1642."

In a postscript he adds:

"The Masters here of those of the Hill there did divers ways importune me to permit some of theirs to go this year thither, insomuch as they have, God forgive them for it, caused a bitter falling out between my sister Peasely and me, and some discontentment also between me and her husband about it, because I would not by any means give way to the going of any of the aforesaid persons."

It was a severe letter. But an adequate explanation of its severity is found in the not unreasonable alarm which Lord Baltimore now felt. Leonard knew nothing of the trial before the peers—the "act of this state," as it is probably described in this letter—neither did he know that the foundations of his brother's rule in Maryland were beginning to tremble. Here, too, was the explanation of Lord Baltimore's subsequent refusal to complete the proposed sale of the Church at St. Mary's, when the governor and the secretary had settled the preliminaries.[7] It was no time to be receiving "garments, olive yards and vineyards, and sheep and oxen and men-servants and maid-servants."

When Lord Baltimore's letter had reached its destination, and Leonard Calvert had read it, and Mr. Territt and Mr. Gilmett had explained its obscure hints, and by word of mouth had told the governor many things which his brother would not venture to commit to paper, Leonard Calvert must have been as thoroughly alarmed as was the proprietary himself. Indeed, so serious was the situation, and so wholly inexperienced did he feel himself to be in meeting the emergency, that his resolution was quickly taken. He would himself leave for a visit to England, and there take counsel with his brother in person. Accordingly as soon as possible after the receipt of this letter Leonard Calvert was on his way to England. The time

[7] Streeter, *Md. His. Soc.*, *F. P.*, *No. 9*, P. 183.

of his departure was not well chosen, the province never having stood in greater need of a responsible and competent head than at this very time. But he was between the Scylla of remaining, without knowing how his brother wanted him to act under the new developments in England, and the Charybdis of going with the prospect of anarchy while he was away. He went, however, and arrived in England in the very midst of the excitement of those troublous times.

Meanwhile the Puritan power, unappreciated at its full strength by either brother, was rapidly rising, before which the Jesuits were to be swept away as easily as dry leaves gathered in the rocky bed of a mountain stream are swept away when the floods in tempestuous torrents pour down into the valley. Leonard Calvert might have learned a useful lesson from those sudden thunder storms of whose terrific grandeur he had often been an interested spectator from the bluff overlooking St. Mary's River, whereon their city was built. Captain John Smith wrote concerning those storms: "The like thunder and lightning to purify the air I have seldom either seen or heard in Europe."[8] A characteristic of them is the timely warning

[8] Smith, *History of Virginia*, Vol. I, P. 114.

they give. The sky is clear and bright, not a cloud in sight. Suddenly just above the horizon a small dark patch is visible in the sky. Presently clouds in great volumes roll and surge upwards, banking themselves in rank above rank until they present a magnificent spectacle. And still all is calm. Not a leaf is turned by the wind, not a drop of rain has fallen. Only the distant roll of thunder, coming nearer and nearer, and the banking clouds growing blacker and blacker, tell of the coming tempest, and warn the traveler to hasten on his way, or seek shelter from the blast. Now it is at hand. Against the darkened sky the leaves of the forest trees are gleaming white, dust whirls about, and great branches are being torn off and flung contemptuously aside. The lightning flashes vividly against the inky blackness of the sky, as if it would rend the very heavens in twain. Echoing crashes of heavy thunder are now following each other in quick succession. The storm at length is at its height. The landscape is deluged with sheets of of rain, and every water course is swollen high with a solid torrent which carries all obstacles before it. An hour afterwards all is calm and peaceful again. The sun shines once more, and the sky glows with infinite gradations of tint and tone.

In the ecclesiastical sky there were signs of just such a coming storm, when Leonard Calvert sailed away from England. Already black clouds were sweeping across the horizon, and the sounds of thunder heard. An experienced eye could now have told Lord Baltimore that if he would retain his hold on Maryland he would be obliged to resort to more anti-Roman measures than anything he had yet attempted or even thought of. Indeed the time was soon to come when he would have to pose as a champion of Puritans, who ridiculed his pretensions to absolute lordship and royal jurisdiction, who scoffed at his religion, and, in the very colony that he had founded, were to disfranchise his co-religionists, and to seize the reins of government for themselves.

CHAPTER XVII.

THE STORM.

1644.

> Deep swelling gusts
> And sultry stillness take the rule by turns;
> Whilst o'er our heads the black and heavy clouds
> Roll slowly on.
> —JOANNA BAILLIE.

While Leonard Calvert was in England the ecclesiastical storm broke over St. Mary's, its breaking being precipitated by the news from England of the remarkable successes of the Parliamentary forces. The Protestants saw that the hour of deliverance had come. They would now look to it that Rome's dominion was at an end. In England the Jesuits lay under a ban, and it was intolerable that in an English colony, and in defiance of English law, they should be permitted to conduct themselves as they had been doing. Was it for this that the Maryland adventurers had left kinsfolk and friends? For this that their fathers had gone through the fires of Smithfield? Had the yoke of Rome been broken off their shoulders in England, and not wherever England's flag waved? Degenerate sons of mighty sires were they, and unworthy of the traditions of their race, if they calmly bore this wrong any longer.

Yet without a leader protestant resentment might have smoldered for a considerable period before bursting out into flame. But that leader was at hand. Baltimore's arbitrary proceedings ten years before were now to bear their unwholesome fruit. Ever since the battle on the Pocomoke, when Baltimore had seized Clayborne's property on Kent Island, Clayborne had been biding his time. At last it had come, and he could now take sweet vengeance upon his enemy. Anticipating by some weeks the ultimate downfall of the king he immediately put himself at the head of the disaffected among the colonists, and with the aid of one Richard Ingle, the captain of a ship engaged in trade with the province, he made war on his ancient foe. Instantly Maryland affairs were in the utmost confusion. The principal officers of the government were hopelessly at variance. Ingle, proclaimed a traitor to his Majesty, his vessel seized, and an attempt made, though unsuccessful, to accomplish his arrest, was more embittered than ever. Meanwhile the surrounding Indians, taking advantage of the dissensions among the settlers, were becoming alarmingly hostile.[1] Altogether the condition of the province was exceedingly critical. In the midst of the trouble Leonard Calvert arrived from England. But he was powerless to bring order out of chaos, and before the end of the year—1644— Clayborne had the supreme satisfaction of coming into possession of Kent Island. This was, however, only the beginning of his successes. He looked forward to greater achievements. In the following spring St. Mary's was attacked by the Protestants, whose discontent Clayborne had focused? Without a struggle the city was captured, and Lord Baltimore's authority in Maryland ceased. On its ruins Clayborne established his own. In all this, and much more in events of far greater moment that followed this, as it is very easy to see, Clayborne had a model beyond the seas. In the person of the Lord Protector the late Secretary of Virginia had found both his exemplar and his strongest encouragement to persevere.

The downfall of the proprietary government caused a panic among the Jesuits. The more prudent sought safety in flight, recognising that they

---

[1] Streeter, *Maryland Two Hundred Years Ago*, P. 33 and 34.

had fallen upon evil times. Even the governor fled the province. The priests, who were naturally regarded as the head and front of the offending, before they could follow the governor's example, were seized and confined, to be sent in chains to England at the first opportunity. Their people were dealt with less harshly. But some among them were banished, while others were heavily fined. Probably those who were thus treated had been more or less prominently identified with the performances of Thomas Copley. But if we may depend upon the statements of the Jesuit report made in 1670—just about a quarter of a century later—we shall see that in 1646 there were Roman Catholics in Maryland who, so far from feeling it necessary to hide themselves in dens and caves of the earth, were not afraid to follow a custom they had established when they were in power, of honoring the night of July 31st—the festival of St. Ignatius—with a salute of cannon. "Mindful" runs the record, "of the solemn custom, the anniversary of the holy father being ended, they wished the night also consecrated to the honor of the same by continual discharge of artillery." Accordingly they kept up the cannonade throughout the whole night. At the time there happened to be in the neighborhood "certain soldiers, unjust plunderers, Englishmen indeed by birth, of the heterodox faith; * * * but now aroused by the nocturnal report of the cannon, on the day after, that is on the first of April, rush upon us with arms, break into the homes of the Catholics and plunder whatever there is of arms or powder."[2] The continuous firing of cannon during the night, while the enemy's soldiers were in the neighborhood, implies that there had been no attempt to drive out, or even to intimidate, all the Roman Catholics. It was an attack not on them but on the Jesuit priests. When order was restored Clayborne was undisputed master of the land.

Thus, as so often elsewhere, the Jesuits had proved to be troublers of the peace of the community which had given them shelter. Rule or ruin seems ever to be the only alternative of their presence.

[2] In Plantagenet's *New Albion*, a pamphlet published in 1648, Clayborne's part in the movement, and also its religious character is seen. "I went" says the author, "to Chicacoen avoiding Maryland, for then it was in war both with the Susquehannocks, and all the Eastern Bay Indians, and a civil war between some revolters, Protestants, assisted by fifty plundered Virginians, by whom Mr. Leonard Calvert was taken prisoner and expelled; and the Isle of Kent also taken from him by Captain Claybourne of Virginia." Streeter, *Maryland, Two Hundred Years Ago*, P. 34.

Already lying under the grave displeasure of the lord proprietary they now suffered well merited chastisement at the hands of the angry colonists, who had determined that a government dominated by them should come to an end. Such a condition of affairs had of course from the beginning been an anomaly. Moreover it had been flagrant lawlessness, existing as it did in the face of the lord proprietary's initial injunctions[3] and his oft repeated protests, to say nothing of the charter to which Maryland owed her existence, and the statute law of England herself. Now, however, the day of retribution had come. But as frequently happens under similar circumstances the most guilty escape. Emphatically was this the case in the present instance. Thomas Copley, the fomenter of strife and dissension, without whose help even Clayborne's opposition would have been as harmless as an arrow against an iron-clad vessel, contrived to make good his escape from personal injury, although he did not escape from pecuniary loss, his home at Potopaco being gutted.[4] On the other hand, Father White, the faithful missionary, against whom no evil report lay, was sent to Eng-

---

[3] *Md. Hist. Soc., F. P.*, No. 7, Pp. 94 and 95.
[4] Neill, *Founders of Maryland*, P. 103.

land in irons, there to be tried and condemned as a felon to suffer imprisonment for violating the laws concerning popish missionary priests. Father White's fate was a hard one, all the harder because so undeserved; but it gained for him, we may be sure, the deepest sympathy of the lord proprietary, whose life-long friend he had been, as he had been also the friend of his father before him. On July 4th, 1646, he was found guilty of teaching doctrines contrary to the laws of England. Unfortunately, with his own misfortunes falling fast upon him, Lord Baltimore was powerless to save the good father from that confinement in the penitentiary to which a rigorous obedience to the law now relegated him. His imprisonment was not, however, of long duration. In January 7th 1648 the House of Commons granted his release from Newgate.[5]

Yet observe here what a clear light is thrown by this incident upon the contention that Maryland was given to Lord Baltimore as a refuge for persecuted Roman Catholics. Granting this claim, never did a Christian government behave in a more tyrannical, arbitrary and iniquitous fashion than did the English government towards Father

[5] *Ibid*, P. 104.

White and his fellow sufferers. With Gallio-like indifference it had allowed an apostolic missionary to be ruthlessly torn from his people, and had then both accepted full responsibility for this act, and had proceeded further to punish him by long imprisonment for exercising a ministry, which, though prohibited by law from exercising in England, yet by its own authority and consent, he had full liberty to exercise in Maryland. Surely to have inveigled Roman Catholics to Maryland by promises of full toleration of their opinions, and then to imprison them for accepting the offers made them, was the very refinement of cruelty, beside which the giving to children a stone when they have asked of us bread is mercifulness itself. Can anyone really believe that the English government had ever regarded Maryland as a refuge for Romanists? Does not Father White's own conduct, and that of his brother ecclesiastics, in first traveling to Maryland under assumed names, and then, as long as it was possible to do so, hiding their priestly status under the style and title of laymen, altogether discredit that contention. Men protected by law have no need to act in that way. That the Jesuits did so act shows that they were fully conscious that they were lawbreakers and that even in Maryland they preached their doctrines at their peril. Father White and his colleagues at any rate did not foresee the rise and extraordinary growth of the Calvert cult and the legendary origin of Maryland.

Lord Baltimore had no time to spend in profitless regrets. There was no predicting to what the Maryland insurrection might lead. For a time it was of course only too evident that he had lost his province. It was even an unsolved problem whether he would ever recover possession of it. The indications were so far from favorable that Lord Baltimore himself gave up all hope. Writing to his brother he bade him gather together the wreck of his private property, and then abandon his ill-starred enterprise. That ill success which had dogged his father's commercial undertakings seemed to be following him also. He was utterly in despair. There was much to justify a pessimistic view. Instead of becoming brighter, the fortunes of King Charles—with which his own were so indissolubly bound up—were daily becoming more desperate. The royal cause was plainly doomed. And when, on the twelfth of June following, the battle of Naseby was fought which resulted in the capture of the king by the Parliamentary forces,

THE STORM.

and the coming into power of Oliver Cromwell, as Lord Protector of England, Baltimore's fate seemed doomed also. Everything was against him. In Maryland the threatened invasion of the Indians had taken place and they were now making war upon his people.[6] At home Parliament had just handed over the whole care of the colonies, his own included, to the Earl of Warwick. Evidently the only thing left for him to do was to quickly save what he could out of the wreck, and abandon his ill-starred enterprise—hence his despairing letter to his brother.

Meanwhile, one little ray of sunshine shot across the darkened sky. Although affairs were so hopelessly forlorn there came just one cheering message from Maryland. Paying no attention to the letter in which Cecilius had ordered him to gather together what he could and abandon the lost cause, Leonard had struck a vigorous blow for his brother's province, which had proved eminently successful. By the help of the Virginians he had come again into possession of St. Mary's, and this without the shedding of blood! After two years experience of other rulers the colonists were glad to come again under the rule of the Calverts.

[6] Sparks, P. 215.

In this there was nothing strange or unexpected. By the banishment of the Jesuits, and the overthrow of Roman influence, the colonists had accomplished their aims. With the exception of Clayborne and Ingle none of Baltimore's enemies were animated by any motives of private hatred and vengeance against him personally. It is important to bear this fact in mind because it explains not only the sudden collapse of this rebellion, but of a more serious one later on. The colonists' rebellion was over when Romanism was crushed. Clayborne's hostility was life-long, and only to be satiated by the death or total discomfiture of Lord Baltimore himself. Hence it was that with the defeat of the priests the whole population came again under Baltimore's rule. For their quarrel was with Rome, and with Rome only. They doubtless even felt that they were helping the proprietary when they were fighting the Jesuits, and they no doubt congratulated themselves that what he had ineffectually tried to do by legislation, Conditions of Plantation, and in other ways, they had in a few hours achieved for him.[7] With Clayborne's undying hostility they had little or no sympathy. But alas! there was no

---

[7] Episcopalians up to the year 1650 were faithful supporters of Lord Baltimore's proprietary claims. Streeter, *Maryland Two Hundred Years Ago*, P 39.

sunshine in England. Events were running on rapidly to that dark day when King Charles passed to the scaffold as an enemy of his country.

Shortly after the province came back again into the hands of its rightful lord the young governor's course was run. At the early age of forty-one he passed away, on the 9th of June 1647. In the main he had been faithful to his brother's interests, and there was probably none who did not sorrow over his untimely death. But it would be a misuse of language to write of him as "a great and good man.[8]" Perhaps it would be equally unfair to think of him as weak and incompetent. Yet his own relative, George Evelyn, the commander of Kent Island, asked of him contemptuously "Who was his grandfather, but a grazier? What was his father? What was Lord Calvert himself at school, but a dunce and a blockhead.[9]" Great men to be sure have come forth with such reputations behind them, but it must be admitted that it is rather an unpromising foundation on which to raise a splendid name and reputation. Leonard Calvert did his best, and according to his ability he served both his brother and Maryland well. But he was not a

[8] Davis, *The Day Star*, P. 174.
[9] Streeter, *Evelyn*, P. 6.

brilliant success as a governor. Not only did he take his religion from Rome but unfortunately he took his politics also. He was simply the tool of the Jesuits, and being such it was natural that they had no great opinion of him. From his brother's account Leonard thought more highly of them than they did of him.[10] So it came about that, in the contest between his brother and the Jesuits, he could not always be relied upon to stand by his brother's orders. This was of course a serious draw back. An ideal governor would have been absolutely independent in his political opinions. At any rate he would have carried out his patron's instructions, whatever his own religious convictions might have been, and this he had not done.

Will it however be believed that he lies in a nameless grave? Of his sepulchre, like that of Moses, no man knows unto this day. A few years ago the State of Maryland erected a monument to his memory, setting it up on the site of the future city of St. Mary's, where he made his agreement with the Yaocomico Indians for the purchase of their lands.

On each side of the square base inscriptions run as follows:

[10] *Calvert Papers*, *No. 1*, P. 217.

THE STORM. 307

Leonard Calvert,
second son of
George Calvert,
First Baron of Baltimore,
and
Anne his wife.
Led the first colonists to Maryland
November 22, 1633—March 3, 1634.
Founded St. Mary's
March 27, 1634.
Died
June 9, 1647.
by his
Wisdom, Justice and Fidelity
he fostered
the infancy of the colony,
guided it through great perils
and dying left it at peace.

The descendants and successors
of the men he governed,
here record
their grateful recognition
of
his virtues.
November—MDCCCXC.

To
the memory of
Leonard Calvert,
First Governor of Maryland,
this monument is erected
by
The State of Maryland.

Erected
on the site of the
Old Mulberry Tree
under which the
First Colonists of Maryland
assembled
to establish a government,
where the persecuted and oppressed of
every creed and of every clime might
repose in peace and security, adore
their common God, and enjoy the
priceless blessings of
Civil and Religious Liberty.

The description of Leonard on this stone is on a par with epitaphs generally, and only serves to show how little descriptions of the kind can be relied upon, almost justifying Byron's sneer: "Never believe an epitaph." This monument, which is in form a marble shaft, raises itself aloft amid the beautiful surroundings of trees and sparkling water, which almost encircle the bluff whereon the adventurers built their city. Beneath the very shadow of the parish church of St. Mary's Parish it stands, in the graveyard where some of the colony's earliest governors lie buried. No where else could it so appropriately stand, for its very presence there is symbolic of the fact that the foundations of Maryland were laid by Anglican Churchmen, who today, as in time past, hold possession of what will ever be holy ground to the Marylander, as the birth-place of the State, though not the starting point of the Church. To Kent Island in the Chesapeake we must look for that.

CHAPTER XVIII.

A NEW DEPARTURE; THE PROGRAMME.

1648—1650

" Now join your hands, and with your hands your hearts,
That no dissension hinder government."
—SHAKESPEARE.

The condition of public affairs in his province in the closing weeks of the year of grace 1648 certainly presented to Lord Baltimore, even if it did not actually suggest itself, the opportunity of a splendid *coup-d'-état*. The situation was in fact the same, in a less exalted sphere and on a humbler scale, as that which had existed in England after the deaths of Queen Mary and Cardinal Pole. Queen and cardinal had stood side by side, working harmoniously for the subjection of England to the papacy, and when together they passed away there opened out before the nation a vision of needed reforms accomplished with such perfect ease, and with such general manifestations of popular approval, as to lead even opponents to acknowledge that God was manifestly directing the affairs of the English Church and nation, bringing light out of darkness, and order out of chaos. So in Maryland the chief actors in recent events had all been removed. Leonard Calvert had been called to

"Where beyond these voices there is peace."

Secretary Lewger had sailed for England with the intention of remaining there. Kent Island had no commander, and the priests, whose power had received such a shock under Clayborne's rule, had not as yet ventured to assert themselves again. It seemed, indeed, as if the old order in Maryland had been so completely changed that there was not even a memento of it left behind.

Thus the hour had come for Baltimore to propitiate the new rulers of England, who, if left alone, were only too likely to strip him of all he owned in Maryland. To avert such a catastrophe as this he decided upon a plan of action for the government of his province which contained features of so radical a nature as to involve a complete reversal of all the methods which had hitherto been followed in Maryland. He would make Maryland thoroughly protestant in its sympathy and in its religion. By so doing he would both swamp Jesuitism, and also place himself in a position where he could propitiate whichever party in the church should eventually bear the supreme rule.

His programme looked to the carrying out of four distinct measures :

(1.) The appointment of Protestants to the highest offices in the province.

The times demanded that governor, secretary and commander should all alike be protestants. Accordingly removing Thomas Greene, a Roman Catholic, whom Leonard Calvert ere he died had named as his successor, the vacancy in the governorship was filled up by the appointment of Colonel William Stone. The vacancy in the secretaryship was filled by the appointment of Thomas Hatton ; while Robert Vaughan was made commander of Kent Island. The choice of Stone was a particularly politic one. He was well known as being in entire sympathy with the Parliament, and devoted to its interests. As King Charles was now lying in prison it was no slight advantage to Baltimore to have such a representative in Maryland : he was worth more to him than an army.

There is reason to think that this change from the appointment of a Roman Catholic to a Protestant governor was not made by Lord Baltimore without some fear and hesitation, as if, in appointing Stone, he was taking a leap in the dark. In the excitement of the times he was afraid his Protestant governor might take to persecuting the Romanists. Although he himself was not a zealous Roman Catholic he had no disposition to break with his Church, or be charged with abandoning his co-religionists in Maryland to the tender mercies of the Protestant majority. Evidently fearing, however, something of this kind—a persecution of Roman Catholics carried on under the form and sanction of legislative acts—he proceeded to guard against its possibility. He therefore delayed the appointment of the new governor until he had taken a solemn oath that he would not use his official position to oppress or molest the Roman Catholics left in the province. This thoughtfulness on behalf of the Roman Catholics shows Baltimore in a noble light. He would not visit the offenses of the guilty upon the innocent. All had not sinned. If the fires of strife and dissension had been kindled by Jesuit teachers, with the Jesuits he had his own account to settle. But he would stretch out his hands to help others. It was not a popular thing to do: perhaps not even a wise or politic thing. Still he did it. And so Lord Baltimore required his Protestant governor to take oath that he would not "directly or indirectly trouble, molest or discountenance any Person whatsoever in the said Province professing to believe in Jesus Christ, and in particular no Roman Catholic, for or in respect of his or her Religion."[1]

From the days of Chalmers, who gives the oath without the clause, 'and in particular no Roman Catholic,' it has been usual with some Maryland writers to quote the oath without any reference whatever to this clause, notwithstanding that without it the whole document is as a watch without a mainspring. Lacking that clause it has even been assumed that the oath was exacted by a Roman Catholic lord proprietary on behalf of a down trodden Protestant minority! How such an odd notion ever obtained a moment's consideration is a mystery. It has not even plausibility to recommend it. When the Puritans were rapidly becoming a power in England; when Romanism was more an object of dislike and suspicion than it had ever been since Mary had burned their undying hatred of it into the hearts of the English people; when political considerations had dictated to Lord Baltimore as a measure of self preservation the appointment of Protestants to fill the highest official places in his colony; when the Roman Catholics were but as a few scattered sheep without a

[1] *Archives of Maryland, Council*, P. 210.

shepherd; when the Roman Church herself was utterly discredited and entirely without power; when arrangements looking to the advent into the colony of five hundred Virginian Protestants were actually being made, and when above all the question of depriving Baltimore of his province was being agitated in influential circles in England, there was little need, forsooth, of any anxiety on the proprietary's part lest there should be, on however small a scale, a colonial St. Bartholomew's massacre. Nor did Lord Baltimore fear one. His fears were all the other way. He thought of reprisals on the part of the Protestants of which Roman Catholics would be the victims, and he took precautions accordingly.

Having thus bound over the Protestant governor to keep the peace with the Roman Catholic portion of his people Lord Baltimore felt free to add to the political and financial value of his new governor's appointment by insisting upon his bringing into the province at least five hundred immigrants. Other men for the same service had been liberally rewarded with broad acres and generous shares in the profits of the enterprise, but Stone's reward was the governorship. This condition, inserted into the body of the commission, recorded how William

Stone had "undertaken in some short time to procure five hundred people of British or Irish descent to come from other places and plant and reside within our said province of Maryland."[2] For a country officered by Protestants it was well to have Protestant citizens, and Stone's immigrants were sure to be of that faith; his recruiting ground naturally being Virginia, he having been high sheriff of Northampton county in that state. Not indeed that this was the first time that Baltimore had sought for immigrants from Virginia. "Upon the express assurance, that there would be a modification of the oaths of office and fidelity, and an enjoyment of liberty of conscience," he had already persuaded some Virginians to settle in Maryland.[3] Evidently Lord Baltimore liked the quality. No wonder that a few years later Roman Catholics were only one in thirty of the population.[4] But so important politically considered was this matter of obtaining a large Protestant emigration Lord Baltimore was not willing to leave it entirely in the hands of Stone. In the very same year therefore that we find Stone hard at work raising his quota

---

[2] *Archives of Maryland, Council*, P. 201.
[3] Neill, *Founders of Maryland*, P. 117.
[4] In 1681, See McMahon, P. 232.

of emigrants we find Baltimore as busily engaged in a similar way in England. As the result of his efforts a Mr. Brooke, to whom Lord Baltimore had shown exceptional favor, having given him liberty "to build and erect chapels in any part of the land allotted to him and the advowsons and donations to all such," was soon leading another expedition to Maryland. These newcomers were all of the Anglican faith and their generous treatment in religious matters is in marked contrast with the restrictions placed on the Roman Catholics who emigrated to Maryland. They settled down on the Patuxent River, just opposite the mouth of Battle Creek, in St. Mary's county where the name Delabrooke still survives.

It was at this time, 1650, that a very auspicious event occurred for all the Anglican settlers in the province.[5] This was the arrival of the Reverend Mr. Wilkinson, the first clergyman of the English Church who is definitely known to have settled in the province since the departure, sixteen years before, of the Reverend Richard James. Is it too much to believe that either directly, by personal request, as his father had formerly sought and obtained the services of the Reverend Mr. James

[5] Ridgely, *The Old Brick Churches of Maryland*, P. 51.

for his Newfoundland plantation ; or indirectly, as the result of a special appeal for emigrants of the Anglican faith having attracted the Anglican priest's attention, that Mr. Wilkinson was secured as pastor for the forlorn Church people of Maryland?

We know very little of this Anglican clergyman or his work. Like St. Paul he labored with his hands and was not chargeable to his flock. And like St. Peter he was a married man, his wife Mary, and his daughters Elizabeth and Rebecca, accompanying him into the province. He was in all probability a true missionary of Christ, a faithful pastor of souls. It is well to say this because there is an idea prevalent that the early clergy in Maryland, and in the colonies generally, were men who were far from being consistent members of their profession. Of a later generation this was unhappily sometimes true. But the first missionaries were men of pure zeal, absolute disinterestedness, and of beautiful lives. Of this class Parson Hunt of Jamestown was the type. Of the latter class Coode[6] the professional agitator, ward politician, scheming trader, all things by turns, was, let us hope, a rare specimen.

[6] Why do so many of our most popular writers hold up to ridicule and contempt, if not religion itself, at least the men who represent it? The clergy are always either fools or

(3) The third measure on the proprietary's programme was eventually to become known as "An Act concerning Religion."[7] It passed the House on April 21st 1649 and was confirmed by the proprietary in the year following. As this measure, which in its inception, as also in its provisions, was nothing more than an Act for securing uniformity in religious matters, has since become famous as the "Toleration Act," it becomes necessary to speak of it at some length with a view to its true nature, and its real place in Maryland history, being thoroughly understood.

The Act contains five sections. Of these sections the first four settled the religion of the colony, and laid down severe punishments for disobedience.

hypocrites to them, although but an infinitesimally small proportion of them can with any justice be so described. See, e. g., Winston Churchill, *Richard Carvel*, pp. 67 and 334. Does any one suppose that the Rev. Bennett Allen was the typical Maryland clergyman? And if not, what is the object of representing him as such? In this respect, as in other ways, how immeasurably superior to these writers, is Shakespeare the greatest figure in English Literature. He never played to the gallery, nor ever, even indirectly, brought religion into dispute.

For Coode's character, see Chapter XXI.

[7] *Archives of Maryland. Assembly.* 1637–1664. Pp. 224 and 247. "This famous statute was drawn up by Cecilius himself, and passed the Assembly exactly as it came from him, without amendment Fiske, *Old Virginia and Her Neighbors*, vol. i, P. 309.

Under the first section it was provided that those who denied the Godhead of any person of the Trinity, or uttered reproachful words concerning the Trinity, should be punished with death, and their property confiscated. Under the second section those who spoke reproachfully of our Lord's Mother, or of any of the Apostles or Evangelists, were liable to be fined, imprisoned, whipped. By the third section it was settled that whipping and fining likewise awaited those who styled their neighbors heretics, schismatics, puritans and the like. By the fourth section fines and imprisonments and whippings were decreed against profaners of the Sabbath or Lord's Day. The fifth section was of an entirely different character. Naively confessing that "the enforcing of the conscience in matters of religion has frequently fallen out to be dangerous to commonwealths," it was enacted and ordained that no person should suffer molestation on account of the free exercise of his religion except as had been set forth in the earlier sections.

A strange Toleration Act! With the exception of the last clause, itself contradictory of all that had preceded it, there is nothing tolerant about it. It is really a most disgraceful piece of intolerance.

It is not a bit better than the blue laws of Connecticut, or the martial code of Virginia, the Articles of 1610. There is not a legislative assembly in the world today that would venture to pass such a law, and still less enforce its provisions. Even for the standard of ideas of two centuries and a half ago there is nothing creditable about it. It was a going back into the dark. Not for a generation had any Englishman been put to death for his religious opinions, or his maintenance of them by word of mouth; not in fact since the puritan Archbishop Abbott had put to death two men for Arianism in 1612. But here was an Act under which the penalty for denying the Godhead or any of the three persons of the Trinity was death: minor offenses of a similar character being punishable with stripes and imprisonment. The passage of this Act is actually described "as one of the proud boasts of Maryland," and "one of her greatest glories."[8] Yet neither the Jews nor the Quakers were safe under its shadow, as both seemed to have well understood, Jews at any rate being almost as scarce in Maryland as Roman Catholics in Virginia. Even the mere profession of his faith by a Jew in "the land of the sanctuary" might easily cost him

[8] McSherry. P. 65.

his life. As for the Quakers, in a pamphlet entitled "*The Deceiver of the Nations discovered and his cruelty made manifest, more especially his cruel works of darkness in Mariland and Virginia*" the author says that "the Indians, whom they judge to be heathen, exceed in kindness, in courtesies, in love, and mercy unto them who were strangers, which is a shame to the mad, rash rulers of Mariland that have acted so barbarously to our people, and them that come to visit them in the name of the Lord, that instead of receiving them, rejected them, and made order after order, and warrant after warrant for pursuing, banishing and whipping of them." [9]

Now our Roman Catholic brethren are credited with the honor of having passed this Act under the supposition that they had a majority of their faith

[9] "In 1658, Joseph Coale and Thomas Thurston, preachers belonging to that body, were treated with great severity by the authorities, and compelled to flee that country."
History of the United States, Edmund Ollier, vol. i, P. 77. Compare with the foregoing and the words in the text the following from McSherry's *History*, P. 88: "Here, too, the gentle Friends found peace and refuge. In England, in Virginia, in Massachusetts, and the north, the pillory and the whipping post awaited them, and almost in sight of Plymouth Rock, the gallows were erected for them. Everywhere, save in Maryland, their peaceful creed was proscribed and punished as a crime. There only was their religious worship held publicly and without interruption."

in the House of Assembly.[10] We are, however, obliged to refuse them this doubtful honor, inasmuch as there is every reason to believe that they were merely a small minority in the Assembly, the Anglicans far outnumbering them. Although had they been in a majority no credit was really due to them. In order to appreciate this it is only necessary to remember that on January 30th, 1649, three months before this law was passed, King Charles had been publicly executed, and the Commonwealth had come into power pledged to the extermination of Episcopacy. If, then, under such circumstances the Roman Catholics were its authors it would necessarily shrink into a piece of panic stricken legislation, a mere attempt to pacify Moloch by throwing to the infuriated god the very principle for which the Roman Church had stood, still stands—the Bishops of Rome themselves being witnesses—and probably will ever continue to stand, that force may be used to compel men to accept the truth[11] whenever it can safely be done.

---

[10] Davis, *The Day Star.* P. 160. Lodge, *History of the English Colonies in America.* P. 119.

[11] See Syllabus of Pius ix, March 8, 1861. In this extraordinary document they are condemned who say the Church may not employ force. (*Ecclesia vis inferendæ potestatem non habet.*)

Nor are we left to general principles and the explicit direction of popes to know this. For just how Rome would have treated a genuine proposal to tolerate heretics may be inferred from the treatment even this poor imitation article received which compared with the genuine thing is but as base metal offered in exchange for good. In the very next House of Assembly, when it was proposed to make this Act a permanent feature of the Maryland Constitution there were four Roman Catholics present. To a man these four voted against the measure and that not because it was an intolerant edict and a disgrace to the statute book of their country but because it was too tolerant![12]

As, however, the same claim is sometimes advanced on the ground that Lord Baltimore, its real author, was a Roman Catholic I must ask attention to the fact that Baltimore was in no sense a representative of the pope or the Roman Church; but that he was, on the contrary, an object of dislike and suspicion to a powerful section of that Church. Indeed he himself would have given a very different account of the origin of this measure. He had little thought of its bringing any honor to Rome. He did expect that its effect on the people of

[12] Neill, *Founders of Maryland.* P. 123.

the colony would be to insure a return of quietness, peace and confidence to which, owing to religious differences, they had been too long strangers! For this purpose he was very desirous that it should be widely known. He therefore directed that it should be set up in all the courts of his province and its provisions faithfully obeyed.[13] It is, however, here extremely interesting to note that the legislators of Maryland who passed this measure, just because Lord Baltimore had asked them to do so, as if to show how little they regarded it, on the very same day they agreed to it, wrote him a lengthy letter of which the burden was corn and tobacco and cattle but, never once do they seem aware of having passed a Toleration Act at all![14]

With the history of the Roman Church standing forever in the background the claim of having inaugurated an era of religious toleration in Maryland is very delightful. That Church has never been distinguished for its kindly treatment of "heretics." Attempts have been made in recent times to blame the state for all the wicked burnings, and all the horrible inventions of thumb screws and racks which are laid at her doors by Protestant

---

[13] *Archives of Maryland, Council.* P. 384.
[14] *Archives of Maryland, Assembly.* Pp. 238–243.

historians.[15] But even if the state could be adjudged guilty in the first instance is the Church, its teacher, to go scot free? Can the Church refuse to accept the principle laid down by her Divine Head, "By their fruits ye shall know them"? Spain is, and has been for centuries, a Roman Catholic country, and yet Spain gave to the world the dreadful Inquisition with its fearful record of torture and fire extending over four long centuries. Were the myriad victims of its fierce intolerance all torn from the loving arms of the Church, while she stood by shedding unavailing tears at her helplessness to save them? Was the Bishop of Rome in those old days a mere creature of kings and princes, and even of mobs? And was he really obliged to go in solemn state to St. Peter's, and sing a Te Deum for the bloody work of St. Bartholomew's Day? And, forsooth, was it the state which compelled him to strike the medal which commemorated as a glorious achievement that crowning deed of fearful treachery and monstrous cruelty, of which the blood will never wash out? Oh, that the outspoken frankness and honesty of a member of the Roman Catholic Church recently lecturing to students in Washing-

---

[15] Gibbons, *Faith of Our Fathers*. P. 241, and following pages.

ton were more common, as he used these remarkable words: "History has not pages enough to record the absurdities committed by Christian priests and princes. This is God's lesson to us. It is outlined in the history of every individual of His Church, from the savagery of St. Peter, pulling his sword to chop off the servant's ear, down to the cruel shooting of Hugo Bassi. Why do Catholic writers seek to cover up the horrors of St. Bartholomew, the cruelties of an Inquisition which burned the flesh of human beings made in God's likeness, or the self-sufficient wisdom which refused to recognize the truths discovered by Galileo?" [16]

I do not love to go back in thought to these dark times, but our separated brethren compel me to show that toleration has never been a part of their creed, any more than in earlier days it was a part of our own creed. Nay it is not yet an accepted principle of the Roman faith. Even today Roman Bishops have to take a vow to assail and to persecute all heretics and schismatics.[17] Undoubtedly there are kindly and tolerant bish-

---

[16] See a Hartford, Conn., newspaper, July 12, 1894, quoting Mr. J. B. Walker, Editor of Cosmopolitan.

[17] "Hæreticos schismaticos * * * pro posse persequar et impugnabo." See *Roman Pontifical* P. 63, Ed. Rome, 1818.

ops and priests of the Roman Church in our midst, and certainly their people are often lovely and pleasant in their lives, and we could ill spare their influence for good, but let none of them talk of Rome's theories of religious liberty. Let them not contradict what her chief bishops, and her greatest saints [18] and doctors have proclaimed to the world. Such teaching is false to their Church. The pope himself repudiates it, anathematizes it, casts it out, and rejects it as an unclean thing.[19]

(4) The fourth item on the programme was the issuing of new Conditions of Plantation. This was done July, 1649. It will be remembered that the crucial clauses of the Conditions issued November 10th, 1641 — those directed against the Jesuits — had never been published. Baltimore had quite a free hand. With the priests hiding in exile there was now an open field. A Protestant governor would have no qualms of conscience, nor a Protestant secretary either, upon being summoned to publish Conditions which were hateful to the Jesuits. Accordingly

---

[18] St. Thomas Aquinas says that heretics are to be killed, or as in another passage, "not to be liberated from the sentence of death," (non tamen ut liberentur a sententia mortis) or as in still another passage, "exterminated from the world."

[19] See note 11, page 322.

the proprietary now issued Conditions of which some clauses were more sweeping and drastic than any which had preceded them. There was, to be sure, not so much reason for these restricting clauses now, but who could tell whether they might not soon be needed again. The power at which they were aimed was only scotched, not killed. Moreover there was the Puritan power to appease, and its friendship to gain. Altogether it was a difficult task which lay before the lord proprietary, but no man knew better how to accomplish it than the self-reliant, quiet, determined man who ruled Maryland from beyond the seas.

CHAPTER XIX.

MARYLAND UNDER PURITAN RULE.

1650–1656.

> "A sect, whose chief devotion lies
> In odd perverse antipathies:
> In falling out with that or this,
> And finding somewhat still amiss."
> —BUTLER: "Hudibras."

Lord Baltimore's touting for emigrants in England and Ireland, in Massachusetts and Virginia, was in one respect a marked success. Hundreds of stalwart men in response to his efforts swarmed over the fertile lands which lay on both sides of Chesapeake Bay. Homesteads rose as by magic, broad acres suddenly came under cultivation, where shortly before the primeval forest had stood, and the waters of the Chesapeake, studded with the light craft of the fishermen, no longer wore the deserted appearance of a silent and unknown sea.

But, alas! in the matter of the quality of his emigrants Lord Baltimore's success left something to be desired. They were a motley assemblage. Even Charles II., from his retreat in Holland, described them as "all kinds of schismatics and sectaries and other ill affected persons." This witness was true. They were of all sorts and conditions of men.[1] Bitterly did Lord Baltimore himself complain about the character of some of these settlers which he had been at so much pains to obtain; not hesitating to describe them as "the basest of men, and unworthy of the least favor and forbearance."

The headquarters of the disturbing element were at Providence on the Severn, now Annapolis. To this place had originally come some Puritan refugees from Virginia. Others in the recent influx of population of like political and religious sympathies naturally gravitated thither, until there had grown up quite a flourishing settlement. But its whole tone and spirit was alien to the proprietary. He was a Romanist and they were Puritans. In no long time they began to seek opportunity to resist the proprietary's claims and to jeopardize his rights. This, however, by direct attack was no easy thing to do. Presently realizing the futility of their course, they adopted other tactics. Com-

[1] See *Founders of Maryland*, P. 154.

plaints and murmurings began to be heard on every side. The place became rife with reports of the sufferings of the poor afflicted Protestants. Such reports in face of the fact that the stream of immigration which had been bringing settlers into the colony for years, indeed from the first, was emphatically a protestant stream was manifestly an impudent slander. Probably Clayborne was behind the scenes. Some such supposition as this is in fact absolutely necessary to account for the factious and bitter opposition to which the Lord Proprietary of Maryland was now subjected. But whatever its origin the old tales of persecution were revived, to be eventually poured into the not unwilling ears of sympathizing co-religionists on the other side of the ocean. The poor, persecuted Protestants of Maryland were represented as in an evil case. Unfortunately for the Puritans' reputation for veracity there now were no such sufferers for conscience sake in the country. Promptly following these charges a statement was issued by the governor, signed by himself, the various Protestant members of the Assembly, and a large number of the leading Protestants of the province, affirming that they all enjoyed the utmost liberty, had nothing whatever to complain about, and knew nothing of the existence of such a state of affairs as the Puritans had reported.[2]

A public statement of that kind made by the officials of the colony, who were themselves Protestants, must have sadly disconcerted the group of irreconcilables on the banks of the Severn, who were doubtless hard pressed to know what was the next best thing for them to do. For the burden of their grief was not that they were being persecuted, but that they were not; their difficulty being a similar one to that of the Jews who delivered Jesus

---

[2] Bozman, Vol. II, Pp. 672, 673, and Burnap, Pp. 181, 182.

This statement of Governor Stone and the principal men of the colony, known as the Protestant Declaration, ran as follows: "The declaration and certificate of William Stone, Esq., Lieutenant of the Province of Maryland, by commission from the Right Honorable Lord Baltimore, Lord Proprietary thereof, and of Captain John Price, Mr. Thomas Hatton, and Captain Robert Vaughan, of his Lordship's Council there, and of divers of the Burgesses now met in the Assembly there, and other Protestant inhabitants of the same province, made the 17th day of April, A. D. 1650."

"We, the said Lieutenant, Council, Burgesses, and other Protestant inhabitants above mentioned, whose names are hereunto subscribed, do declare and certify to all persons whom it may concern, That, according to an act of Assembly here, and several other strict injunctions and declarations by his said lordship for that purpose made and provided, we do here enjoy all fitting and convenient freedom and liberty in the exercise of our religion under his lordship's government and interest ; and that none of us are anyways troubled or molested, for or by reason thereof, within his lordship's said province."

to the Roman Governor of Judæ because he made himself a king, whereas everyone knew that his chief offence in their eyes was that he utterly refused to be a king.

It is however, abundantly manifest from the "Protestant Declaration" that Clayborne's opposition found no sympathy among Church people generally, who formed the great bulk of the population.[3] His strength lay only among the more rabid and anti-Romanist section on the Severn ; but with these he was all powerful. Yet disconcerting to its authors as the ignominious break down of the charge of persecuting Protestants must have been, the opposition to Lord Baltimore was not silenced. His enemies now took other ground. No true Englishman, they contended, could take the oath of fidelity which he exacted from those who settled upon his lands. To allow the lord proprietary to describe himself as an absolute lord was to give him the kingship entirely. And what more would he have? Baltimore, with his usual tact, immediately omitted the words which wounded their consciences. To do the Puritans justice their objections were well taken, Baltimore having exceeded his powers in

[3] Ridgely, *Annals of Annapolis*, P. 34.

exacting the oath from any one. The colonists owed allegiance to the King of England whose subjects they were, not to him who was himself a subject. But although their objections were well founded these Puritans were scarcely the men to have advanced them. " They had been made acquainted by Captain Stone, before they came to Maryland, with that oath of fidelity, which was to be taken by those who would hold any land there from his lordship ; . . . . nor had they any objection to the oath, till they were as much refreshed with their entertainment there, as the snake in the fable was with the countryman's beast ; for which some of them were equally thankful."[4] The Puritans were not however satisfied. Never did that old fable of the wolf and the lamb receive such ample fulfilment. One would have thought, considering Baltimore's conciliatory attitude, that even his enemies would have been willing to let him alone. But, alas, men are often ready to incur much greater trouble and expense to injure

[4] In 1655, there were twenty thousand settlers in the province, yet in the battle of Providence only one hundred and seventy-five Protestants were arrayed against one hundred and thirty Roman Catholics. And this was a sort of colonial Marston Moor, where every man who could bear arms, for or against the cause, was expected to be present.

an enemy than they are to gratify a friend, and Clayborne, who was focusing Puritan discontent, could not forget the battle on the Pocomoke and his wounded honor. Ere long an ample opportunity presented itself to be completely avenged on his adversary. This came about through the state of public affairs in England.

As soon as Cromwell had pacified the English royalists, he turned his attention to the royalists abroad. Maryland had never been a royalist colony in the sense that Virginia had. She had latterly in fact espoused the cause of the Commonwealth. It is true that immediately after the execution of Charles I, Thomas Green, the acting governor, had proclaimed Charles II. as king, but this he had done without authority, and upon the return of Governor Stone, who had been absent in Virginia, the act was promptly disowned by the proprietary government.[5] With this sole exception there was absolutely no legitimate ground of complaint against Maryland. She had been faithful to the Commonwealth. So clearly was this the case that Charles II., when without any prospect of ever

---

[5] When Charles II came to the throne, Philip Calvert, Lord Baltimore's then governor, made a great point of the proclamation. *Archives of Maryland, Council*, P. 393.

succeeding to his father's throne, a mere fugitive, had issued his commission assuming to depose Cecilius Calvert and give Maryland to another, because "he did visibly adhere to the rebels of England."[6] Moreover in Maryland herself all was well. The recent legislation concerning religion came in usefully here. It showed how the province had proved to be a refuge for persecuted Puritans from Virginia, as her very enemies must acknowledge, for she had sheltered them. Lord Baltimore was therefore able to make out a good case on behalf of his province. And this he did so well that it was decided by the Privy Council to leave out all mention of Maryland in the instructions to be given for the reduction of the colonies, the feeling being that she needed no disciplining. Nevertheless when the Act was passed the fatal words had been inserted: "For the reducing, settling and governing of all the plantations within the Bay of Chesapeake." Clayborne had been at work. As if to leave no loop-hole of escape he had got himself appointed as one of the four commissioners whose duty it was to see that the work was faithfully done. With Clayborne as one of the commissioners the Privy Council might have saved

[6] Neill, *Founders of Maryland*, P. 126.

themselves any uneasiness on that score. They had appointed a man upon whom they could thoroughly depend to do all that anyone could do. An old writer discussing the motives of the Commissioners, and especially the claim that they were influenced in their treatment of Maryland by religious considerations, says quaintly, "It was not religion, it was not punctilios they stood upon: it was that sweete, that rich, that large country they aimed at."[7] With Clayborne, however, another motive was paramount. He sought vengeance. Losing no time to accomplish his heart's desire he, and his fellow commissioners, forthwith sailed for Maryland. In March 1652 they were at St. Mary's, where they heralded their arrival by deposing Governor Stone, seizing the records of the province, and establishing a new government under six commissioners named by themselves over whom they eventually set Stone as their representative. At last Clayborne had ample satisfaction for the wrongs he had suffered. But to his infinite credit it is to be noted that on the whole he acted with much moderation. Great was the rejoicing among the Puritans in Maryland, great too among the Puritans in

---

[7] *Leah and Rachel*, Pp. 24 and 25; also Longford's *Refutation*, Pp. 4 and 10.

England, at what they regarded as "Babylon's Fall in Maryland."[8]

Thus things remained for about two years. At the end of that time Baltimore, who was doubtless in receipt of frequent letters from his province thought that he could rightly urge Stone to throw off Clayborne's rule and assume his old position as governor. Stone was not convinced it was the wisest step to take, but he followed the directions he had received, and Baltimore presently found himself again recognized as the Lord Proprietary of Maryland. But the step was premature. As soon as Clayborne heard in Virginia of Stone's doings he hastened to Maryland. With his reappearance on the St. Mary's River the spirit of Baltimore's friends was immediately crushed, and they begged the governor not to attempt any resistance. The Roman Catholics especially were anxious that he should not give battle, being convinced that such an attempt could only end in new troubles for them. Stone followed their advice and submitted to the enemy, with the result that Clayborne's yoke was more firmly than ever riveted on the province. But the Roman Catholics did not save themselves by this timely concession. When order

[8] Anderson, Vol. II, P. 173.

was again restored "An Act concerning Religion" was passed, the gift of the new Puritan Legislature, another Toleration Act, for such I suppose we must consider it.[9] Granting religious liberty to the people it did so within somewhat narrower limits than the earlier, and more famous, measure after which it was plainly fashioned; which had evidently inspired it, and the place of which it was clearly intended to fill.[10] The earlier Act had provided that no one

---

[9] *Archives of Maryland, Assembly*, Pp. 340 and 341.
AN ACT CONCERNING RELIGION.
It is enacted and declared in the name of his Highness, the Lord Protector, with the consent and by the authority of the present General Assembly, that none who profess and exercise the Popish Religion, commonly known by the name of the Roman Catholic Religion, can be protected in this province by the laws of England formerly established and yet unrepealed, nor by the Governor of the Commonwealth of England, Scotland and Ireland, and the dominions thereunto belonging, published by his Highness, the Lord Protector, but are to be restrained from the exercise thereof, therefore all and every person or persons concerned in the law aforesaid are required to take notice.

Such as profess faith in God by Jesus Christ (though differing in judgment from the doctrine, worship and discipline publicly held forth shall not be restrained from, but shall be protected in the profession of the faith) and exercise of their religion so as they abuse not this liberty to the injury of others . . . . provided that this liberty be not extended to popery or prelacy, nor to such as under the profession of Christ hold forth and practice licentiousness."

[10] The earlier Act Concerning Religion was repealed by the new legislature. See *Archives of Maryland, Assembly*, P. 351.

professing faith in Christ was to be molested in the free exercise of his religion. Such liberty however, was not to be extended to such persons as Unitarians, Jews and the like, that is all persons who did not believe in the Godhead of Christ. Those who did believe in Christ's Deity, but were otherwise unorthodox, as for example Quakers, with all those who professing orthodox views yet disgraced their Christian profession by unseemly conduct, were likewise placed outside of protection. The new Act, in a similar spirit with these provisions, "provided that religious liberty be not extended to popery or prelacy." Thus the limits, not overgenerous of the earlier toleration measure had already been somewhat encroached upon; those now outside the pale of protection being Churchmen and Roman Catholics, together with the adherents of a few of the many protestant sects which now began to appear in the religious world. All others might without fear of injury profess their faith and practice.

It was not of course pretended by its authors that this was a toleration measure, any more than the authors of the similar Act of 1649 claimed that it was their intention to give religious toleration. It was rather of a punitive character. The Roman

Catholics were punished by it because they were Roman Catholics. The Act provided that the professors of "the popish religion could not be protected in the province, but were to be restrained in the exercise thereof." The Anglicans were to suffer, not because they were Anglicans, for Clayborne himself was one, but for their easy going indifference to Clayborne's interests. His successes had in fact been achieved by the Puritans, the Anglicans having been merely passive spectators. They had "not come to the help of the Lord, to the help of the Lord against the mighty." And so the old Hebrew denunciation which fell upon the village of Meroz, for a like passive indifference in a critical period, was to be their portion. Accordingly into this new toleration statute went a clause which provided that toleration was not to be extended to Anglicans.

Perhaps it was the fact that Clayborne, at least by inheritance and later profession, was a Churchman himself, that the Churchmen were dealt with less severely than the Roman Catholics who were now declared to be not only ecclesiastical, but political outcasts. They had done nothing to deserve this treatment. But then they were friends, sympathisers and supporters of Lord Baltimore. And just then it was a bad thing to be known as a friend of the proprietary. Thus it came about that Churchmen and Roman Catholics were cast out together and their religion put under a ban, and, in the case of the Roman Catholics, even their political manhood taken away.

Meanwhile from his country seat in Wiltshire the lord proprietary had been observing the signs of the times, and to his keen eye the prospects were decidedly better than they were five years before, when he had decided to abandon his province. He had even hopes of conciliating the new ruler of England. He was, in fact, looking forward to being regarded by Cromwell as a staunch Parliamentarian. With his own record as a personal friend of the deposed king, and a Roman Catholic to boot, to say nothing of the record of his father as a thorough going partizan of all those very pretentions of the House of Stuart, which were now overwhelming it with disaster, it was no ordinary feat of political gymnastics which he proposed to perform. But slender as were the prospects of success Lord Baltimore had no option but to attempt it. He had at any rate nothing to lose by defeat, whereas he had everything to gain by success, and he decided to make the attempt. In the spirit of Queen Esther at the Court of Ahasuerus he would do what he could even though with her he should have to say: "If I perish, I perish!" But his case was not hopeless by any means. He even felt himself strong enough to strike. Writing to Stone he exhorted him to fight for his province. Stone again obeyed his patron, and in March, 1655, a bloody battle was fought at Providence in the enemy's country. On the proprietary's side there were about one hundred and thirty men, for the most part Roman Catholics, who appeared on the field flying Baltimore's black and gold flag and shouting the battle cry, "Hey for St. Mary's!" The Puritans numbered one hundred and seventy-five, and to them the captains of two ships lying in the river had promised their help. Shouting the Puritan battle cry: "In the name of God fall on," they rushed to the fight. Instantly the ships opened fire. The St. Mary's men had not reckoned upon this. They were literally between two fires, and from the beginning there was not the slightest prospect of victory for them. But they fought bravely notwithstanding. The battle, however, was soon over, and the Puritans were left in possession of the field. From one of the two captains who had helped them, Captain Heamens of the Golden Lion, we have an account of the battle, and it is he who relates with much satisfaction how they took among the spoil "pictures, crucifixes, and rows of beads, with great store of reliques and trash they trusted in." There were besides a good many bodies of their fellow-men also left on the field, for Stone's force was almost annihilated, but of these Captain Heamens did not take so much account. Stone himself was taken prisoner, with all of his men, except four or five who escaped. Will it be believed that the victors disgraced themselves by putting four of their prisoners of war to death in cold blood, and that they were only just restrained from executing all, although they had surrendered under promise of quarter? General confiscation ensued, followed by a strong petition to the English government urging it to end Maryland's existence, and unite the province again to Virginia from which it ought never, in the judgment of the Puritans, to have been separated.

But "the night is long that never finds the day." The darkest hour is often that before dawn. This very battle, which seemed to crush out every hope Baltimore had was but the bringing in of a brighter day. Clayborne had now done his worst. This victory was his last success. It was neither for the interest of Maryland herself, nor yet for the interest of England, that this state of things should continue, and Cromwell put a stop to it. Referring the whole matter to the Committee of Trades and Plantations, that committee on the 16th of September 1656 decided wholly in favor of Lord Baltimore, with the result that his authority was restored, and he came, not without hesitation and delay to receive him on the part of some of his old enemies, into possession of his province.

Lord Baltimore himself must have marvelled at his success. For it was without doubt, entirely due to his wise and statesmanlike measures that his colony was saved. In this connection the "Reasons of State concerning Maryland in America," bearing date August 1652, are extremely important. They fully explain Lord Baltimore's ultimate success. No doubt in them we read the arguments which he himself used before the Privy Council.[11] That

---

[11] In substance, Baltimore's arguments were as follows:

1. The Commonwealth would have greater power over both if Maryland and Virginia remained separate.

2. In case one was disloyal the other was at hand as a place of refuge.

3. There would be a healthy rivalry between Maryland and Virginia.

4. In Lord Baltimore's presence in England they had good security for Maryland's loyalty.

5. Maryland's dependence on Lord Baltimore was more economical for the Commonwealth.

Lord Baltimore was no ordinary man this remarkable success clearly proves. Any man who could emerge with honor from such a precarious and even compromising position as that in which he had stood commands our admiration and our respect. Consider what he had done. A Roman Catholic, at a time when to be a Roman Catholic was to be politically a traitor, and ecclesiastically entitled to no sympathy at all; a landlord, whose property had been bestowed upon him by a king whose own lawlessness and indifference to public sentiment had cost him his throne and his life; a landlord too, whose Roman Catholic tenants had brought the administration of his vast estate everywhere into great disfavor; a landlord, moreover, whose own record in the matter of his dealings with a part of his estate had been by no means free from blame; yet it is this same man who when tried on a frivolous pretext before the bar of his peers, and by a hypocritical and hostile government, comes to the front to receive at the hands of that same government his

---

6. The Commonwealth would bring itself but contempt if it rewarded Lord Baltimore's well known fidelity to its cause by doing anything prejudicial to his patent, his colony having been faithful when all other colonies, New England only excepted, had proved faithless.

See *Archives of Maryland, Council*, Pp. 280, 281.

sceptre of sovereignty again. It were a pity that even on the wider scale of a kingdom such talents had not found an outlet. One wonders what might have been the history of England herself if in the critical times of Charles I. or James II., Cecilius Calvert had been summoned to the throne. That the giving back of the sceptre of Maryland into his hands as the hands best fitted to wield it was itself an act inconsistent with the position of a government that had abolished kingship, only increases our admiration of him. Even Clayborne ought to have congratulated him upon attaining such wonderful success. In the facility with which he could acknowledge king or lord protector, monarchy or commonwealth, according to whichever should be uppermost, Lord Baltimore has been somewhat severely arraigned, even by Protestants, as "that aristocratic Mr. Facing-both-ways,"[12] a sort of forerunner of the famous Vicar of Bray. But that versatile eccelesiastic, claiming for himself a certain consistency among all his tergiversations, for he would live and die the Vicar of Bray, emphatically denied the impeachment. So with Lord Baltimore. He, too, was consistency itself. Whatever king might reign, he would be Lord Proprietary of Maryland.

[12] Prowse, *History of Newfoundland*, P. 159.

CHAPTER XX.

LORD BALTIMORE ENJOYS HIS OWN AGAIN.

1656-1675.

> "And the night shall be filled with music,
> And the cares that infest the day
> Shall fold their tents, like the Arabs,
> And as silently steal away."
> —LONGFELLOW: "Day is done."

Not for a full year after the decision of the Committee of Trades and Plantations in his favor did Lord Baltimore come into undisputed possession of his province. He obtained his rights in St. Mary's at once. But the Puritans, as if no voice had gone out against them, still held possession of the northern parts of the Chesapeake, and there ruled with a strong hand. They retained also the the records and the great seal of the Province. Finally, however, an agreement being reached between their leader and Lord Baltimore, they yielded to the inevitable, and the rebellion of six years standing came to an end. From this time until Lord Baltimore's death, November 30th, 1675, save for an incipient rebellion headed by his own governor, Josias Fendall, when Charles II. came to the throne, there was a long period of rest which Lord Baltimore diligently used to push forward by every legitimate means the material advancement of his colony, particularly by sending out new emigrants to develop its untold resources. In this he succeeded so well that during the twenty years which followed the fall of the Puritans the population of Maryland increased from ten thousand to twenty thousand.

The new settlers were not all Church people. "A considerable number of them were Presbyterians from Scotland, and here indeed was the cradle of Presbyterianism in the United States.[1]" Scarcely any of the emigrants were of the Roman Church, it may be that none of them were—the members of that Church already in Maryland having had too unpleasant an experience of the country to warrant their describing it to their brethren as "the land of the sanctuary." It thus resulted that the Roman Catholics were not even at this early period, according to the most generous estimate, more than a fourth of the total population of the province.

[1] Allen, *History of Maryland*, P. 37.

But Romanism was not yet a dead issue. A piece of very decided interference with individual liberty, bordering perilously on actual persecution, occurred as late as 1657 on the part of a Jesuit father named Fitzherbert. This priest, like his brethren, had entered Maryland under an assumed name, being recorded on the ship's books as "Francis Darby, Gent."[2] Discarding, almost immediately on his arrival, the prudence which he had showed himself to possess, it was not long before one of the Marylanders—a Mr. Henry Coursey—felt it his duty to draw Lord Baltimore's attention to his doings as one who was apparently bent on becoming a worthy successor of Mr. Copley, who had recently died, and whose mantle had evidently been bequeathed to him. This gentleman, writing to Lord Baltimore, said, "Since I wrote my last to you, I have received a message from Mrs. Gerrard, which is that Mr. Fitzherbert hath threatened excommunication to Mr. Gerrard, because he doth not bring to church his wife and children. And further, Mr. Fitzherbert said that he hath written home to the heads of the Church in England, and that if it be their judgment to have it so, he will come with a party and compel them.

[2] Neill, *Founders of Maryland*, P. 129.

I told Mr. Fitzherbert of it, about a year since in private, and also that such things were against the law of the country. Yet, his answer was, that he must be directed by his conscience, more than by the law of any country. I do not my Lord, trust myself upon any business of quarrel, but it is peace and quietness I desire. And I hope your Lordship has no other cause than to wish the same, and so I refer the consideration of it to you.[3]"

On October 5th, 1658, Fitzherbert was brought to trial on the charge of having threatened Thomas Gerrard that, if he "did not come and bring his wife and children to his church, he would come and force them to the church, contrary to a known Act of Assembly for the Province." Fitzherbert in his defence pleaded first the "Act for Church Liberties," holding that as in Maryland every Church professing to believe in God the Father, Son, and Holy Ghost was accounted Holy Church, he had full liberty to preach and teach his creed; and, in the next place, that the "Act concerning Religion" guaranteed him freedom from molestation in the free exercise of his religion. Fitzherbert was acquitted. But if we may judge from the evidence in our possession neither the letter nor the spirit of

[3] *Ibid*, P. 132.

the Acts he appealed to warranted his use of physical force to supplement his spiritual exhortations, nor justified his understanding so literally his position as a member of a militant Church. Yet neither he, nor his accusers, strange to say, appear to have paid any attention to this phase of the case, their difficulty being to ascertain whether he had, or had not, a right to freely profess and practise his religion in Maryland, and urge others to profess and practise it too. Properly enough his judges found that he had this right. But Thomas Gerrard, his wife and children had the same right also.

In connection with this priest may be told the story of Mary Lee, who was put to death as a witch. This unfortunate woman was a passenger on the same vessel that carried Mr. Fitzherbert to Maryland. On the way thither the voyagers encountered very heavy weather, as doubtless at the outset the superstitious sailors predicted that they would, owing to the presence on board of his reverence. The Jesuit, not unreasonably looking at the case from quite a different standpoint, subsequently reported that owing to their vessel being storm-tossed for fully two months, an opinion arose that they were suffering from the malevolence of witches.

This idea getting abroad among the sailors they forthwith seized "a little old woman suspected of the very heinous sin of sorcery, and, guilty or not guilty, slew her."[4]

The whole story of the tragedy is more fully related in the provincial records where Mr. Henry Corbin, a young merchant from London, and a passenger on the same ship, describes the proceedings to the Governor and Council of Maryland. This witness said that, two or three weeks before they reached the Chesapeake, it was rumored among the sailors that Mary Lee, one of the passengers, was a witch. On the sailors asking the captain to have the woman tried upon this charge he at first refused. But as the ship daily became more leaky, having sought the advice of Corbin himself, and a Mr. Robert Chipsham, another merchant on board, he decided to allow an examination in order to allay the fears of the seamen. But before this could be done two of the seamen, without orders, searched her body, and having found, as they afterwards declared, witch marks upon her, fastened her to the capstan for the night. But the next morning the marks "for the most part were shrunk into her body." Whereupon the sailors asked Corbin to

[4] *Excerpta Ex Diversis Litteris Missionariorum*, 1654, P. 9.

examine her. At this point the woman confessed herself a witch. From her own testimony there was of course no appeal. Seeing what was coming, and feeling helpless to prevent it, but protesting against their treatment of the poor creature the captain retired to his cabin, while the sailors, notwithstanding his protest, took and hanged her from the yardarm, afterwards casting her body into the sea.[5]

During these latter years of Lord Baltimore the Anglican Church in the province was in a sad plight, a plight which was not at all improved by the departure in 1662 of Cornwaleys, the hero of many a battle for the people and a staunch Churchman, and the coming into office, as governor, of the proprietary's son Charles, who, though by no means so good a politician as his father or grandfather had been, and under whose rule therefore Church affairs were not likely to be greatly improved. Had Lord Baltimore only seen his way to persevere in his original good intention of providing the Maryland Church people with religious privileges, the country might have become an ideal colony for those days, and, at the same time, his own hands would have

[5] Neill, *Founders of Maryland*, P. 128.

been immensely strengthened. But instead of doing this he adopted a *laissez faire* policy which had, as its logical result, a state of affairs which must have sorely troubled his lordship. By it Maryland had become a veritable cave of Adullam in religious matters. Of her it might now be truly said:—

> Sure, when Religion, did itself embark
> And from the East, would Westward steer its bark
> It struck; and splitting on this unknown ground,
> Each one thence pillaged the first piece he found.
> Hence, Amsterdam, Turk, Christian, Pagan, Jew,
> Staple of sects, and mint of schism grew;
> That bank of conscience, where not one, so strange
> Opinion, but finds credit and exchange.[6]

Of course such a state of things could not fail to produce serious discontent among those of the Marylanders who regarded themselves as entitled to some special consideration as men whose civil and ecclesiastical rights had been protected by their charter. Moreover the appointment of a Roman Catholic governor, even though he was the proprietary's son, could not but be an exceedingly unpopular measure. Indeed to many it would not appear otherwise than as a mark of bad faith. During the critical times of the Commonwealth Lord Baltimore had made large capital out of the fact that his officers were Protestants. His enemies

[6] *Ibid*, P. 154.

therefore could hardly be accused of being hypercritical if they had begun to regard the appointments of those times as a mere ruse to gain the good will of Cromwell, and which having served its purpose was now thrown aside with as little ceremony as a man flings away a last year's almanac. Still there was perhaps no justification for this view. It was only natural that Lord Baltimore should appoint his own son to that office. But all the same the appointment was not without its perils, although its evil results were not to be seen in Lord Baltimore's own day. In his son's day, however, they fell as an avalanche falls on an Alpine village, bearing away in its mad course houses and public buildings and men and women and little children, until nothing is left to mark the spot where awhile before a beautiful village, nestling quietly beneath the mountain, had added its own lovely beauty to the picturesque scene.

The time came at length when Cecilius Calvert was to be gathered unto his fathers. For over forty years he had governed Maryland well, though not without serious mistakes. But when one remembers that he never saw Maryland, and that the most serious of his mistakes, his antagonizing of Clayborne, may be said to have been inherited, one is rather inclined to marvel, not that he made a few mistakes but that he did not make many more. His tenure of Maryland fell in times which were most exacting in their demands for true statesmanship and farseeing sagacity, yet he did not fall short of these requirements. His last years were happily passed in undisputed possession of his vast province, which he was now passing on to his son and successor, at peace with itself, and immensely improved in value. At last that call had come to which none may turn a deaf ear. Doubtless he was ready to go. He knew that he had lived out the alloted space of human life, and had filled a great part in human affairs, though he could not have foreseen the future greatness of the State he was building. But what of all now !

> "The boast of heraldry, the pomp of power,
> And all that beauty, all that wealth e'er gave,
> Awaits alike the inevitable hour,
> The paths of glory lead but to the grave."

That hour had come. The invisible messenger on the pale horse was at the door. The greatest of the Barons of Baltimore had run his course.

It is unfortunate that we possess so little of any thing which Cecilius Baltimore wrote. Although we well know from what we have, what manner of man he was. Yet had we nothing else of his own to guide us, one glance at his picture would assure us we were looking on the face of a man who could not fail to be a power among his fellows. There is no possibility of mistaking the meaning of those features, or of failing to learn the lessons they teach. Side by side in the rooms of the Maryland Historical Society in Baltimore hang the portraits of five out of the six Barons who once ruled Maryland. Of them all Cecilius' picture is by far the most striking. Those who are familiar with his portrait as preserved in Bancroft's History will be apt to think of him as a cavalier whose face showed few signs of strength or greatness, a face betokening the pensive dreamer to whom the practical realities and solemn duties of life were altogether unknown. But looking at that other picture we shall see the real man. No cavalier he, or a simple dreamer either, but a Puritan endowed with all the sturdy independence and displaying all the energetic life of the Puritans. Alone of his house he is portrayed there in no gay courtier's dress, but in a quiet garb such as Quakers wear, and in that true lifelike picture we see a face strong, determined, thoughtful—one not to be forgotten. In that gallery of portraits Cecilius Calvert is manifestly king. They say,

"When beggars die, there are no comets seen;
The heavens themselves blaze forth the death of princes."

It may be so. But without the signs in the heavens to bear witness to it we should have known the greatness of Cecilius, Baron of Baltimore.

After the death of Cecilius, Charles his son naturally succeeded to the province over which he had been set as governor.[7] A description of Maryland at this time from the pen of one of the clergy, the Rev. John Yeo,[8] writing to the Archbishop of Canterbury, gives a most dismal view of the state of religion, and of the moral condition of the colony. Maryland, to Mr. Yeo, was positively a

---

[7] For many years, indeed until quite recently, it has been usual to record Cecilius as having been succeeded in the Barony by one John, Lord Baltimore. There was no John. His existence was a myth. His creation by the historians has been quite satisfactorily explained. But an odd feature of the error is that in Johnson's *Universal Encyclopedia*, revised in 1895, John still keeps his place among the Barons of Baltimore, being enrolled as third on the list. But perhaps there is nothing really noteworthy about this trifling creation of an additional baron when one sees how much equally veracious information concerning the real barons is yet solemnly retailed as sober truth.

[8] Yeo's letter, written from the "Patuxant River, in Maryland, 25th day of May, 1676," is given *in extenso* by Anderson, Vol. II, P. 611. In his letter, Mr. Yeo speaks of "Cecilius, Lord Baron Baltimore being dead, and Charles, Lord Baron Baltimore being bound for England" that year, and he suggests that the Archbishop should try and obtain from their new proprietary a suitable provision for the clergy of the Church.

very hot-bed of evil, as he tells the Archbishop that for ten or twelve counties, with their twenty thousand souls, there were but three clergy of the Anglican Church. Besides there was "noe care taken or provision made, for the building up Christians in the Protestant Religion, whereof not only many daily fall away either to Popery, Quakerism, or Fanaticism, but also the Lord's day is prophaned, religion despised and all notorious vices permitted ; so that it has become a Sodom of uncleannesse and a pest-house of iniquity."

But what else could have been expected in a new country among people far removed from the restraints of home and religion—when schools there were none, and when there were only two or three churches widely separated—served by only as many clergy—but that God's day should have been profaned, that evil of every kind should have been rampant, and that men should have acted as if the God they had served on the other side of the ocean had no power to help or bless them in Maryland. Happy indeed would it have been for all if in that new land, some voice had gone forth in their midst like that of Joshua of old ; "As for me and my house we will serve the Lord."—happy most of all for the third Lord Baltimore whose responsibilities as proprietary were just beginning. But this word was never spoken. And the path of the men of Maryland, and the path of Maryland's proprietary, began from the first to diverge more and more.

CHAPTER XXI.

THE CHURCH OF ENGLAND ESTABLISHED AND ENDOWED.

1675—1692.

> Founded in truth ; by blood of martyrdom
> Cemented ; by the hands of Wisdom reared
> In beauty of holiness, with ordered pomp,
> Decent and unreproved.
> —WORDSWORTH.

Upon Charles Calvert succeeding to the Lord Proprietaryship of Maryland he immediately prepared to return to England. Arriving there in the following year he found that his presence was very timely, Yeo's letter of the 25th of May, 1676, being in the hands of the Bishop of London—to whom as the bishop interested in the colonies the archbishop had referred the letter—and by whom he was at once called upon to meet its statements. Lord Baltimore replied that the Act of 1649, confirmed in 1676 tolerated and protected every sect, an answer which was hardly to the point as the charge was not that the Church in Maryland was being persecuted, but that it had not the means of subsistence. However, after quoting the Act, the lord proprietary addressing himself to that grievance, informed the bishop that "four ministers of the Church of England were in possession of plantations which offered them a decent subsistence." He was, moreover, under the impression that in an Assembly, such as that of Maryland, it would be extremely difficult, if not impossible, to induce it to consent to a law that should oblige any sect to maintain other ministers than its own." It will be here observed from his use of the word sect that Charles was not acquainted with the position of the Church in Maryland as an integral portion of the Church of England.

The matter came finally before the Privy Council which decided that Lord Baltimore's position was not well taken. The Council probably reminded him of the conditions of his charter, and of the duties it imposed upon him, bidding him not to forget that to the services of their national Church his Maryland tenants were justly entitled. It was therefore fitting that he should see to it that they were not left as sheep without a shepherd. Nor was this so strange a predicament for a Roman Catholic proprietary to find himself in as some have thought.[1] His charter had created that obligation for him; but if he found it burdensome to his conscience to comply with its provisions, there was an easy way out of the predicament. He could readily throw it up, and refuse any longer to hold a position which he deemed incompatible with his profession of Roman Catholicism. As long as he did not choose to avail himself of this privilege, the Privy Council was abundantly justified in insisting that "he should propose some means for the support of a competent number" of the clergy of the English Church in that province from which he was drawing a princely income as a gift from the English Crown.

Presently Charles returned from England, but on his arrival in Maryland he forgot all about the ruling of the Privy Council, and the warning he had received. At any rate, with the exception of passing laws for the suppression of vice, and the better observance of Sunday, he did nothing at all. He would have acted with more wisdom if he had done what was required of him. But the man who could cut off his own son's annual allowance, and leave him dependent upon charity,[2] merely because

[1] Fisher, *Men, Women and Manners*, Vol. II, P. 195.
[2] Benedict Leonard Calvert abjured Roman Catholicism,

he had become an Anglican, was not likely to be found providing clergy for his Anglican tenants, though his not doing so would be a distinct breach of trust. Rather was he more likely to be found giving to his co-religionists whatever advantages his official position enabled him to give. We shall not therefore be at all surprised to find that soon after he had been accused of neglecting the spiritual interests of the Church people committed to his care, it was alleged he was showing undue partiality to Roman Catholics. There seems to have been no great reason for the accusation, nevertheless there was enough truth in it—so the English Government considered—to justify, and in fact to require, its taking the extreme position of ordering that all public offices in Maryland should be given to Protestants, "the feeling that the country was being governed in the interest of a small coterie of papists having rapidly increased."[3]

The third Lord Baltimore was a decidedly differ-

"much to the wrath and disgust of his aged father, who at once withdrew his annual allowance of four hundred and fifty pounds. Benedict was obliged to apply to the Crown for a pension, which was granted by Anne and continued by George I. until on February 20, 1715, the situation was completely changed by the father's death." *Old Virginia and Her Neighbors*, Fiske, Vol. II, P. 168.

[3] Fiske, *Old Virginia and Her Neighbors*, Vol. II, P. 155.

ent man from his father. Cecilius Calvert had contrived to keep on good terms at Court and to receive judgment after judgment in his favor. His son, not having his father's gifts, found little pleasure in king's courts. He loved the plain life of a colonist in Maryland infinitely better than he loved the fashionable life of an English nobleman. But however soothing this may be to the feelings of the patriotic Marylander it was not the best thing for Lord Baltimore. Possibly that old refusal to permit Cecilius to go out with the first expedition had been an unalloyed blessing. It had saved the second lord proprietary from being a colonist only. It had kept him in touch with the rulers in Church and State. With these officials Charles, the third Lord Baltimore, had no dealings at all, and in the end he lost Maryland.

In the meantime evidence of his continued neglect of Church people accumulated, such at least being the import of a letter from a devout Churchwoman to the Archbishop of Canterbury, enclosing a petition "To the Most Reverend the Archbishops and the rest of the Right Reverend the Bishops, on behalf of herself and others, his Majesty's subjects, inhabitants of the Province of Maryland, showing that the Province was without

CHURCH OF ENGLAND ESTABLISHED. 367

a church or any settled ministry, to the great grief of all his Majesty's loyal subjects there, and praying his Majesty that a certain parcel of tobacco, of one hundred hogsheads or thereabouts, of the growth or product of the said Province, may be custom free, for and towards the maintenance of an orthodox divine, at Calvert Town, in the said Province, or otherwise allow maintenance for a minister there." Praying furthermore that their "Lordships would vouchsafe to contribute towards the building of a church at Calvert Town."[4] Shortly after this petition was received, on the 29th of September, 1685, the Reverend Paul Bertrand sailed to Maryland."[5]

Charles Calvert never probably understood the difficulties of the Maryland Churchmen. He went on his blundering way, his life very much like the swirl of a bat in the dusk, profiting neither by past mistakes, nor friendly warnings and advice. But he could not help realizing that his proprietaryship was not a distinct success. And so when the death of Charles II. came in 1685, followed by the accession of James II., he probably regarded the change as a godsend in his misfortunes. James, as a

[4] Neill, *Founders of Maryland*, Pp. 160-163.
[5] *Ibid*, P. 163.

Roman Catholic could surely understand him and his position better, and would sympathize with him more readily, than the merry hearted monarch had done who seemed but a trifler at the best. But, alas, for human hopes and expectations. If Charles II. had chastised him with whips James II. would chastise him with scorpions. Barely had the new king been seated on his throne ere he commenced proceedings to annul all the colonial charters then in existence. But as the Maryland Charter was unlike every other, in that it was held by a Roman Catholic, Baltimore might reasonably have considered his interests quite safe, James being the only Roman Catholic king who had ever sat upon the English throne.[6] In this hope Lord Baltimore was to experience grievous disappointment. James viewed Baltimore's rights with even greater hostility than Charles had ever done, and in his attack on the colonies his special animus was directed against Maryland. The virulence of his attack was inspired and directed by Father Petre,

---

[6] Before Elizabeth's reign the Roman Catholic Church did not exist in England, its presence there being due to the act of Pius V. in 1570, who, in that year, sent the second Italian Mission to 'evangelize' England. Thus it was that Queen Mary, although in full sympathy with the Bishop of Rome, and acting under his orders, was a member of the English National Church.

CHURCH OF ENGLAND ESTABLISHED. 369

the king's Jesuit confessor, who was "the principal instrument in seeking to deprive his Lordship of his government."[7] It was not an open enemy that did Lord Baltimore this dishonor. But there were reasons for it.

Maryland had made a record for a long and determined opposition to the Jesuit society. Had it not been for the temporizing policy, first of Cecilius and now, though to a much lesser extent, of his son, Maryland might have been a Roman Catholic land. The society's agents had done and suffered much to bring that about, but just when they had reached forth their hands to pluck the fruit of their labors and their self-denial, they were thwarted by the lord proprietary himself. To use their own words: "Even occasions of suffering had not been wanting from those from whom rather it was proper to expect aid and protection."[8] Hence the special hatred of Maryland at the English Court. In the judgment of the king and his Jesuit confessor, Maryland should be punished for the record she had made for herself. But ere the proceedings had well begun which, were to terminate in the ending of Baltimore's rule the doughty James had

[7] Hawks, P. 57.
[8] *Md. Hist. Soc., F. P. No. 7, Letters 1642*, P. 88.

fled the kingdom, having no desire to provide the world with the spectacle of another royal execution.

For a time Charles Baltimore, who had been in England since James' accession, breathed more freely, though he realized that the flight of King James meant the coming of William of Orange. Indeed, with something of the old energy and tact which his father had been wont to display, he hastened to submit himself to the new ruler of England, and promptly sent a message to announce his action to the authorities of his province. Unfortunately the messenger died on the way, and as neither his commands, nor even any information as to his attitude towards the new government reached Maryland, his officers were uncertain what course to pursue. Consequently while others colonies north and south were raising the Orange standard Maryland took no part in the demonstration, and made no sign.

This circumstance was just what the enemies of the proprietary desired. His religion had always been a source of irritation to them, and now more than ever in view of King James' recent performance. Somehow or other a story was started to the effect that the Roman Catholics, with the aid of the Indians, were about to massacre the Protestants. It was a foolish tale, without a particle of truth, but it gave a demagogue named John Coode, a man of profligate character, but who, notwithstanding his antecedents, had actually obtained, ordination during a visit to England, an excuse to found an "Association to protect the Protestant religion and the sovereignty of King William and Queen Mary," and to organize a band of armed men with a view to seizing the government at St. Mary's. This done he published a statement impeaching the rule of the lord proprietary. In that document he asserted that Baltimore "had been building up his own power in the colony at the expense of the sovereignty of the Crown, and to name or own the king's power was sufficient to incur the frown of his lordship. He had affronted the king's officers of customs, had forcibly detained one of them, and another one had been murdered by an Irish papist. He had oppressed the people, established popish idolatry instead of the churches and chapels of the ecclesiastical laws of England, given the most fertile lands to Romish churches and forfeited the lands of the Protestant ministry. He had vetoed the best acts passed by the assembly, disposed of Protestant orphans to be brought up in

Romish superstition, separated a young woman from her husband, and committed her to the custody of a papist, imposed excessive fees, seized Protestants in their houses by armed forces of papists, and committed them to prison without warrant, allowed no redress for outrages and murders committed by Catholics, and used every means to divert the obedience of the people from the new Protestant king and queen."

"His agents, the priests and Jesuits," the declaration continued, "had used solemn masses and prayers for the success of the popish forces in Ireland and the French designs against England, and on every side could be heard protestations against their majesties right to the crown, and vilification of their persons. For these reasons the people of Maryland had taken up arms to vindicate and assert the sovereignty of King William, and to defend the Protestant religion." [9]

How far the charges were well founded will ever be a question. They were doubtless grossly exaggerated. But that there was a solid substratum of truth in them we cannot doubt, the mass of the people being unquestionably with Coode. It is

---

[9] Fisher, *Men, Women and Manners*, Vol. II, P. 199. See also Hawks, P. 65, Chalmers, P. 332.

unfortunate that an investigation into the truth of these charges, which was to have been held by the Privy Council, and which indeed was actually begun, was never completed. King William, by an arbitrary exercise of power, quashed the proceedings, and took away Lord Baltimore's position and powers as Lord Proprietary of Maryland, leaving him, however, in possession of his rents and revenues, and of the ownership of the lands which properly belonged to him. Eventually the province did come again into the possession of the Barons of Baltimore, but it was not until 1715, twenty-five years afterwards, when Charles was dead, and when the family had returned to the faith of their forefathers.

Following upon this arbitrary act of deprivation the king appointed Sir Lionel Copley as royal governor in place of the deposed proprietary. The new governor at once convened the Legislature, which drew up a loyal address thanking the king and queen for having delivered them "from the arbitrary will and pleasure of a tyrannical popish government under which they had so long groaned." In perfect accord with this, they next recognized, by the first Act which they passed, the royal authority of William and Mary. Their second measure was, "An Act for the service of Almighty God and the service of the Protestant religion." By this law it was declared that the Church of England in the province should have and enjoy all her rights, liberties and franchises, wholly inviolable, as they then were, or thereafter should be, established by law; that the several counties should be laid out into parishes; that the free-holders of each parish should meet and appoint six vestrymen; that a tax of forty pounds of tobacco should be laid on each taxable person in the province; that the sheriff should collect the same; and that the vestries of each parish should apply the proceeds of this tax to the support of ministers, or in the event of there being no ministers, to the building or the necessary repairs of the church, or other pious uses in their discretion. The vestries were next made bodies corporate to receive and hold property, and the ten counties of Maryland were divided into thirty-one parishes, as follows: The County of St. Mary into the parishes of William and Mary, and King and Queen. Calvert County into Christ Church, All Saints', St. Paul's and All Faith. Charles County into William and Mary, Port Tobacco, Nan-je-moy and Piscataway. Anne Arundel County into Herring Creek, South River,

CHURCH OF ENGLAND ESTABLISHED. 375

Middle Neck and Broad Neck parishes. Baltimore County into St. Paul's, St. Andrew's, St. George's and St. John's. Cecil County into South Sassafras and North Sassafras. Kent County into Kent Island and St. Paul's. Talbot County into St. Peter's, St. Michael's and St. Paul's. Dorchester County into Great Choptank and Dorchester. Somerset County into Somerset, Coventry, Stepney and Snow Hill parishes.[10]

Thus was the Church of England established and endowed. It was not of course a popular measure. The Roman Catholics keenly resented it. So did the Puritans,—now entirely separated from the Church—perhaps even more keenly still. They resented both the establishment of England's National Church, and the endowment to which they, in common with its own sons, were called upon to pay forty pounds of tobacco per man, a provision which was not entirely popular with those most interested in it, the clergymen themselves, for there was nothing in the Act to stipulate that the tobacco paid should be of a certain quality. Hence the parson was not uncommonly paid in unmarketable stuff, which could neither be sold nor used.

[10] Return made to Governor and Council. See Hawks, P. 73.

Historians frequently mistake the character of this act of establishment. Regarding it as a piece of intolerance towards other bodies of Christians they speak of it as an act of oppression. But it should be born in mind that it really did nothing more than make Maryland in Church matters what all along she had legally been by her charter, a part of England. It merely enforced the teaching of the charter. Save in the matter of the poll tax it put the Puritan and the Romanist in no worse position than they were in England. And of this none had much right to complain since all religious parties then believed in Church establishments; though it must be admitted that the establishment of the Church in Maryland was of a more definite and formal character than that of the Church in England. In England owing to the fact that the Church had existed before the state, and had in reality established the state, such an Act as that which passed in Maryland would have been an anachronism and an absurdity.

It is to this action of the royal Governor and the Legislature of Maryland in 1692, that Maryland today presents the spectacle, almost unique in America, of the Episcopal Church strong in the country districts. I was myself once Rector of one of Maryland's country parishes, a parish which covered an area of some sixty square miles. It was one of these old colonial parishes which owed its existence to the Act of 1692. It had its church erected in conformity with the requirements of that Act. Within its boundaries there was not then, and there is not now, another resident minister of any denomination, and there were over two hundred communicants. The strange delusion that the Roman Catholic Church is altogether in the ascendency in Maryland can readily be dispelled by a visit to just such a parish as this with its own rector, and even with its colored curate to attend to the people of the colored race.

St Mary's City had now seen its day. It had become exceedingly inconvenient, as the capital of the country, situated as it was at the extreme end of the province. And so the Assembly decided to sit henceforth at Annapolis. St. Mary's fought bravely against the change, for she knew it meant death to her. But opposition was useless. Nothing that her people could do availed to alter the mind of the new authorities. St. Mary's had stood for the old state of things; Annapolis was to stand for a new and better state. Accordingly the change was made and St. Mary's ceased forever to be of any importance save to the antiquarian and to the historian. Today a few scattered homes, so far apart as scarcely to be visible two at a time having in their midst a lovely church and a school for girls, state-supported, constitute St. Mary's City. In the presence of the school the historian will love to see a beautiful appropriateness. It was to St. Mary's that a daughter of the Emperor of the Piscataway Indians was taken by Leonard Calvert, and his kinswoman Margaret Brent, for education.[11] But its inaccessibility necessarily militates sadly in many different ways against its real usefulness.

So entirely have the former glories of St. Mary's departed and its importance dwindled away, that as the steamers, plying between Washington and Baltimore, steam up the St. Mary's River to land freight or passengers at the site of the ancient capital, the boatmen simply announce that the steamer is at 'Brume's Landing.' That is all. No city, no village, only a wharf, a landing place, nothing more. There is something pathetic in this entire passing away of a place, which though never great and populous, was yet for sixty years the centre of the political and ecclesiastical life of Maryland. But *sic transit gloria mundi*. Words these which

[11] "*A Scion of Nobility*," William Hande Browne.

have a peculiar interest to our Roman Catholic brethren throughout the world. For at his coronation every Bishop of Rome, as the thin ashes of a handful of lighted flax fall at his feet, hears them spoken with full and sonorous voice by one who bids him well remember how soon all earthly glory fades. Many among us will perhaps see much to justify the appropriation of these same words to conclude a sketch of Religion under the Barons of Baltimore, with special reference to the claim, universally made, and hitherto all too generously allowed as just and right, that the Roman Church once proclaimed Religious Toleration in Maryland.

FINIS.

INDEX.

A

ACT for Church Liberties, 233-4. Establishes Roman Catholic Church, 236-8. At variance with Magna Charta and the Maryland Charter, 239.
ACT Concerning Religion known as the "Toleration Act" passed 1549, 318. Confirmed by the Proprietary the following year, 318.
ACT of Toleration a rule of intolerance, 319.
ACT Concerning Religion, passed 1634, repeals previous Act, 339.
ADVENTURERS to Maryland:—Influenced by mundane considerations, 134-140. Were mostly members of the English Church, 142-3. Sailed 1633, 146. Arrived in Maryland, Feast of the Annunciation, 1634, 167.
APOSTLE of the Indians of Maryland, Father White, 196.
ASSEMBLY, HOUSE OF:— Working of the first Legislature, 231. Recognized royal authority of William and Mary, 373. Established Church of England, 374. Decided to remove to Annapolis, 377.
AVALON, CHARTER OF, 37-57. Issued to Sir George Calvert, 1623, 50. Modelled on the feudal palatines of Durham, 51.

B

BANCROFT withdraws the statement of his first edition, 15-16.
BERTRAND, Rev. Paul, sailed to Maryland A. D. 1685, 369.
BROOKE leads an expedition of Anglican immigrants, 316.
BURNAP admits that the Act for Church Liberties established the Roman Catholic Church, 237.

C

CALVERT, SIR GEORGE:—First Baron of Baltimore, 1-7. Preacher of religious toleration a fiction, 11. Buys Vaughan's estates in Newfoundland, 38-39. Charter of Avalon issued to him 1623, 50. Visited Newfoundland 1627, 61. Visited Newfoundland 1628, 63. Leaves Newfoundland for Virginia, 77. Refuses to take the Oath of Supremacy, 81. Returns to England, 92. Obtains charter for territory south of Virginia, 98. Charter annulled, 98. Secures new charter for territory north of Virginia, 99. Dies, 101. True place in history, 107.
CALVERT, CECILIUS:—Grantee of charter, 111. Never visited Maryland, 121-129-130. Offers special inducements to adventurers, 134-140. Demands removal of the Jesuits, 262. Petitions Sacred Congregation for removal of the Jesuits, 262. Issues new Conditions of Plantation, 265. Makes concordat with the Jesuits, 269. Summoned before the House of Lords, 277. Makes overtures to the Puritans of Massachusetts, 281. Letter to his brother Leonard, A. D. 1642, 283-9. Gives up Maryland as lost, 302. Determines to make Maryland Protestant, 310. Requires Governor Stone not to oppress Roman Catholics, 312-3. Confirms, 1650, Act Concerning Religion, 318. Restored to his authority by by Commonwealth, 345. Dies 1675, 357. His place in Maryland History, 358.
CALVERT, CHARLES:—Son of Cecilius succeeds to his father's titles, 359. Reminded by Privy Council of the conditions of his charter,

C

363. Alleged to be showing undue partiality to Roman Catholics, 365. Submits to William of Orange, 370.

CALVERT, LEONARD :—Founds the Province of Maryland, 1-6. Enters into communication with Indians, 173. Rebuked by his brother Cecilius for granting additional lands to the Jesuits, 287-8. Visits England, 291. Arrives in Maryland 1644, 296. His authority in Maryland ceased, 296. Regains St. Mary's by the help of Virginians, 303. Dies A. D. 1647, 305.

CHARLES, Second proclaimed King by acting Governor, 335.

COODE, JOHN :— Impeaches the rule of the Lord Proprietary 1689, 371.

CHURCHES to be consecrated according to ecclesiastical laws of England, 122-7.

CHURCH :—The first church building erected in Maryland, on Kent Island, 175.

CHURCH OF ENGLAND men build a church at St. Mary's, 197. Build a church at Poplar Hill, 199. Ministered to by clergy from Kent Island and Virginia, 202-3. Established in Maryland, not a popular measure, 375.

CLAYBORNE, William :— Secretary to the State of Virginia, 92. Sailed to England when Sir George Calvert went to England from Virginia, 92. Secured revocation of Sir George Calvert's charter for territory south of Virginia, 98. Sails for Virginia, 98. Notified by Leonard Calvert that he must relinquish all dependence upon Virginia, 180. His contention with Lord Baltimore, 180. Ends disastrously, 183. Makes war on his ancient foe, 295. Gains possession of Kent Island, 296. Establishes his authority in St. Mary's City, 296. Fosters strife at Providence, 333. Appointed commissioner for governing Chesapeake Bay, 336. Sets out for Maryland 1651, 337. And his fellow commissioners depose Governor Stone and set up a new government, 337. Victorious at Providence, 343. Crushed by decision of Trades and Plantations, 345.

CROMWELL refers Maryland matters to committee of Trades and Plantations, 345.

C

COPLEY, Thomas, arrives in Maryland 1637, 203. The evil genius of Maryland, 204. Claims 6,000 acres for sending out adventurers, 208. Commences aggressive work, 209. Excludes Anglicans from political office, 212. Escapes personal injury, but not pecuniary loss; appeals to Lord Baltimore, 251. Secretly acquires land from King Pathuen, 259.

CORNWALEYS, Captain :—Reminds the first Legislature that they are under English laws, 231. Sends letter of complaint to Lord Baltimore in reference to Act of Church Liberties, 235. A wiser counsellor than Copley, 254.

F

FITZHERBERT, a worthy successor to Copley, 350-2. Threatens Thomas Gerrard, 351. Suggests malevolence of witches as cause of bad weather, 352.

FLEET, Captain Henry, from Virginia, points out site for St. Mary's City, 173-4.

H

HATTON, Thomas, a Protestant, appointed Secretary, 311.

HARVEY, Sir John, Governor of Virginia, pays a state visit to St. Mary's, 177.

HAWLEY, Jerome, sailed to England, 183.

HISTORIES in our schools, untrustworthy, 17.

HOLY CHURCH and Roman Church interchangeable terms, 238.

I

INDIANS evangelized, 186-7.

INGLE, Richard, aids Clayborne, 295.

INSTRUCTIONS of Lord Proprietary, 148-171.

J

JAMES the Second commenced proceedings to annul the Maryland Charter, 368.

JAMES, Rev. Richard, an English clergyman sent by Sir George

INDEX 383

J

Calvert with his emigrants to Newfoundland, 46. Stationed on Kent Island, 47. Died, 1638, 47. Widow, dispossessed, 210.
JESUITS, sentiment towards their Protestant countrymen, 193-4. Proselytism, instances of, 216-19. The first to introduce slavery into Maryland, 214. Claim the power of working miracles, 219-222. Persecute Protestants, 222-224. Refuse to sit in first legislative assembly, 225-6. Dispute Lord Baltimore's title to lands not ceded to him by the Indians, 259. Triumph over Cecilius Calvert, 269. Break the concordat, 271. Panic-stricken at the downfall of the proprietary government, 296.

L

LEE, Mary, hanged as a witch. 353.
LEWGER, John, Secretary to Maryland, arrived in Maryland 1637, 260. Not a Romanist of the Copley type. 260. Opened an anti-Jesuit campaign in the House of Assembly, A. D. 1640, 261.

M

MARYLAND, history opens at the Court of King James, 21. Charter of, 113. Extent of territory granted, 114. Terms of charter, 119. Charter differs from Charter of Avalon, 121-22. Churches to be consecrated according to ecclesiastical laws of England, 122-27. Charter revoked by William the Third, 373.
MATCH, the Spanish, 2.-30.
MEMORIAL to Leonard Calvert erected by Maryland Government, 306-7.

N

NEWFOUNDLAND visited by Norsemen under Eric the Red, 41. Rediscovered by Cabot, 1497. 41. Claimed for Queen Elizabeth by Sir Humphrey Gilbert, 41. England's first colony, 42. Parcelled out by trading companies, 42. Visited by Lord Baltimore, 1627, 61. Abandoned by Lord Baltimore, 1629, 64.

O

OATH OF SUPREMACY:—Refused by Sir George Calvert, 81. Meaning of, 82-3. Fidelity to Lord Baltimore, 334.

P

PETITION to Anglican Hierarchy for clergy for Maryland 1686, 366.
POCOMOKE, battle of, 183.
POTT, Governor of Virginia, to Privy Council in reference to Calvert's refusal to take the Oath of Supremacy, 89-90.
PROVIDENCE:—The headquarters of the new emigrants, 330. Battle of, 343.
PROTESTANT Declaration set forth by Governor Stone and others, 332.

R

RALEIGH, Sir Walter, the founder of the English Empire in America, 21.
RELIGIOUS service at the landing of the adventurers, 167-8.

S

SMITH, Captain John, Governor of Virginia, explored Chesapeake Bay in 1608, 91.
STOURTON, Rev. Erasmus, chaplain of John Guy's company to Newfoundland, 46; Complains to the King that mass was said openly at Ferryland, 69.
STONE:—A Protestant appointed Governor in place of Green, a Roman Catholic, 311. Undertakes to procure five hundred immigrants for Maryland, 315. Puts out Protestant Declaration 1650, 332.
ST. MARY'S:—Chosen as the site of the Capital, 173. Ceases to be the Capital, 378.

T

TOLERATION, Religious, unknown in Sir George Calvert's day, 9. Acknowledged by Cardinal Vaughan, 74. Acknowledged by Archbishop Ireland, 74.

V

VAUGHAN, a Protestant appointed Governor of Kent Island, 311.
VESTRIES made corporable bodies to receive and hold property, 374.
VIRGINIA:—Visited by Sir George Calvert, 77. Tendered oath of supremacy to Sir George Calvert, 81. Governor Pott writes Privy Council respecting Sir George Calvert's refusal, 89.

W

WHITE, Father: his two accounts of voyage of Ark and Dove, 151. Apostle of the Indians, 196. Sent to England for trial, 299. Released from Newgate, 300.
WILKINSON, Rev. Mr., an Anglican clergyman, arrives in Maryland, 1650, 316.
WILLIAM III. deprived Charles Calvert of his proprietaryship, 873. Appointed Sir Lionel Copley royal governor, 373.

ERRATA.

On page 113 read "commemorated" for "memorialized."
On page 201, third line, del. comma.
On page 239 read "Charta" for "Charter."

www.ingramcontent.com/pod-product-compliance
Lightning Source LLC
Chambersburg PA
CBHW030424300426
44112CB00009B/847